The PET DOCTOR

The PET DOCTOR

YOUR TOTAL
GUIDE TO DOG
AND CAT CARE

MORTON B. CAPLAN
MSc, DVM

Whitecap Books
Vancouver/Toronto

The information in this book is true and complete to the best of our knowledge. All
recommendations are made without guarantee on the part of the author or Whitecap
Books Ltd. The author and publisher disclaim any liability in connection with the use
of this information. For additional information please contact Whitecap Books Ltd.,
351 Lynn Avenue, North Vancouver, B.C., V7J 2C4.

Edited by Linda Ostrowalker
Cover and interior design by Warren Clark
Cover photograph by Chris McCallan
Interior illustrations (pp. 44, 53, 54, 55, 99, 110, 122) by Joseph Sherman.
Medical illustrations (pp. 155, 166, 180, 184, 185, 191, 211, 225, 247) are courtesy of
Hill's Pet Nutrition, Inc.

Typeset by Warren Clark

Printed and bound in Canada

Canadian Cataloguing in Publication Data

Caplan, Morton.
   Pet doctor

   Includes bibliographical references and index.
   ISBN 1-55110-250-1

   1. Dogs. 2. Cats. I. Title
SF426.C36 1994   636.7'0887   C94-910363-2

Acknowledgments

I wish to thank all my colleagues and friends who suggested topics for inclusion. My own pets have provided me with the joys and wonders of pet ownership: Alistair, a domestic short-haired tabby cat, who lived from May 1977 to November 1992; Blue, a beautiful black and brindle Labrador/Shepherd, who joined my family at the age of one year and died at the ripe old age of fourteen in May 1992; and the always playful and happy Aimée, a gray Bouvier/Sheepdog, who came into my life as a little ball of fluff in June 1986. She taught me the joys of raising a puppy and has grown into a gracious and loving companion.

My sincere and heartfelt appreciation goes to Harvey Brownstone for his inspiration and encouragement while I was writing this book. His tremendous talent at editing the text, tirelessly reading and rereading every line to ensure that it was easy to understand, is humbly acknowledged. This book would not have been possible without him.

Dr. B. H. Grahn, (D.V.M., Diplomate, A.B.V.P. of the Department of Veterinary Internal Medicine, Western College of Veterinary Medicine, University of Saskatchewan), reviewed the manuscript. His comments are gratefully acknowledged. A very special thanks goes to Linda Ostrowalker for her superb contribution to the final editing of the book.

To all my clients and friends,
both two-legged and four-legged,
who, over the years, have allowed
me the privilege of serving them
in my chosen profession.

Contents

CONTENTS

Preface

Although as a youngster I never had a dog or cat, I was fortunate to have had contact with other people's pets, and so my fascination with animals began. After obtaining degrees in biology and zoology, my inspiration for becoming a veterinarian stemmed from observing my cousin Harriet caring for the West Highland White Terriers that she bred. After graduation from veterinary school, I completed an internship and residency program in small animal medicine and surgery. I finally established my own clinic in downtown Toronto, and have been privileged to put into practice my own personal philosophy of veterinary medicine, which is very simple: cautious interventionism.

I recall "pearls of wisdom" my teachers would point out: rare diseases don't occur frequently; when you hear hoofbeats in the hallway, don't look for zebras; treat diseases that are treatable; be forthright with your clients and don't be afraid to admit that there may be something you don't know. I use these axioms regularly in my practice. For example, when presented with a cat that is vomiting, I take an x-ray to rule out the possibility of a foreign object, and then I offer treatment for the most common cause of vomiting in cats (hairballs). I will investigate more extensively if the animal does not respond, and I will only hospitalize an animal if I am doing something for it every day that the family cannot do at home.

Every pet owner can attest to the existence of the natural phenomenon known as the "human-animal bond." This book is a reflection of the perspectives and insights on the human-animal bond that I have developed over the years as an urban veterinarian. My aim has been to present a comprehensive pet care guide and helpful reference source for dog and cat owners, using examples from my practice to illustrate the important principles of responsible pet ownership. I have tried to explain the *reasons* for the courses of action that veterinarians suggest, as I believe there is a higher level of compliance when procedures are understood.

In my discussion of medical conditions, I have sought to explain, in lay terms, how these conditions develop, how they can be diagnosed, and options for treatment. Wherever possible, I have also provided a prognosis as to whether the condition is curable or controllable, and whether it is generally progressive or stable. This is not meant to be a voluminous veterinary textbook dealing with each and every condition that could possibly affect a cat or dog. Rather, I have presented the most common conditions seen in everyday veterinary practice. There are some rare diseases that may have to be diagnosed and/or treated by a specialist.

No book can ever be a substitute for proper professional advice and assistance tailored to the individual case. However, it is my sincere hope that this book will provide a solid foundation of basic principles of responsible pet ownership.

Responsible
Pet Ownership

1

The Human-Animal Bond

Pets are perceived by most people as much more than items of property; they engage us in real relationships, and in some cases give much more than they take. In recent years, psychiatrists, psychologists, social workers, and veterinarians have documented the many positive aspects of pet ownership. The special link between people and animals is referred to as the "human-animal bond." This bond is defined as a mutually beneficial association between people and animals, with physical, emotional, intellectual, spiritual, and philosophical aspects. Anyone who comes home after a difficult day and feels tension melt away with the wagging of a dog's tail, or the sound of a cat's purring, is benefiting from the human-animal bond. Single people and seniors have someone with whom to share their lives. Children have a devoted companion who gives unconditional love and affection.

Pets are generally considered by their owners to be family members. In one North American report, four out of five dog owners acknowledged the existence of an emotional tie between their pet and some family member. Another study found that 98 percent of pet owners talked to their pets; 80 percent viewed their pets as people, not animals; 80 percent believed that their pets were sensitive to their feelings; and 28 percent confided in their pets.

In recent years, studies into the therapeutic value of companion animals have flourished all over the world. In many countries, dedicated individuals—from pet owners to trained therapists—are taking dogs, cats, and other small animals to visit hospitals, seniors' homes, and jails. Animals are being used to develop rapport with Alzheimer's patients, withdrawn children, and others who have retreated into themselves.

Many studies have revealed that interactions with a pet can improve both mental and physical well-being. When people speak to each other, blood pressure almost always rises, sometimes into the hypertensive range. In contrast, when people talk to pets, their speech pattern is usually slower, softer, and higher pitched, and word groupings are shorter than in conversations with people. This speech style is associated with lower blood pressure. Even the mere presence of an animal, without any physical or verbal contact, can lower blood pressure. The act of looking at a tropical fish aquarium can significantly reduce blood pressure in both hypertensive and normal subjects. Maybe that is why so many dentists' offices have aquariums!

Coronary patients with pets are more likely to live longer than those without pets. The simple act of petting a dog reduces the risk of heart attack by lowering blood pressure, heart rate, and anxiety levels. Pets also give emotional support. Dogs (and most cats) love without reservation. They are 100 percent on your side, never doubting, never criticizing.

Pet owners consistently score higher than nonowners in feelings of life satisfaction, self-esteem, and overall well-being. Pets may even propel careers: a 1984 survey of one hundred chief executive officers of "Fortune 500" companies revealed that 94 percent had a dog or cat as a child and 75 percent were currently pet owners. The incidence of pet ownership in this group was significantly higher than in the general population.

Other studies indicate that pets influence family cohesiveness. Family members are more understanding of each other and reach consensus more frequently if they are pet owners than if they are not.

Research indicates that pets help their owners cope with major life crises, such as divorce, death, job loss, and illness. Pets are a comforting, constant friend in time of need, and give a bereaved person a reason for going on. When we care for others, including pets, we feel needed and appreciated. Often people without children manifest their need to nurture by caring for their pets.

A dog can inspire physical exercise by serving as a walking or jogging partner, extending the time each day that the owner spends in physical activity.

Pets and Seniors

Many studies have found that elderly people with pets tend to be more self-reliant and optimistic than nonpet owners of the same age. For the elderly, a pet can mean the difference between despair or withdrawal and continued interest in life. Pets help keep an elderly person mentally alert; the responsibilities of feeding and grooming a pet give the owner a sense of purpose. Seniors with pets have a higher survival rate than nonowners after suffering severe physical shock such as angina or heart attacks. Pets also serve as catalysts to encourage interpersonal relationships between the elderly and those caring for them. The love, care, and attention, both given and received, can go a long way to facilitating a nurturing and supportive environment.

Countless sociologists have commented on the sense of isolation experienced by senior citizens in Western culture. When institutionalized, it is often necessary for older people to surrender many of the things that have given their lives comfort and meaning, such as a relationship with a treasured pet. While caring for a pet has been proven to increase life expectancy, those forced to give up their pets late in life often lose the will to live and die soon after parting with them. Fortunately, many seniors' facilities now allow resident pets, or are establishing animal visitation programs.

Pet Visitation Programs

Many institutions have established pet visitation programs, where volunteers bring animals to visit residents. These programs have demonstrated time and again that the presence of pets can result in increased social competence, life satisfaction, and a sense of well-being in patients. Animals can bring people out of themselves and relieve depression.

Several years ago I volunteered to take part in the visitation program at a chronic care hospital. I had two large dogs, an elderly, quiet one and a well-behaved but very active and excitable one. I felt the older dog would be ideal for the visitation program, but the organizer said the younger dog would interact better with the patients. She was correct. My older dog sniffed each patient once, then went to sleep in a corner. The younger dog, however, engaged everyone's attention by licking faces, retrieving balls thrown by patients, and generally showing her appreciation for pats and dog biscuits! She provided the stimulation and excitement the patients craved. Even those patients who were unable to speak had very expressive eyes as they interacted with Aimée on whatever level they could.

Pet-Facilitated Therapy Programs

Pet-facilitated therapy programs use animals as adjuncts to psychotherapy and rehabilitation, providing more intensive and prolonged patient contact than a pet visitation program.

Some prisons permit inmates to adopt pets as a way of reducing aggressive behavior and improving morale. Even the most difficult inmates become more tractable when given the responsibility of caring for a dog, cat, or bird. Animals also assist in group therapy for drug addiction and behavioral disorders.

The Community Association for Riding for the Disabled (C.A.R.D.) provides horseback-riding programs for children and adults with physical or intellectual disabilities. This organization recognizes that there are considerable psychological and physical benefits to be derived from horseback riding. For example, tightness of the inner thigh muscles, characteristic of patients with cerebral palsy, is relieved by the gentle stretching required to sit astride a horse. Improved balance and strength are other physical benefits of riding. One study even demonstrated that riding could enhance speech and language development! Feelings of mobility, freedom, and independence are experienced when riding a horse. Confidence and self-esteem come with learning to control and care for a large animal, while interaction with instructors and other students builds social skills. For people who feel "different," the nonjudgmental affection and loyalty of an animal may make all the difference in the world.

In some institutions, pets help autistic patients to communicate and express themselves. Programs using animals to rehabilitate patients with mental handicaps have existed in Europe for over a century, but have only recently gained widespread acceptance in North America. Studies show that many psychiatric patients who were previously withdrawn and incapable of caring for themselves became more communicative and social when caring for dogs. The necessity of attending to their animals' needs, and the affection given by the dogs in return, seemed to break through long-standing barriers of isolation and apathy. Many patients improved sufficiently to be discharged.

In another study at a hospital for the criminally insane, patients who had the responsibility of caring for pets showed a marked decrease in suicide attempts and violent behavior. Animals seem to open the lines of communication between staff and patients, helping to establish the trust that is essential to successful therapy.

Pet-facilitated therapy, however, is not without its own problems. The loss of a companion animal—a painful experience for anyone—is potentially devastating to someone already suffering from depression.

Animals for People with Physical Disabilities

A special aspect of the human-animal bond is the use of trained service animals to assist people with disabilities. Dogs are often trained to guide the blind, or to assist people with hearing impairments or physical disabilities. Tiny capuchin monkeys have been trained to feed and care for their paralyzed owners. All of these worthy companions literally become a physical extension of the person.

A guide dog is trained to be its master's eyes; they work as a team. I have had the opportunity to care for three guide dogs so far in my career, and I have the utmost respect for their unquestioning devotion and loyalty.

"Hearing ear" dogs help give their owners confidence and freedom. In this partnership, the dog signals a variety of sounds inside and outside the home—everything from the morning alarm clock to a baby's cry, a telephone call, or a life-saving fire alarm. Unfortunately, these highly trained dogs are not getting the widespread recognition they deserve, perhaps because, unlike the guide dog population, hearing ear dogs are not walked on a special harness and are not of any particular size or breed.

The newest specially trained service dog is the "handi-dog," trained to act as the arms and legs of people confined to wheelchairs. These dogs can carry packs, open doors, retrieve objects on command, and protect their owners in hazardous situations. Handi-dogs can push the button to summon an elevator, and pull a wheelchair over difficult spots. But the animal's most important function may be social. Many wheelchair users have difficulty approaching others, and some people often feel awkward about initiating contact. The dog, however, serves as an "ice-breaker," giving people something to talk about until personal conversation becomes comfortable.

Even without training, some dogs seem to have an innate capacity to sense when their owners are in distress. A 1993 British survey of thirty-seven dog owners who were epileptic found that the dogs seemed to know in advance when the owners were about to have a seizure, and some even fetched help. All the dogs were untrained, yet all responded to their owners' seizures.

Pets and Children

Pets have a positive influence on childhood development, contributing to the child's need to love and be loved. Sharing secrets with a nonjudgmental confidant can be very important to a child's psychological well-being. Children who understand that their animal friends need food when they are hungry, water when they are thirsty, rest when they are tired, and shelter from heat and cold, have taken a giant step toward acquiring the most important attributes a person can ever learn: self-lessness and compassion. Tasks associated with pet care provide children with an excellent opportunity to learn responsibility. In addition, through pets, children are exposed to the natural cycle of life: pregnancy, birth, old age, and death.

Pets also provide a healthy sense of ego satisfaction for children. A child can train a pet, and derive a sense of achievement from its obedience and good behavior. Studies have shown that children who have had high-quality experiences with companion animals generally show more empathy and concern for others (both human and animal) than children who have not had a close relationship with a pet.

To ensure that a child reaps all the benefits of life with a pet, the child must be taught respect for the animal and how to play with it safely. However, they must also learn that strange animals may not be as trustworthy as their own pets; a child should never approach an unknown animal without first asking an adult.

Human Socialization

Pets also facilitate ordinary human socialization. One study reported that people find it easier to approach others if they first establish contact through an animal. Thus, someone walking a dog is more likely to engage in a conversation with others than someone walking alone. Another researcher refers to dogs as "social lubricants"; he found that pet owners speak to more people and have longer conversations when they walk a dog than when they walk alone. Although 60 percent of these interactions took the form of a simple greeting ("Hello"), 40 percent consisted of genuine conversations. This researcher also noted that female walkers tended to hold longer conversations with male walkers than with other female walkers. I have several single friends who swear that the best way to meet other singles is to take a dog to a park on a sunny day! Another study concluded that people in the company of their pets appeared to others to be more attractive, happier, friendlier, and more intelligent than people without pets.

≈

The benefits of pet ownership are virtually limitless. Animals help us maintain our mental and physical equilibriums. They divert us from worrying about our own problems and stimulate us to be more active. They make us laugh and help us to maintain a sense of humor. They offer us security, succor, esteem, understanding, forgiveness, fun, and laughter, and most importantly, abundant and unconditional love. We are the richer for having pets in our lives.

2

Acquiring a Pet

There are many factors to consider before deciding to bring a pet into the family. First, are you committed to having an animal dependent on you for perhaps the next twenty years? If so, what type of pet would best suit your lifestyle—a dog, a cat, or some other furry or winged creature? Some people are more naturally attracted to one type of animal than another.

As a veterinarian I am always thrilled when people ask my advice before acquiring a pet. Consultation with a veterinarian combined with background information from additional sources, such as breeders, animal shows, pet owners, and reference books, can make the experience of choosing the right pet for your household an enjoyable one. Discussing with children the commitment they must be willing to make to help care for the pet helps to set the stage for a healthy caring environment in which the new animal will thrive.

Choosing the appropriate time to bring a pet into your household is vital, especially if it is a puppy or kitten. Holiday gatherings and birthday parties are *not* good times! The young animal that has been taken from its mother and siblings by strangers needs to be introduced to a household calmly and reassuringly. If you are giving a pet as a gift, I recommend giving an "I.O.U. ONE PET" at the party, and getting the animal at a subsequent quiet time, when the new owner will be able to spend at least a few uninterrupted days with his or her new companion.

Should It Be a Dog or a Cat?

Your living accommodations should be taken into consideration before deciding whether to get a dog or a cat. If you live in an apartment or townhouse complex, are you allowed to have a pet? Are you concerned about the noise that your pet may make? If you live in a high-rise building, are you prepared to meet the extra challenge, during the housebreaking period, of teaching the dog that it must not relieve itself in the hallways and elevators, but must wait until it is all the way outside?

If you want to have a dog, is there a nearby exercise area where you can take it for a safe run, or will it be restricted to walks on a leash? If you live in a house, do you have a fully enclosed "escape-proof" backyard? What about your lifestyle? Are you away from home for extended periods of time? Cats tend to be more independent than dogs and can, if necessary, be left alone for several days if provided with sufficient food and water. This is not, however, a recommended practice. A cat that has been left for a lengthy period of time may be lonely and seem aloof and rather peeved when you return. Dogs, on the other hand, are usually conditioned to go outside at specific times of the day. If you are unexpectedly delayed, or if you are on rotating shift work, you may be greeted upon your return by a hungry, lonesome dog, and possibly by a mess if nature called during your absence. There is also a chance that a dog left alone will chew on the furniture. However, an erratic work schedule doesn't necessarily preclude you from having a dog, as there are pet-walking services available. Look in the Yellow Pages of the telephone directory under "Pet Services" or "House Sitters." These individuals should be bonded so they can be entrusted with a key to your house; if you are going to be late getting home, a telephone call to the service will ensure that your dog will be taken out.

Although dogs can be trained to relieve themselves on newspaper on the floor, this is practical only for small breeds, due to the volume of urine produced by larger breeds. Also, it is generally not advisable to leave even a "paper-trained" dog unattended for long periods of time as dogs are social creatures and need human company.

If you will be leaving an animal at home alone, you should ensure that your home is "pet proofed." A discussion of this topic is found in Chapter 3, "Protecting Your Pet From Harm." Are you prepared to incorporate these precautions into your routine?

Generally speaking, having a dog means exercise, both for you and your pet. If you like to take walks several times a day, a dog might be a suitable pet for you. However, remember that inclement weather will not stop the call of nature or your dog's need for exercise, even if the dog disagrees! Our larger dog, Aimée, hates to go outside when it is raining (not that I blame her), and she will hold her urine for hours. It takes major coaxing on our part to convince her to go outside for one final urination at bedtime.

Choosing the Breed and Sex

Although the selection process for dogs and cats is almost identical, you will have far fewer choices of breed and pet size with cats. You must decide between selecting a purebred or mixed breed, young or mature animal, male or female, short-haired or long-haired animal.

It is important to select a breed of dog or cat that suits your particular situation. Very large breeds of dogs, such as Great Danes and Saint Bernards, need large areas of living space, but generally do not require as much activity as smaller breeds. The lifespan of different breeds of animals also varies greatly. The very large breeds usually live only eight or ten years, while the very small breeds (such as Chihuahuas and Toy Poodles) can live to be twenty years old. Many cats will live up to sixteen years, with the occasional cat surviving to the age of twenty-two or even twenty-four years.

Although every animal has its own unique personality, it has been my experience that certain breeds exhibit general character traits. Knowledge of these breed characteristics can give you an idea of how a particular dog might fit into your household. For example, a dog that was developed to be watchful and defensive, such as the Rottweiler, should make an excellent watchdog. A dog developed for herding sheep, like the Border Collie, should be good in a family situation, where the individual people, in effect, become the dog's "flock."

The "social" breeds—the herding, working, and some of the sporting dogs—are, as a general rule, more obedient and more easily trained than the breeds that were developed to work independently, such as hounds and terriers. Certain types of dogs are by nature very active and excitable (for example, Irish Setters and Springer Spaniels); others tend to be calm and complacent (for example, Retrievers and Newfoundland dogs). If you enjoy hunting or taking long walks you might be interested in one of the hunting, sporting, or herding breeds. Hound dogs (for example, Beagles and Bassets) are often quite noisy; how will this affect you and your neighbors? The Basenji dog is supposedly mute and won't bark; it will, however, make squealing-type sounds.

If you have a young family, you might prefer a large gentle dog (such as a Bouvier or Retriever) that can withstand the constant handling of a child, rather than a delicate breed (Chihuahua, Maltese, or Shih Tzu) or an aggressive, dominant breed (Rottweiler or German Shepherd). Families with children need to select a breed that can withstand the commotion of a boisterous household. Many larger breeds have a special rapport with children and have the additional advantage of being able to walk away if the play gets too rough!

Some breeds tend to be natural guard dogs (German Shepherd, Doberman). However, those seeking a watchdog can pick from any size noisemaker. A small bark can alert a family just as well as the sound of a large dog. One mistake too many people make is choosing a dog for protection that is otherwise unsuited to their situation. A puppy that grows into a sturdy, solid, well-muscled dog might not be suitable for a frail person to take for walks. Similarly, a petite or timid person might have difficulty training and controlling a powerful breed such as the Rottweiler. It may be amusing to watch, but it can also be frightening to be pulled down the street by an undisciplined dog that weighs almost as much as its owner, especially if the sidewalk is icy!

Many of the terrier-type dogs (for example, Scottish Terriers, Irish Terriers) are natural diggers (the name is derived from the French verb "terrier" meaning "to dig"); if you have a prize rose garden, make sure the dog does not have access to it! Terriers are fearless, feisty dogs that were developed to oust and eliminate animals such as foxes or badgers from their burrows by enthusiastic digging and staccatolike barking. The spunk and courage needed for the hunt also make terriers excellent watchdogs.

Most scenthounds, such as Bloodhounds or Basset Hounds, have "nose-brains," meaning that they are ruled by their noses rather than their eyes. The sense of smell in these dogs far surpasses that of humans—they can sniff out a jackrabbit in the next county! In contrast, sighthounds, including the Borzoi and Irish Wolfhound, have keen vision and an inborn passion and need to run.

The sporting companions (for example, German Short-haired Pointers and Weimaraners) display an urge to hunt, point, flush, and/or retrieve, and are highly energetic, demanding exercise no matter what the weather.

The main duty of the herding breeds, such as the Bouvier and Belgian Sheepdog, was to herd and gather sheep and cattle. These dogs sometimes had to defend their charges against predators or thieves. Thus, most herding dogs are easy to train and bond closely with their families.

Some dog breeds, such as Rottweilers, Afghans, and Chow Chows, are very strong-willed and might not be suitable for first-time pet owners because they are notoriously difficult for inexperienced people to train.

There is also a financial component to consider. A large dog costs more to feed and medicate than a miniature breed. A bottle of pills to treat an infection in a Great Dane might cost three times the amount required to treat the same infection in a small Poodle. Similarly, the cost of boarding or grooming a large dog will be greater than that for a smaller breed.

Personally, my favorite dog breeds are Golden Retrievers and Black Labradors. They are intelligent, sturdy, and generally easy to handle. On the other hand, I have met very few Pomeranians or American Eskimo dogs that I could approach and examine in confidence since they are usually "one-person" pets and do not readily accept strangers.

Some cat breeds (including the Siamese and Burmese) are renowned for being vocal; can you live with a Siamese cat that "talks" frequently (actually, it's more like a whine)? Other types of cats, such as the Abyssinian or Persian, are usually very affectionate. Breeders of Bombay cats describe them as intelligent and sociable. Some people prefer to have a more exotic and unique breed, such as a Tonkenese or Oriental Shorthair. I once had a client who wanted a very large solid cat and so she bought a male Maine Coon cat, and it grew into one of the largest cats I have ever seen—it weighed thirteen kilograms (28 lb.)!

The amount of time required to brush, comb, and groom a dog or cat should also be considered. Some dogs need frequent clipping; if you are not going to trim the dog yourself, you will have to pay a professional dog groomer.

For people with allergies, certain breeds of cats (for example, the Rex) and dogs (Soft-coated Wheaten Terrier or Bichon Frise) are recommended; these nonshedding animals have fur coats with little or no dander or undercoat.

Some animals are more likely than others to develop certain medical conditions. For instance, ear infections are very common in Poodles and Cocker Spaniels. Dachshunds often have back problems. Large breeds such as German Shepherds are apt to develop hip dysplasia (a degenerative hip disease) and other joint problems. Irish Setters and Schnauzers are prone to developing blindness due to atrophy of the retina. Bedlington Terriers can develop a certain type of liver disease. West Highland White Terriers and Poodles often develop allergies, which can cause itchiness that requires constant medication to keep it under control. If you are interested in acquiring a purebred dog of a specific type, speak to breeders about possible medical conditions or inherited problems their dogs might be prone to developing.

If you do not have your heart set on a specific breed, a mongrel or mixed breed might be suitable. The dominance of certain breed characteristics in a mongrel might give you some indication of the general behavioral trends that may emerge in that animal's personality.

One final point about breeds. Some pet stores offer mixed breeds such as "Cock-a-poo" (Cocker Spaniel mixed with Poodle) or "Peke-a-poo" (Pekingese mixed with Poodle) and represent them to be purebreds, thereby charging a high price. These animals are *not* purebreds, and should not be mistaken as such.

You must also decide whether the sex of your pet is important to you. Walking a male dog generally involves frequent stops to allow him to "label" his territory by urinating on trees, fire hydrants, and other vertical surfaces. Male cats may spray urine to mark their territory, although this is rare in neutered cats. Male cats can develop very serious, life-threatening urinary problems, although the risk of this occurring can be minimized if the cat is maintained on a premium-quality diet.

Make sure that the pet you have selected is of the sex you want. On several occasions I have had the rather unusual experience of having to inform a client that his or her new male cat or dog is actually a female, or vice versa, even though the client was told the animal's sex by staff at the animal shelter or pet shop. This is one of the reasons I always recommend that a newly acquired pet be brought to the veterinarian for an initial examination as soon as possible.

Where to Get Your Pet

Pets can be acquired from a pet store, breeder, private source such as a newspaper advertisement, or from an animal welfare organization. The cost of the pet will vary accordingly.

If you are looking for a purebred animal, a breeder should be consulted. If your veterinarian cannot recommend a breeder, there are magazines such as *Dogs in Canada* and *Cat Fancier* that list the breeders of different types of dogs and cats, as well as their general breed characteristics. Even if a breeder in your area does not currently have any animals, he or she might know of someone else who does. Professional breeders generally take pride in their animals, and will only consider prospective purchasers who demonstrate an intention and ability to provide good homes for their pets. Some people are reluctant to approach a breeder because they fear the price of a pet will be excessive. Although the price may be a little higher, an animal obtained from a breeder usually conforms more closely to the breed standards and, more importantly, is almost always healthier (and, therefore, ultimately less expensive) than one purchased at a pet shop.

Some people with pets to give away or sell place notices in stores and newspapers. If you are interested in a pet from a private home, visit the family and observe the surroundings and the condition of *all* the animals. Do they seem happy and healthy? Do not accept a puppy or kitten that appears sickly just because you feel sorry for it. Even if you are offered an ill animal for free, be aware that this may be a costly and heartbreaking acquisition, although it might ultimately be rewarding.

The local humane society or animal shelter is another possible source for your chosen pet. These animals are often there on "borrowed time" and you definitely will feel a tugging on your heartstrings as you gaze into the animals' hopeful eyes, knowing that if they do not find a home shortly, they will miss the opportunity to live a full life. Many shelters have adult dogs that are already housebroken and trained. This can be a real advantage—just ask anyone who has lived through a puppy's "chewing stage"!

One cautionary point about adoptions from animal shelters. Remember that these pets have no history—that is, no one knows for sure their breed compositions, or more importantly, the type of life experiences they have had before coming to the shelter. However, in my experience, most animals that have been adopted from animal shelters have become wonderful and loving pets.

You might also telephone your veterinary office to see if they know of any animals available for adoption. Sometimes veterinarians know of litters of puppies or kittens ready to leave their mothers, or even adult cats and dogs that are available for a variety of reasons—perhaps because their owners are moving or someone in the family has developed allergies. Occasionally, when seeing-eye dogs or police dogs are retired from service, private caring homes are sought for their twilight years. After years of devoted service, these animals deserve special homes. A call to your local Institute for the Blind or police force might allow you the chance to share your life and home with a retired service animal.

Puppies and kittens are also available at pet stores. Too often, these animals come from puppy or kitten "mills" or "farms," where the adult females are bred every time they come into heat and the litters are raised in crowded, stressful, and often unsanitary conditions with poor nutrition. As soon as they are old enough to be weaned, the young animals are given their first vaccinations and packed into a small kennel for transportation to a distant pet store. Puppy mill animals often have genetic, congenital, or other health problems that emerge later on in life. Often the breeding animals are selected not for their temperament or physical characteristics, but rather for the number of offspring they can produce. The puppies may be incubating a serious disease such as parvovirus or distemper. Although a puppy or kitten obtained from an animal shelter might also have medical problems, in my experience these animals are in better condition than those obtained from pet stores supplied by puppy and kitten mills.

If a particular breed is suddenly increasing in popularity, the puppy farms will try to produce more of these animals as quickly as possible (sometimes by inbreeding), resulting in a greater chance of physical or personality problems. Several years ago, I started to see a number of Cocker Spaniel puppies that were quite neurotic and difficult to handle. Sure enough, they had been purchased at pet shops supplied by puppy mills! More recently, many Bichon Frise puppies have exhibited undesirable behavioral traits, such as excessive nervousness or snapping.

If you are considering buying an animal from a pet store, insist on an assurance that the animal has not come from a mill. In addition, find out what type of guarantee comes with your purchase. You should be able to have your new pet thoroughly examined within forty-eight hours of purchase by a veterinarian of your choice and returned for a full refund if the animal is found to be unhealthy. Some pet stores may offer to pay for a visit to a veterinarian of *their* choice. If the doctor is paid by the pet store, there is a conflict of interest, making it unlikely that he or she will recommend that the puppy or kitten be returned, even if major medical or congenital problems are discovered. For this reason it is illegal in many jurisdictions for the pet store to specify which veterinarian must be consulted for a prepaid checkup.

Another obvious way to acquire a pet is to adopt a stray or "foundling" animal. Often at the end of the summer, pets that have been cared for in cottage country will be abandoned because the family is unwilling to bring them back home and commit to caring for them further. This is despicable. Clients once brought me a young cat that they saw tossed from a car as they were waiting for a bus; they decided to adopt it. Such animals need and deserve a good home.

Animals sometimes find their own way into your life. At my first clinic we often kept the front door open when the weather was warm. One afternoon I heard some strange meowing in the cat ward. Sitting on top of the bank of kennels and demanding food and attention was a lovely orange cat that had wandered into the clinic. My assistant adopted "Scruffy" and gave him a good home. On another occasion, I went to a friend's house to give the first vaccinations to a litter of nine Bouvier/Old English Sheepdog puppies. I couldn't resist the temptation to adopt one of them, and that is how Aimée joined our family.

Choosing the Individual Pet for You

Selecting a pet should be governed by more than simple chance if you are fortunate enough to be choosing from a litter of animals. Certain personality traits will become evident if you watch the interaction of the puppies or kittens, both with each other and with you. Some animals are, by breed and personality, more dominant than others. A dominant individual will push the others away from the food. It will climb over its littermates and begin growling at them at an early age. A more submissive individual will give way and back down from the dominant one. The submissive puppy or kitten will roll over and bare its belly, or it may crawl away rather than walk.

The degree of dominant or submissive behavior that is desired will depend upon your circumstances and needs, and the relevant factors are similar to those described earlier in the discussion of breed types. Puppies that exhibit an even balance of both dominant and submissive behavior are usually quite easy to train, and are therefore suitable for most households, including those with children, senior citizens, and people with disabilities. A submissive puppy, on the other hand, will need to be trained using very gentle methods and much positive reinforcement. This puppy could be suitable for a quiet household.

In choosing a puppy or kitten from a litter, you should first sit quietly and watch all the animals interacting with each other. As a general rule, you do not want to adopt the pet that is shyly huddled by itself in the corner of the room. Nor should you want the one that is bullying the others. Hold each animal on your lap and watch its reaction—avoid the one that immediately resists and tries to jump down. The one that seems most comfortable is probably the best one for you.

A very effective personality test involves turning the young dog or cat onto its back in your hands. This is a submissive posture and reflects how the animal will relate to you as the head of the family. The pet that is quite complacent in this position will probably turn out to be a "people-oriented" animal, anxious to recognize you as someone in control who can be trusted. If the pet struggles incessantly and won't stay on its back, it has a strong stubborn streak. This animal will try to rule the household and there is a good chance that it will be difficult to handle. I always conduct this personality test in my office the first time I am introduced to a new kitten or puppy. I warn the clients if I suspect that the animal will be difficult to handle and, unfortunately for the clients, I have seldom been wrong. I relied on this quick test to help me pick my dog Aimée from her littermates, and it worked perfectly.

Choosing a Name

Once you have selected your pet, you should give it a name. In my practice I find that most of my patients have been named before they meet me. However, one time a client had not as yet named her cat. I remarked that the animal was a "No Name," and that is the label that stuck! On another occasion, when I said it was a no name, the client replied, "As in generic," and "Generic" became the cat's name. Another client with two unnamed cats then decided to call them "Gen" and "Eric." The name chosen for your pet may reflect the aspirations you have for your new friend. This can be seen in the "regal" names such as Duke, Baron, Queenie, Princess, etc., or in naming the pet "Baby." A deceased pet may be memorialized in the name of a new pet. For example, when a Sheltie named "Tuppence" died, her family named a new Sheltie puppy "Tuppence Two," which soon became abbreviated to "Tupptou." Some names are chosen because they appeal to the client's sense of humor: a cat named "Mouse" or "Monkey," a black cat named "Snowball," or a dog named "Fluffy" or "Turtle." Other names can be derived from the cartoons: Bart, Dawg; or from the movies: Tramp, Benji, Lassie. People sometimes like to play with the spelling of the pet's name: "Bartholo-mew" for a cat, or "Phydeau" for a dog. I have seen pet names derived from the names of the owners: "Dami" from David and Michelle, "Shenin" from Sheldon and Nina.

Some people feel that even if they cannot afford an expensive car, they can still have a pet called "Porsche" or "Mercedes"! Pairs of names are often amusing, such as "Remy" and "Martin," "Chip" and "Dale," or "Sonny" and "Cher." Some animals are named after sports celebrities or entertainers, like "Babe Ruth" or "Elvis." Others are named after well-known fiction characters, such as "Rhett" and "Scarlett," or "Lucy" and "Ricky." Breeds of animals that have their origins in certain countries are often named to reflect their heritage. For example, Dachshunds named "Hans," "Heidi," or "Krista"; Poodles called "Mimi," "Fifi," or "Bébé"; Scottish Terriers called "Meghan"; Old English Sheepdogs named "Dudley" or "Higgins"; Borzois called "Nakita" or "Tolstoy"; Bouviers called "Beau"; Afghan dogs named "Omar" or "Sharif"; and, of course, Siamese cats named "Sushi," "Chang," or "Tao."

Your pet's name may result from lengthy family discussions or a spontaneous decision. Whatever the method, remember that your pet will have its name for the rest of its life, so be sure you are pleased with your selection!

3

Protecting Your Pet From Harm

Outdoor Perils

Many families allow their cats and dogs to roam at large outdoors, exposing them to many dangers. Some people argue that keeping a cat exclusively indoors is unnatural; I disagree. It is far more "unnatural" for a pet to be hit by a car or suffer other types of injuries. I also do not believe that a dog should be tied up in a backyard or shut out of the house on a small balcony for hours on end. Similarly, a cat does not deserve to be locked out. When I walk my dog, I frequently see cats huddled on window ledges or outside the front doors of their homes, meowing pitifully to be allowed inside to escape the cold of winter.

For the sake of safety, dogs should always be walked on a leash. A dog that is walked without a leash might run across the road if it sees a squirrel, a cat, or another dog, and be hit by a car. There are very few, if any, exceptional dogs that never break training under any circumstances. Why take a chance? Remember, accidents are never supposed to happen, but they do, resulting in serious injuries or death for the pet, and unforgettable grief for the owner.

Other Animals

Other animals are a major source of harm for pets that are allowed to go outside unsupervised. Dogs frequently fight with other dogs. When a large dog picks up and shakes a smaller one, it may cause severe injury to the latter's internal organs, as well as painful separation of the skin from the underlying body wall muscle. Even if only a small puncture wound is visible, the damage caused by the separation of the skin from the muscle layer can be very extensive. Surgery is required to clean and disinfect the underlying tissue and reattach the area of separation.

Roaming dogs and cats run the risk of injury from wild animals, such as porcupines, skunks, raccoons, snakes, and even toads. I remember one client who would bring in his two Saint Bernard dogs every few weeks, loaded with porcupine quills. The dogs never seemed to learn from these painful encounters to avoid such animals. Finally, the family decided to fence in their acreage in an effort to keep the dogs away from the porcupines. Unfortunately, even after the fence was erected, the dogs still occasionally managed to get their faces full of quills!

Porcupine quills are usually embedded in the dog's legs, paws, nostrils, skin near the eyes, and even around the mouth and in the tongue. A general anesthetic, or at least heavy sedation, is needed to allow the doctor to remove the quills. Each quill must be seized with forceps and gently pulled out. If a quill breaks off and disappears beneath the skin, it is lost and cannot be removed until it works its way back up to the surface.

Anyone whose animal has been sprayed by a skunk will attest to the difficulty of removing the scent from the pet. The skunk's spray is also very irritating to the eyes. The suggested methods of removing skunk odor are discussed in Chapter 8, "Grooming Your Pet."

Although Coonhound paralysis is a poorly understood neurological condition affecting hunting dogs, in most cases there is a history of a raccoon bite. Generally, there is a weakness in the hind legs that may progress to the entire body so that the animal is unable to move. Often the dog cannot even lift its head, and may have difficulty swallowing and a change in the bark. If the dog does not die from respiratory paralysis, with supportive nursing care it may completely recover in three weeks to three months, although recurrences are possible.

Toad poisoning occurs in dogs and cats that attack and bite—or even just "mouth"—two species of *Bufo* toads. While all toads secrete substances that are repulsive to animals that mouth them, *Bufo* toads secrete a particularly poisonous chemical that mimics the heart drug digitalis. The signs produced include copious drooling, difficulty breathing, and convulsions. Signs develop within a few minutes following contact, and death can occur in as little as fifteen minutes. Treatment consists of washing the animal's mouth with an abundance of water, and administering drugs to reduce salivation, to control convulsions, and to counteract the effects on the heart.

The danger of your pet contracting rabies is very real in areas where rabies is present in wildlife, including foxes, bats, and skunks, as most rabid wild animals lose their natural fear and will approach humans and other animals.

Frequently, a cat will develop infected bites and scratches after defending its territory against other cats. Such abscesses usually must be treated by a veterinarian.

Outdoor cats are often chased up trees by dogs. It might take hours before the cat ventures back down, and it might get seriously injured if it falls or comes into contact with hydro-electric wires.

Humans

Unfortunately, free-roaming pets are exposed to dangers from another species of animal, namely, humans. Roaming cats, as well as dogs that are left unattended outside of stores, are frequently stolen. When this happened just before Christmas to a very unique-looking Siberian Husky dog that had an eye problem, the owner enlisted the assistance of the local Toronto media, stressing that without special eye drops, the dog would go blind. Happily, the dog was returned in time for the holidays. Tragically, most pet owners whose animals are stolen are not as fortunate.

Although animals can slip out accidentally, I feel that leaving them outside unsupervised is irresponsible; there is a good chance that the pet might never return home. Even if the pet is not stolen, it might wander off and get disoriented and lost. If the pet is lucky, it will get adopted as a foundling by a loving, caring family, although the original owner will forever be left wondering what happened. If it is wearing some identification, it might be returned home, but this is rare.

We have all heard stories of pets returning home after a long disappearance. Cats and dogs have been known to take months to travel vast distances back to their previous homes if the family has moved. Unfortunately, these instances are infrequent; in the vast majority of cases, an animal that goes missing is never seen by its family again.

The Environment

The outdoor environment is full of dangers for cats and dogs out on their own. For instance, the pet might eat rotten food or garbage, as well as poisonous materials, set out either by accident or malice. The pet will usually experience vomiting and diarrhea from eating rotten food. If your dog has eaten something unknown while it was outside, feed it several slices of bread until it can be examined by a veterinarian. If the dog ate a bone, the bread should coat it, preventing any sharp points from damaging the stomach. If a large amount of fat was eaten, the bread will lessen the chance of it being absorbed. But remember to check with your veterinarian even before symptoms of illness develop. The dangers of ingesting foreign objects is discussed further in this chapter, in the section entitled "Indoor Perils."

Most rodent-control products, as well as many insecticides and weed-control chemicals, can be harmful to pets. Metaldehyde, or "slug bait," is a poison that is commonly used to kill garden snails and slugs. Unfortunately, dogs are also attracted to the bait, which contains a toxin affecting the nervous system. The symptoms begin with lack of coordination and a slight degree of muscle tremor. Within one to two hours, the muscle tremor may worsen to a point that the dog cannot stand, and it may have convulsions. Usually it will have to be anesthetized for twelve to seventy-two hours to control the muscle spasms; this also gives the veterinarian an opportunity to wash any remaining poison out of the dog's stomach. Dogs normally recover from metaldehyde poisoning with no signs of residual damage. Cats do not seem to be attracted to slug bait.

Another serious outdoor threat to your pet is environmental temperature extremes. Dogs tied up outside in the hot summer weather are very susceptible to heatstroke. Even if you leave your dog in the shade, the sun moves across the sky during the day, and your pet may soon be in the blazing heat of the sun. It is even more dangerous to leave a pet in a parked car on a warm day, even with the window open, as the temperature inside the car can rise very rapidly. A breeder of West Highland White Terrier dogs once brought a litter of puppies to my office for their first vaccinations. She didn't mention that she had left an adult dog in the car. After the puppies were vaccinated, we enjoyed playing with them in the office for a short while. When the breeder returned to the car, she found her older dog in a state of collapse from heatstroke.

The symptoms of heatstroke, namely, rapid panting, a staring expression, and fever—which may rise as high as 43°C (110°F)— develop very quickly. Both the force and rate of the heartbeat are increased, and as the condition progresses, the dog will have difficulty breathing, and vomiting may occur. If not treated promptly, heatstroke is fatal. Rapid and heroic measures are necessary if the dog is to be saved, since body temperatures above 41°C (106°F) can be tolerated for only a few minutes before severe damage to the nervous and circulatory systems will occur. The quickest way to reduce a dangerously high body temperature is to plunge the dog into ice-water. The next best treatment is to spray the animal with cold water and place it in front of a large electric fan. Ice packs applied to the head may also be effective.

Close attention must be paid as the body temperature is lowered. It should be stopped when it reaches 39.5°C (103°F), as further cooling may be followed by a subnormal temperature. The patient should be closely watched for twelve to twenty-four hours, as collapse or coma may occur after cooling, indicating irreversible brain damage. I have treated three Husky dogs, among other breeds, for heat-stroke, and one of them began convulsing the day after its temperature had been stabilized. Unfortunately, it passed away shortly afterwards in spite of continuing treatment.

Extremely cold temperatures will cause hypothermia in a dog that has not been acclimatized to gradually lowering outdoor temperatures. If a dog has been kept outdoors for prolonged periods during the fall, the cool temperatures will stimulate the growth of a thick coat and a layer of fat beneath the skin, enabling it to withstand cooler weather. However, it is still very important to provide an outdoor dog with shelter from the wind. A dog that is used to being indoors cannot withstand long periods outdoors in cold weather.

Cats that are left outdoors for prolonged periods in very cold weather may get frostbitten ears. Usually, the affected tips of the ears will turn hard and leathery, and may become curled, or even fall off. The frostbitten tissue may also become infected. Your veterinarian will determine whether soothing ointments should be applied to such areas.

Unneutered male dogs that are forced to lie outside on the snow for long periods of time often get frostbitten scrotums. If this skin irritation is severe, soothing antibiotic balms may be necessary to prevent infection.

Swimming pools pose another potential danger to your pet. The slippery sides make it very difficult for an animal that has fallen into the water to get out of the pool. It is even more serious when an animal falls into a pool that is covered with a vinyl blanket; the animal can easily slip underneath the edge of the blanket and drown. A cat was brought to my office one time during the winter after its family fortunately saw it slip beneath the pool cover. The cat was suffering from shock and severe hypothermia, but we were able to save it by gradually warming it up.

In extremely hot or cold weather, cats like to sleep under the hood of a car, often on top of the engine block. In cold weather, the engine of a recently driven car will provide some warmth. In warm summer weather, the metal engine block will be cool if the car has not been used for a while. The danger occurs when the engine is suddenly started with the cat lying on the engine block; the moving fan and fan belt will severely injure the cat. You can prevent this type of accident by getting into the habit of knocking loudly on the hood of the car before you start the engine. The cat will be startled by the noise and run away.

In the winter, salt is often used to melt snow and ice from the roads and sidewalks. Many dogs will show signs of sore paws shortly after walking through a patch of salt. Some small dogs will refuse to move any farther. In my experience, dogs with very little fur between the pads on their paws are affected by salt much more than dogs with a lot of fur between the pads. The fur seems to protect the pads from actual contact with the salt.

If your dog's feet are sensitive to salt, try to walk it along the edge of the sidewalk or on the snow. When your pet comes inside, wipe its paws gently with a damp cloth. You can also purchase rubber boots to protect your dog's feet from the snow, ice, and salt. Some styles of boots fall off easily, but there are some with straps over the dog's back to keep the boots in place. To accustom your dog to wearing boots, let it walk around the house in them, while you praise it profusely.

Some owners protect their dogs from the cold with a T-shirt or a coat. A large Dachshund was brought to my office one cold winter day dressed in a fleece jogging suit, complete with attached hood! I am sure that these winter clothes are beneficial to short-haired dogs, and most seem to enjoy wearing them. Purchase clothing for your dog that is easy to put on the animal. Velcro straps and fastening strips are very useful to hold the coat in place, and they make the task of dressing the dog quite simple.

There are many mechanical injuries that can afflict pets. They can get their tails caught in doors. I have seen cats that have had their legs or tails caught in wildlife traps. Cats have been injured by lawn mowers. Bullet wounds are not uncommon in stray dogs and cats. I often wonder how many of these injuries are accidental and how many are deliberately caused by malicious, sick people.

Automobiles are a source of peril to animals on the street. Although cats and dogs can run across the street at high speed, they are frequently struck by cars. The injuries resulting from a car accident may be minor, just stunning the animal for a brief moment, or they may be extensive and potentially fatal. An injured animal might lie by the roadside or it might crawl off to a sheltered area where it won't be found in time to save its life.

When Your Pet is Lost

You should have a contingency plan to follow if your pet disappears. But first, unless it was actually seen running away, be certain that it is, in fact, gone. Close all the windows and doors and then thoroughly check the entire house. The mere fact that a door has been left open does not necessarily mean that the pet has run away; it might be sleeping under a bed!

Have posters and fliers made, including an up-to-date picture of your pet and a complete description. Some people suggest adding the words "needs medication," to motivate a person who finds the pet to contact you rather than keep it.

Post the fliers on telephone poles, convenience store windows, bulletin boards in grocery stores and laundromats, and anywhere else you can think of. Ask local schools if they will post the flier on their bulletin boards—children often see stray animals at school playgrounds.

Contact the animal control agency and local humane society. Remember that many people, even some workers in animal shelters, may not be experts on various breeds. Is it a Papillon or a large Maltese, a Norwegian Elkhound or a Husky, a Border Collie or a mongrel? Remember, too, that some people's descriptions of an animal's coat color may vary considerably from yours. The average person may not be familiar with terms such as "brindle," "merle," "ticked," or "harlequin." If an animal that even remotely fits the description of your pet has been picked up, go and check it out. If there is more than one humane society in your area, contact all of them. One family in Toronto kept checking with the animal control agency in the area where they lived, but, unfortunately, their dog had been found in a neighboring area and they were not reunited with their pet.

Contact local animal hospitals, as a veterinarian might have treated your pet for an injury. If the animal was adopted by someone, it might have been taken to the nearest animal clinic for a checkup. Post a flier in veterinary offices; other pet owners might be sympathetic and watch for your missing animal.

Check with radio stations about airing a "missing pet" bulletin. Place ads in the "Lost and Found" section of local newspapers. Be sure to keep watching the "found" column in case someone advertises your pet. Ask your letter carrier, neighbors, storekeepers, and police to keep an eye out for your missing pet in their travels around your neighborhood.

If you advertise a reward, it might be prudent not to mention the amount. If it is generous, a person might try to convince you that he or she has found your pet. If your animal was stolen, the thief may weigh the amount you are offering against the price for which the pet could be sold elsewhere.

Are there any circumstances that might make your pet's disappearance into a human interest story? Sobbing tots, ailing owner, unusual cat or dog—these factors might persuade the local newspaper to publish a feature story, which always is more interesting to the general public than simple "lost pet" ads. The fact that the Husky referred to earlier in this chapter disappeared during the Christmas season and would go blind if it did not receive its eye drops sparked the media attention that led to the dog's return.

If your pet is a registered purebred, check with the local kennel club and other groups supporting your pet's specific breed. Many people inform these organizations if they have found a purebred animal.

Continue to check with the animal pound and humane societies. Pets have turned up many months, or even years, later. If you do find your lost pet, please notify the animal shelters, veterinary clinics, and other organizations you had previously contacted.

Preventing a loss is better than searching for your pet. Ensure that the gate or pen is locked before your dog is let outside. One evening, I did not notice that the electricity meter-reader had left the back gate open; when I put my dog outside, intending to leave it in the backyard for a few minutes, it went for a walk by itself. Luckily, it returned home unharmed several hours later.

Your pet should always wear an identification tag such as a city license or a rabies tag. Engrave your telephone number on the back of the tag in case the record office is closed at the time someone finds your pet. Some pet collars have small pockets for the owner's name, address, and telephone number.

Cats that go outside should wear identification collars that are elastic or "break-away." If these collars get caught on a tree branch, they will unravel or stretch, allowing the cat to escape. The collar and identification will be lost but there is no danger that your cat might be strangled or remain trapped by its collar.

Even an indoor cat should wear a collar with some identification, just in case it escapes outside. Adjust the collar so that you are able to fit one finger between the collar and the animal's neck. I have seen loose collars slip into a pet's mouth while remaining around the animal's neck. If this were to happen while you were not at home, the pet would be extremely uncomfortable and distressed.

Many purebred dogs have been tattooed with a number by the breeder in an ear or on a flank. If the tattoo is legible, make sure you have a copy of it at home. Many municipalities have tattoo programs carried out by veterinarians. Ask your veterinarian about the availability of this method of identification. I once found a beautiful Himalayan cat at a construction site near my home. Fortunately, it had a tattoo in its ear; it took just a few telephone calls to find out who had the appropriate records and to contact the grateful owner.

An increasingly popular way to identify animals is by implanting a microchip beneath the pet's skin on the left side of the neck. This relatively simple technique, which has no side effects, is being endorsed by many humane societies. Most veterinary offices and animal control agencies have scanners that can read the electronic information number contained within the microchip. This information is fed into a 24-hour retrieval network and the owner can then be contacted (the owner must keep the network apprised of his/her current address and telephone number). Unfortunately, there is no way of knowing in advance that the pet has a microchip; everyone involved with stray animals must get into the habit of scanning each and every animal for a microchip. Hopefully, some time soon, every animal that has been implanted with a microchip will have a universally recognized identifier (such as an "M" tattoo in the left ear), to alert the finder to the existence of the microchip.

If you really care about your pet, do not let it go outside without a leash. Domesticated dogs and cats are not equipped to cope with the many perils of the great outdoors, and they depend on their owners to act in their best interests. Please don't let them down!

Indoor Perils

Although there are many risks of danger to an animal outdoors, perils exist for pets even within the confines of the home. As with young children, animals can get into serious mischief in unexpected ways. Remember, prevention is more effective than treatment. Look carefully around your home and think of everything and anything that your pet could possibly get into, and take steps to prevent accidents, illness, and tragedy.

"High-Rise Syndrome"

"High-rise syndrome" occurs when indoor cats attempt to become outdoor cats by venturing out onto apartment balconies or window ledges. Their families explain: "I told him not to jump"; "When he fell two weeks ago he didn't get hurt" (this time he fractured a leg); "He never fell from the balcony before." I am always dumbfounded by the apparent lack of concern of some pet owners, and this sentiment is surpassed only by a profound feeling of sadness for the unfortunate animal whose family could have easily prevented a terrible accident.

You should assume that if your cat is allowed onto the balcony, sooner or later it is going to attempt jumping up onto the railing. Any family that really cares about its pet *must* "cat-proof" the balcony by installing fencing or netting from floor to ceiling to keep the pet confined while allowing access to fresh air. Some of my clients have held their cats over the edge of the balcony and made them look up and down, thinking the cats would perceive their precarious position and be very careful to stay away from the edge. Only time will tell if this actually works, but I would not advise anyone to rely on this method of teaching such an important lesson to a cat.

Cats can fall from apartment windows when the screens are removed for cleaning. One family saw their cat jump from the floor right up and through the open window; to the owner it seemed as if the cat was committing suicide. It must be devastating to witness such a tragic and unnecessary accident.

The damage to high-rise syndrome cats is extremely variable. Some cats that have fallen from a height of six or seven storeys have received only minor injuries, while others have sustained considerable internal damage and broken bones. Of course, some variability is due to the type of landing surface. Bushes, soggy flower beds, or tall grass may break the animal's fall and prevent substantial injury, whereas a concrete surface can cause severe injury or death. The distance of the fall is also important. Strange as it may seem, if a cat falls from a relatively short height—for example, four or five floors—it might be more severely injured than if it falls from a height of seven or eight floors. A longer fall gives the cat time to land feet-first, as well as allowing it to arch its body and spread its limbs to act like a parachute, slowing it down to some degree.

Another way in which indoor cats can end up outdoors was related to me by a client whose indoor cat repeatedly developed abscesses from fighting with other cats. As there were no other cats in the home, I could not understand how it was finding adversaries. The family explained that when the cat was allowed to roam the hallway, it would sit in front of the elevator. When the elevator door would open, the cat would venture inside and get off on the ground floor, where it would go right out the front door! The mystery was solved. Neighbors would see the cat outside and bring it back to its family, complete with fresh wounds from fighting with street cats.

Electrical Wires

Although all indoor pets are surrounded by different types of perils, it is usually the younger animals that get into mischief. Kittens and puppies are attracted to wires, including electrical, telephone, and cable television wires. While an animal can be electrocuted while chewing through electrical wires, more commonly it will receive a strong electric shock and suffer a mouth burn; sometimes the electric shock will cause severe difficulty in breathing. If you suspect that your pet has received an electric shock, you should have it examined by a veterinarian right away.

The best way to prevent such injury is to remove the temptation. If you cannot conceal the wires, there are several deterrent products available in pet stores to prevent biting and chewing. Cats usually avoid the smell of citrus products; try rubbing citrus peel onto the electrical wires. You could also add some black pepper, tabasco sauce, or cayenne pepper to petroleum jelly and spread this paste on objects to deter cats and dogs from chewing or playing with them.

Swallowing Foreign Objects

"Foreign objects" refers to nonfood items that are dangerous when swallowed by a dog or cat. Symptoms such as vomiting, lack of appetite, depression, and abdominal discomfort may indicate that the pet has swallowed a foreign object. An x-ray will reveal a metallic or bony object directly, as well as a distended intestine or an unusual gas pattern caused by other objects invisible on an x-ray.

Among the objects that I have removed from pets' digestive tracts are: coins, washers, erasers, thumbtacks, needles, rocks, pieces of bark, pipe cleaners, twist ties, pieces of toys, pieces of corn cob, and pieces of glass from broken light bulbs. In one memorable case, a dog swallowed some bread dough that had been set aside to rise before baking. I gave the dog a chemical to make it vomit the large mound of dough, which had already begun to rise in the stomach!

Animals sometimes help themselves to items from the garbage, either inside the home or outside in the street. A few times each year, a dog or cat is brought to my office because it is reluctant to eat, and has been pawing at its mouth. An examination may reveal a small chicken bone or a small flat rib bone wedged against the roof of its mouth. If the animal is cooperative, the bone can be removed without too much difficulty.

Another source of temptation (and trouble), particularly for cats, is thread or fine string. Thread often gets caught beneath the animal's tongue when it is swallowed. Sometimes we are lucky enough to notice the string wrapped around the back of the cat's tongue, although often it will be too deeply embedded in the tissue. On x-ray, the intestine usually appears bunched up like an accordion. The motion of the intestine causes the thread to cut into the intestinal lining, greatly weakening or actually perforating it. This causes the cat to vomit every time it eats. Even if the veterinarian is fortunate enough to be able to cut the thread in the cat's mouth, it is rarely possible to pull out the remainder by hand; the thread is gripped too tightly by the intestinal lining. Delicate intestinal surgery is required to remove all the thread.

If the cat has swallowed all of the thread, leaving none wrapped around its tongue, the thread may become embedded in the lining of the intestine, which will cause vomiting. Again, surgery is necessary to remove the thread from the intestine.

Cats do not necessarily learn from such an experience. I operated on one feline patient to remove some thread it had pulled from the back of a scatter rug. A few months later, it developed the same symptoms. Surgery was performed again and this time I removed thin strands of elastic, which had come from the material used to hold hockey pads in place!

There are times when an owner has seen a sewing needle in the back of a cat's mouth. Sometimes I have been able to grasp the needle with an instrument and remove it, but sometimes it slips down the cat's throat. I take a cautious approach in treating a cat that has swallowed a needle. After assuring myself that no thread is caught in the cat's mouth, I feed it a bulky meal in the hospital. I follow the progress of the needle through the digestive system by taking repeated x-rays. Within twenty-four to forty-eight hours, the needle will usually be found in the stool. If, at any time, the x-rays show that the needle is not progressing, I perform immediate surgery to remove it.

Appliances

Household appliances such as microwave ovens and clothes dryers are very dangerous for pets that might be curious enough to venture inside them. Make sure that a playful kitten or puppy has not jumped inside the dryer while you are putting clothes into it. Be certain that children are clearly instructed never to dry a wet cat or dog in either appliance; a microwave oven is lethal within seconds and a dryer can cause severe injury or death within minutes.

Keep your pet away from the stove when you are cooking. If you are inattentive for even a second, an animal could burn itself while sampling food that is cooking, or it could be injured by knocking over a hot frying pan or pot.

Don't get into the habit of leaving the refrigerator door ajar. A curious kitten could easily venture inside and be trapped when you shut the door.

Houseplants

Some cats seem to require the extra fiber provided by grass to help them vomit a hairball, or to help them have regular bowel movements. Grass seed purchased at pet stores can be grown at home for a cat.

Houseplants can be dangerous for pets, particularly cats that like to chew on the leaves, stems, and flowers. Curious young pets are more likely to chew plants, particularly during the teething stage, than are adult animals. Most plants will cause vomiting, although sometimes plant material will just pass through the digestive system and be excreted in the stool.

The sap from some plants, including dumb cane, *Poinciana*, and poinsettia, is irritating to the cat's mouth and will cause excessive drooling or mouth sores. The leaf blade of rhubarb is toxic and the foliage of potato and tomato plants can produce severe stomach upsets. The iris also causes severe irritation of the digestive system, while foxglove, oleander, and lily of the valley contain chemicals affecting the heart. *Rhododendron* and *Amaryllis* can cause nausea, vomiting, abdominal pain, and diarrhea.

The nervous system is affected by other plants in many different ways. Marijuana and morning glory contain hallucinogens. The chinaberry tree and yellow jasmine cause convulsions. Belladonna, deadly nightshade, and jasmine can produce a rapid increase in body temperature, causing collapse. Cats are extremely attracted to spider plants, which can be hallucinogenic if the leaves are chewed. After my cat would munch on a spider plant leaf, it would sit and stare at things that were not there!

In my experience, plants can cause other problems in cats, even if this has not been reported in the current literature. A client once told me that her cat had undergone a personality change; it became very aggressive, persisted in attacking her feet, and was no longer the nice cat that it used to be. She was even considering having it euthanized. My questioning disclosed that the only recent change in the household had been the introduction of a new exotic green plant, the name of which she did not know. Even though no one saw the cat eating the leaves, I suggested that the plant be removed on a trial basis; once the plant was removed, the cat's behavior returned to normal.

Another client's kitten was having very loose, foul-smelling stools. All the usual tests, diet changes, and medications did not improve its digestion. The owner finally noticed that the kitten was nibbling on a green plant (again, the client was not familiar with the type of plant). Although I told her that plants usually cause vomiting rather than diarrhea, she decided to remove the plant from the kitten's reach; its stools improved almost immediately. This was confirmed shortly thereafter when the kitten succeeded in sneaking into the room with the plant and the digestive problem recurred.

Following is a list of potentially harmful plants that are often found in homes and gardens. These plants must be avoided if there are cats in your home (dogs, once past the teething stage, rarely chew on plants). Even if just parts of a plant (bark, leaves, berries, and so on) might be poisonous, this list rules out the entire plant.

Common Plants Poisonous to Cats

Alocasia	Bayonet	Bleeding heart	Cactus
Amaryllis	Beargrass	Bloodroot	*Caladium*
Apricot	Belladonna	Bluebonnet	Castor bean
Arrowgrass	Bird-of-paradise	Boxwood	Cherry
Avocado	Bittersweet	Buckeyes	Chinaberry
Azalea	Black-eyed Susan	Burning bush	Christmas rose
Baneberry	Black locust	Buttercup	*Chrysanthemum*

Clematis	Hellebore	Lupine	Rhubarb
Cornflower	Hemlock	Marigold	Rosary pea
Corydalis	Holly	Marijuana	Rubber plant
Crocus, autumn	Horsebeans	Mistletoe	Scotch broom
Crown-of-thorns	Horsebrush	Mock orange	Skunk cabbage
Cyclamen	Horse chestnuts	Monkshood	Snowdrops
Daffodil	Hyacinth	Morning glory	Snow-on-the-
Daphne	*Hydrangea*	Mountain laurel	mountain
Deadly night-	Iris	Mushrooms	Spider plant
shade	Ivy	*Narcissus*	Staggerweed
Death camas	Jack-in-the-pulpit	Nightshade	Star of
Delphinium	Jasmine	Oleander	Bethlehem
Dicentra	Java beans	Peach	Sweet pea
Dumb cane	Jerusalem cherry	Peony	Tansy mustard
Eggplant	Jessamine	*Philodendron*	Tobacco
Elderberry	Jimson weed	Pimpernel	Tomato
Elephant's ear	Jonquil	*Poinciana*	Tulip
Euonymus	Jungle trumpets	Poinsettia	Tung tree
Evergreen	*Lantana*	Poison ivy	Virginia creeper
Ferns	Larkspur	Poison oak	Weeping fig
Flax	Laurel	Pokeweed	Wild call
Four o'clock	Lily	Poppy	*Wisteria*
Foxglove	Lily, spider	Potato	Yellow jasmine
Golden glow	Lily of the valley	Privet, common	
Gopher purge	Locoweed	*Rhododendron*	

Household Chemicals, Medicines, and Foods

Household chemicals can be very harmful to pets. For example, if your cat walks through some detergent or bleach that has been spilled on the floor, its skin may be burned. Then it will lick off the substance as it grooms itself, and probably become ill. There might be severe irritation or burning of the mouth, vomiting, or diarrhea. Turpentine is also very irritating to the skin and must not be used to remove paint from an animal.

Lead poisoning, usually caused by the consumption of paint containing lead, affects both the digestive and nervous systems in dogs. Although most paints today no longer contain lead, I recently treated a dog that had chewed layers of paint from a door in a very old building. Lead causes intestinal muscle spasms and very pronounced abdominal pain, with the dog whining, being restless, and assuming abnormal positions. The nervous symptoms cause the dog to show extreme sudden excitement, running wildly about while barking continuously, followed by convulsions.

Left untreated, lead poisoning is often fatal, but, fortunately, effective therapy is available. Several drugs can be used to combine with the lead in the body to prevent its absorption and allow it to be excreted. Treatment must be carried on for several weeks. In the case I treated, the dog had a relapse after two weeks, and the treatment had to be continued for an additional two weeks.

Cats are rarely poisoned by lead since they are very selective eaters and seldom gnaw on or ingest nonfood substances. However, both dogs and cats are attracted by the sweet smell and taste of antifreeze (ethylene glycol), which is extremely poisonous. The ingestion of even a small quantity will cause rapid and severe irreparable damage to the kidneys. One spring, I treated a Collie whose kidneys had completely shut down after it drank water from the toilet in the family cabin before the toilet had been drained of antifreeze.

Another common household poison is warfarin, contained in rat or mouse bait. Warfarin interferes with the normal clotting of blood. The pet might be found dead with no previous signs of illness after suddenly bleeding to death internally. In less acute cases, some bleeding might be seen from the animal's nose, or from its gums after it has chewed its food, or there might be blood in the urine or stools.

There are several different active ingredients that can be found in rat poison, and the prognosis for your pet depends upon which product was swallowed. The name of the poison involved would be of great assistance to your veterinarian in initiating treatment. If you live in an apartment and your unit is being treated by an exterminator, let them know that you have a pet and find out exactly what product is being used and where it is being placed. One client let her dog play in the basement storage area of her building, not knowing that rat poison had been put down there. Fortunately, she saw the dog eat the bait and we were able to contact the pest control company to ascertain the chemical used and the best antidote.

A new nonpoisonous product that is used to catch mice is a very sticky pad coated with a substance to attract rodents. The mouse's mouth and paws stick to the pad and the animal eventually dies. Aside from being a very cruel way of eliminating rodents, this product can cause problems for pets. I once had to remove one of these pads when it became stuck to a curious cat's fur!

Food left unattended can be very tempting to a dog or cat, and they will sometimes go to great lengths to help themselves. One time when I was out of town and my cat Alistair was staying with neighbors, she knocked a defrosting chicken off the counter and onto the floor, where the two resident dogs were able to join her for a feast! Luckily, this time they only developed upset stomachs. The consequences could be much more serious, since bones can severely damage a pet. One of my clients left his dog in the car with a bag of groceries that he had just purchased, including a foil-wrapped barbecued chicken. Although he was gone only a few minutes, he returned to find that the dog had completely devoured the chicken—bones, wrapping, and all. The dog required intestinal surgery to remove the bones and foil wrapping.

Remove temptation. Don't even leave butter in an uncovered dish on a table or countertop—your pet will get an upset stomach from eating it. Make certain your garbage container is securely closed.

Chocolate is very harmful to dogs and cats and ingestion of even a small amount can cause convulsions and death. Other types of people-food, such as liquor, carbonated drinks, spicy foods, and sweets, can cause stomach upsets.

Some medicines for people can be harmful to animals. Cats and dogs are very sensitive to aspirin, which should be given only on the advice of a veterinarian. The pain reliever "acetaminophen" is poisonous to cats. Digitalis, whether for humans or prescribed for your pet, is very toxic if taken in larger than prescribed amounts for heart conditions.

4

Your Pet and Your Vet

Choosing a Veterinarian

One of the first things you must do after acquiring a pet is choose a veterinarian, and the best reference is by word of mouth. Ask your friends where they take their pets, if they are pleased with the service they receive, and whether they would recommend their veterinarian. As well, you must consider the location and hours of operation.

However, the most important factor is what I call the "comfort level": the degree to which the pet owner has confidence in, trusts, and feels a rapport with the veterinarian. Sometimes new clients visit my clinic and chat with me before bringing in their pets—this is a form of "comfort-level interview." Once a comfort level exists, many clients will continue to bring their pets to the same veterinarian even after moving a considerable distance from the animal hospital. These clients understand the importance of continuity and consistency in the medical care of their pets.

Some animal hospitals receive patients by appointment, while others have open clinic hours during which clients may "drop in" with their pets. While open clinic hours might be convenient, you can never predict how long you will have to wait to be seen. Some veterinarians run more than one practice, and use one office as a "feeder" clinic, transferring all hospitalized patients to a central facility. The location of this central facility is a relevant factor if you wish to visit your pet while it is being hospitalized.

Some clinics have only one veterinarian while others have several. In a multidoctor practice it might be easier to get an appointment and the hours of service might be longer than in a solo practice. However, a different doctor might treat your pet on each visit, and some people dislike this. Prior to engaging my services, a client left his cat for surgery in a multidoctor practice where he had been dealing with the same doctor for months. Unfortunately, the cat passed away in the hospital shortly after the surgery and the client was given the sad news by telephone from a veterinarian he had never met. This upset him, because he was left with the impression that his cat had not been cared for by the doctor he knew. In a solo practice, your pet will always be seen by the same doctor except when he or she is away, in which case there might be a "locum" or fill-in doctor on duty, or you may be referred to a nearby practice.

Ask your prospective veterinarian how after-hours emergencies are handled. Some veterinary hospitals are staffed twenty-four hours a day, some have a doctor "on call," and others refer after-hours urgent cases to an emergency clinic that is open only at night, on weekends, and on holidays. If you take your pet to an emergency clinic, bear in mind that you have no credit rating there and the staff do not know you. A significant deposit will probably be required before the pet is admitted, and payment in full must usually be made before the pet is discharged. The fees charged by emergency clinics are usually higher than those charged by regular veterinary offices; after all, the staff is being compensated for working all night, and the equipment is more sophisticated than at a regular daytime facility. When your pet is released from the emergency clinic, you will be given a report sheet to take to your regular veterinary office for follow-up care.

Some clients prefer the services of a house-call doctor. House-call veterinarians are equipped to examine, diagnose, treat, and vaccinate pets in your home. If surgery, hospitalization, or x-rays are required, the pet will be taken to a hospital with which the veterinarian is associated. House-call veterinarians are identified in the Yellow Pages of the telephone directory under "Veterinarians."

If you decide to use the services of a house-call veterinarian, have your pet ready at the appointed time and be prepared to assist the doctor with the examination. One time I made a house call to a small apartment where two cats needed to be vaccinated. When I arrived, however, only one cat came to greet me and the other could not be found. After the first cat was vaccinated, the owner and I spent twenty minutes searching for the elusive patient but to no avail. The client told me later that the cat had wedged itself behind some books in a bookcase!

Another time, when I arrived at a client's home to vaccinate one of his two cats, the client put the eight-kilogram (18-lb.) cat on the kitchen table. I showed him how to properly restrain the cat for the examination, but when I put my stethoscope to the cat's chest, it gave a little hiss, and the frightened owner jumped back, releasing the cat. The cat retreated to a corner and became extremely aggressive. Meanwhile, the other cat, who did not need vaccinations that day, came out of the bedroom and stood near us hissing as well! At that point I packed my supplies and wished the owner luck; if he could not control his cats in his own home, there was nothing further I could do. So, if you are using the services of a house-call veterinarian, make sure that your pet is confined before the doctor arrives.

In rural areas, many veterinarians operate "mixed" practices, treating horses and other farm animals in addition to cats and dogs. If you live in the city, you will probably bring your pet to an "exclusively small animal" practice; there are even "cat only" and "dog only" hospitals. The "small animal" designation includes all house pets, regardless of size. In other words, a small animal veterinarian will treat a Great Dane but not a small goat! Most small animal practitioners are "generalists" who deal with all aspects of your pet's health needs, just like family physicians in human medicine. There are times, however, when a pet's condition may require treatment from a doctor who has a high degree of skill and expertise in a specific field, such as internal medicine, ophthalmology, neurology, dermatology, orthopedics, reproduction, or animal behavior. Specialists work in veterinary schools and in private practices in large cities. Your regular veterinarian will monitor the follow-up care recommended by the specialist; close liaison between the two doctors will ensure a high quality of continuing health care for your pet.

The First Visit

You should take your pet to see a veterinarian within a day or two of adoption, to spot any serious problems before you become closely attached to the animal. I once examined a miniature Poodle that had just been purchased from a breeder. I casually pointed out that the puppy had a severe underbite, where the lower jaw extended far beyond the upper jaw. I had wrongly assumed that the breeder had made the client aware of this. The client was upset to learn of this deformity even though I tried to assure her that, aside from not being a show-quality puppy, the dog's quality of life would not be affected. The client could not be convinced; she said that she had recently undergone painful jaw surgery, and she could not bear to have a dog with a jaw problem! She returned the puppy to the breeder, who called me to express her extreme displeasure, stating that she had simply forgotten to mention the jaw condition to the purchaser, and that I should not have pointed it out. I explained that I had a duty to disclose *all* my findings to my clients; if at some point the purchaser had taken the dog to another veterinarian who mentioned the condition, it would have appeared that I hadn't thoroughly examined the puppy.

On another occasion I examined a Rottweiler puppy that had just been purchased from a breeder. My examination disclosed a heart murmur, probably due to a deformity that was congenital (present at birth), but without extensive testing I could not know the severity or prognosis for the condition. As the dog was intended to be a working dog, any type of heart problem would probably seriously affect its performance and longevity. The breeder immediately allowed the client to exchange the puppy for a healthy one.

At the pet's first visit to the veterinarian, it will be thoroughly checked for fleas, ear mites, respiratory infections, and other conditions that are best treated early, especially if there are other animals at home. The veterinarian will also review any vaccination certificates you may have and advise how to best schedule the remaining inoculations. All your questions regarding training, feeding, and proper care can be discussed at this visit. Write down your questions in advance so as not to forget any. If no vaccinations are due with this visit, the pet will experience a pleasant examination, lots of attention, perhaps a tasty treat to eat, and no needle jabs!

The Routine Physical Examination

When your pet is brought to the veterinary office for its annual vaccinations, it will also be given a brief but thorough physical examination. I begin my examination by checking the eyes and nose for clearness and discharges. I examine the mouth and note the condition of the lips, tongue, teeth, and gums. I feel the neck for any swellings, then look into each ear for evidence of discharge, parasites, or infection. I listen to the heart and lungs with a stethoscope, then feel the abdomen to assess the liver, kidneys, spleen, and various segments of the intestine. I feel the glands in the back of the knee and then check the external genitals. The skin and coat is then inspected for its general condition and for parasites. After checking its temperature, I conclude by weighing the pet. If the family has a particular concern, I will ask questions to pinpoint the problem area, and then conduct a more specific physical examination.

When to Bring Your Pet to the Veterinarian

Apart from vaccinations, regular checkups, and elective surgery, there are myriad problems for which veterinary care might be required for your pet. Some people are very reluctant to bring their pets to the veterinary office, even when they suspect that their pets are ill. I once had a client who repeatedly called my office to "report" on her cat's condition (it was listless, vomiting, and not eating), but would not bring it in to be examined, despite my constant urging that she do so. This is usually the type of owner who will wait until the pet is at death's door, then bring it to the veterinarian and expect an immediate cure with a pill!

Although some problems can be resolved over the telephone, in most cases I find that if a situation, however minor, is of sufficient concern to prompt a telephone call for advice, it merits an appointment with the veterinarian. Ideally, the animal should be examined when the symptoms are first noticed, as this is when the chances for a full recovery are greatest. As a general rule, the longer a pet is ill, the longer the recovery period (if recovery is even possible), and the more expensive the treatment.

Sometimes an owner will bring a pet to see me because it "just doesn't seem right." This type of owner is so closely bonded with the pet, and so in tune with its moods and behavior, that any pattern of deviation, however slight, is immediately recognized, even if the owner cannot identify the exact problem. Never be embarrassed or hesitant about taking your pet to the doctor if you feel it isn't acting normally. I have come to respect the intuition of my clients, because I have found that they are usually correct when they feel something is wrong. With detailed questioning and a thorough physical examination, I am usually able to hone in on the possible problem. If no problem is discovered at this stage, the owner will be asked to continue to monitor the pet, and to bring it back if the condition persists. Some illnesses are elusive, and several examinations and tests may be necessary over a period of time before the problem is identified.

Here are some indicators you can use to determine whether your pet might need veterinary attention.

1. Does it have a fever? The normal body temperature of a dog or a cat ranges from 38°–39°C (100.5°–102°F).
2. Is there a change in appetite—either excessive eating or a lack of interest in food?
3. Is the pet having difficulty eating, chewing, or swallowing?
4. Is there a foul smell or bleeding from the gums or mouth?
5. Is there any sneezing or nasal discharge?
6. Is there any coughing or gagging, vomiting, or diarrhea?
7. Have you noticed a change in the pet's water intake?
8. Is there a change in bowel movements or in urination (frequency, color, loss of housetraining)?
9. Is there a discharge or clouding of the eyes?
10. Is there a smell or discharge from the ears, or is the pet bothering its ears?
11. Have you discovered any lumps, sores, loss of fur, or foul odor on the pet's body?
12. Is the pet scratching, chewing, or licking itself excessively?
13. Does the animal seem to be in pain when you touch a certain spot?
14. Does it show any lameness, or reluctance to jump up or climb stairs?
15. Is there a change in the pet's energy level, or shortness of breath after exercise or when it is at rest?

If your pet displays any of these symptoms, you should make an appointment with your veterinarian for a proper diagnosis of the problem.

Emergency Situations

A seriously injured animal in extreme pain may bite. Wrap a cat or a small dog in a coat, towel, or similar restraint. For most dogs, you can make a muzzle using a belt, leash, or strip of cloth; wrap it around the dog's mouth twice and tie it behind the ears. This is illustrated in Figure 4.1.

Immediate veterinary attention is required if your pet is faced with any of the following emergency conditions.

Bleeding: Bright red pumping blood indicates a severed artery; darker seeping blood indicates a severed vein.

Treatment: Apply direct pressure over the bleeding site; use a fair-sized piece of cloth (such as a towel or shirt) or, if necessary, your bare hand, and press

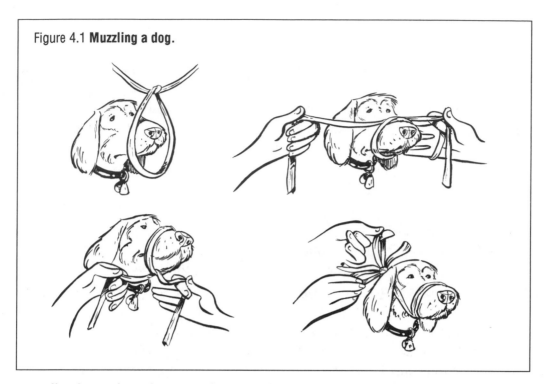

Figure 4.1 **Muzzling a dog.**

firmly against the wound. Try to keep the area clean, but in situations of profuse bleeding cleanliness is less important than time. Maintain the pressure until the bleeding stops or the veterinarian takes over. If bleeding is on a limb, apply a tourniquet by tightly twisting a leash or strip of cloth above the wound. Release pressure every five to ten minutes for a minute or two.

Bloat or torsion: Usually occurs in deep-chested dogs. There will be a sudden enlargement of the chest and abdomen, especially on the left side. Dog will try to vomit with no success, and will appear to be in pain, very weak, and in shock. This very serious condition is discussed further in Chapter 14, "Diseases of the Digestive System" in the section on "The Stomach," page 169.
Treatment: Transport the animal to a veterinarian immediately.

Blocked bladder: Usually occurs in male cats. Cat will try to urinate without success, and act distressed. The abdomen may become obviously distended. This condition of extreme emergency is discussed further in Chapter 15, "Diseases of the Urogenital System." See the section on "Feline Urologic Syndrome," page 190.
Treatment: Transport the animal to a veterinarian immediately.

Drowning or electrocution: Be sure the electrical current is off before you touch the animal.

Treatment: If the animal is unconscious, use cardiopulmonary resuscitation (CPR). Lay the pet on its right side and perform cardiac massage with the heel of your hand just behind the left armpit. Press against the chest rapidly, about 120 times per minute. At the same time, have another person hold the jaws shut and place his or her mouth over the front of the pet's muzzle, covering the nose and mouth. Blow air forcefully into the nostrils for two or three seconds, then release. If you are alone, begin the heart massage, stopping occasionally to perform artificial respiration.

Foreign objects: If an object is lodged in the throat, and your pet is choking or fainting, do not wait for veterinary help.

Treatment: Use the "Heimlich Maneuver"—clasp your arms around the animal just behind the last rib. Press sharply upward to eject the object from the windpipe and out of the mouth.

Hyperthermia or heat stroke: Dangerous overheating, which may occur when the pet is left even for a few minutes in a closed, parked car. The animal may be panting and frantic with anxiety, or comatose. Hyperthermia is discussed further in Chapter 3, "Protecting Your Pet From Harm." See the section on "The Environment," page 23.

Treatment: Immediately immerse the animal in ice water to bring its temperature down to 39.5°C (103°F). Do not allow temperature to drop any lower! Seek veterinary help at once.

Shock: Usually occurs following an accident or injury. Characterized by any combination of: fast, shallow panting; anxiety; glazed eyes; semiconsciousness; marked weakness; faint, fast pulse inside the animal's midthigh; membranes of gums and inner eyelid linings a dead white color.

Treatment: Wrap the pet in a warm blanket and transport to veterinarian immediately!

Trauma: A pet that has been hit by a car or that has fallen from a great height should immediately be checked by a veterinarian even if there are no apparent signs of injury. The doctor will treat any shock, look for signs of serious internal injury or fracture, and treat any external injury.

Wounds: Skin tears, though seldom serious, should be stitched within twenty-four hours to aid healing and prevent infection and scarring. However, time is of the essence with deep or large wounds, wounds involving the eyes, or wounds that expose internal organs.

Treatment: If there is no bleeding, cover the area with a clean, damp cloth. Do not try to scrub or remove dirt since this may cause bleeding. Wounds in the chest cavity must be covered carefully and pressure must be applied at all times to prevent lung collapse.

Diagnostic Tests

Various diagnostic procedures may be performed to determine the exact nature of your pet's illness. **Radiographs** or **x-rays** outline some of the internal organs and bones. An x-ray is taken while the pet is held in position on a table. Occasionally the animal is sedated to allow more accurate positioning.

If a digestive disorder is being investigated, a barium preparation might be given by squirting the fluid into the pet's mouth with a syringe. A series of x-rays is then taken to follow the movement of the barium from the mouth to the stomach and intestine. If a foreign body is present in the digestive tract, it is usually highlighted by the barium. This test will also show if there are ulcers, or if there is a delayed emptying of the stomach or intestine due to a tumor or other obstruction. Barium can also be given as an enema, to identify tumors or thickenings in the large intestine or rectum.

The functioning of the kidneys and urinary system can be tested with x-rays taken after a dye has been injected into a vein; this is called an **intravenous pyelogram** or **IVP**. Problems with the intervertebral disks in the back are identified by injecting a dye into the spine and taking an x-ray called a **myelogram**. A **CAT scan (Computer-aided Axial Tomography)** is a sophisticated x-ray system producing a three-dimensional image of the brain to identify a structural problem in the skull, such as a tumor or a fluid-filled brain cavity.

Ultrasound tests use sound waves to produce an image of the internal organs to identify abnormalities. The heart and chest can also be examined with **echocardiography**, which uses sound waves to produce an image of each part of the heart while it is beating.

The major advantage of x-rays and ultrasound tests is that these "noninvasive" procedures do not involve any surgery, and therefore the animal is in no danger and experiences very little discomfort.

Endoscopy is conducted by inserting a long, flexible tube with a cameralike attachment into the animal's body after it has been anesthetized, so that the veterinarian can see various structures. The endoscope can be passed through the mouth to study the lungs or digestive tract, or it can be inserted in the rectum to check the lower intestine. It can also be put into the abdomen through a small incision to view other internal organs. The endoscope can be equipped to take biopsies and samples of fluid for analysis.

Exploratory surgery is another important diagnostic procedure, especially when it is suspected that internal organs are involved. Although traditionally considered to be a last resort when other attempts to conclusively identify the problem have failed, exploratory surgery can be an expeditious way to pinpoint the exact problem and hopefully fix it at the same time.

An **electrocardiogram** (**ECG**) can be taken to check the functioning of your pet's heart. The animal is awake and held on its side, and a small wired clip is attached to each leg. The ECG may be produced in the office and interpreted by your veterinarian, or it may be transmitted by telephone to a veterinary cardiologist for analysis.

Blood tests provide information about the functioning of many body systems. A blood sample is taken from either the front leg or the neck, and sometimes the needle site is shaved to make it easier to find the vein. As with people, most animals tolerate blood tests quite easily. A CBC (Complete Blood Count) checks the red blood cells for signs of anemia or abnormality, while the white blood cell count will indicate if infection or leukemia is present. Tests performed on the chemicals in the blood can detect endocrine imbalances as well as problems with the kidneys, liver, or muscles, to name just a few. Blood tests can also detect antibodies, indicating that your pet has been exposed to or is suffering from a particular disease such as feline leukemia, feline infectious peritonitis, canine heartworm disease, or canine lyme disease.

If abnormal cells are found in a blood test, a **bone marrow biopsy** should be performed. After the animal is anesthetized, a large needle is inserted into the hip or the top of the leg bone, and a sample of the bone marrow is withdrawn for examination under a microscope. This will reveal if the problem involves the production of blood cells, most of which normally occurs in the bone marrow.

A **urine test** can be very informative in identifying kidney, prostate, and bladder problems. Usually the pet will be catheterized by passing a soft flexible tube up the urinary passageway (the "urethra") into the bladder, where an uncontaminated urine sample can be obtained. Sometimes a free-flowing sample will suffice: a container is held underneath the animal as it is urinating. If the pet is relatively relaxed and cooperative, a urine sample can also be obtained by gently pressing on its bladder. Or, if the bladder can be felt by the veterinarian, a needle attached to a syringe can be inserted through the belly wall to extract a urine sample. This procedure, called **cystocentesis**, is most veterinarians' "method of choice" because it allows for the most accurate analysis of the urine obtained.

If a neurological problem is being investigated, an examination of the fluid surrounding the brain and spinal nerves (cerebrospinal fluid) can be conducted by means of a **CSF tap**. The patient is anesthetized and a fluid sample is withdrawn through a needle. A microscopic examination of this fluid can yield much information regarding an inflammation, infection, or tumor in the brain. A similar procedure, called an **abdominal tap**, can be performed to extract fluid from the abdomen to identify problems such as internal bleeding, feline infectious peritonitis, and circulatory problems.

Hospitalization

If your pet is admitted to the hospital either for medical care or diagnostic tests, you can rest assured that the standard of care and attention it will receive will rival (if not exceed) that provided in the best human hospitals. The veterinarian(s) and trained support staff will check your pet frequently to monitor its vital signs and temperature, administer fluids, provide medication, change bandages, and conduct any other procedures required.

Sometimes feeding a hospitalized animal can be a challenge. Special prescription diets or a concentrated food will be offered, and, if warranted, the patient may be force-fed (food is actually put into the mouth), or fed using a stomach tube inserted through the mouth or nose. These last two options are only used if the animal is not vomiting and if it is imperative that the pet receive some nutrition. One of my patients with severe liver disease recovered and began eating on its own after being fed through a stomach tube for six days.

Hospitalization is stressful for animals just as it is for people. Each hospital has its own visitation policy and every case should be considered individually. When the animal sees its family, it may get very happy and excited, thinking that it is going home—until the visit ends and it is left alone again, feeling abandoned. Its condition could deteriorate, and for this reason, visits are sometimes discouraged.

However, there are times when a hospitalized pet may refuse to eat for no medical reason, or may just seem to pine for its family. In this case I often suggest a family visit. If the patient responds positively to the visit, I will ask the family to encourage the pet to eat. Even if the pet won't eat during the visit, I have seen numerous cases where a pet's appetite and general condition improved greatly following a family visit.

Years ago, I performed surgery on a Terrier-Chihuahua with a severely fractured leg. The dog would not eat until the owner visited it and played a teasing game, pretending to eat the food himself! Another time, a kitten was hospitalized for two months due to severe burns received in a house fire. The owner visited at least once a day and cuddled the kitten for an hour or two, continuously talking softly to it. I am convinced that this loving attention helped the kitten to endure uncomfortable dressing changes and expedited its remarkable recovery.

Sedatives, Anesthesia, and Surgery

Sedatives can be given either by injection or tablet to calm the patient in a variety of situations, such as prior to surgery, during thunderstorms and fireworks (some pets get very upset at the loud sounds), prior to an airplane flight or long motor trip, and prior to grooming if the animal is very nervous. Sedative tablets take several hours to take effect. *Never* give your pet a sedative intended for human use unless you are advised to do so by your veterinarian.

As with surgery on human patients, various types of anesthesia are used to ensure that animals are not in pain during certain procedures. A local anesthetic is used to "freeze" or block the feeling from the specific area where minor surgery, such as the removal of superficial skin growths, is to be performed. Local anesthesia is also used for a cesarean section delivery. If a general anesthetic were used, the newborns would absorb the anesthetic and be very sleepy upon delivery; they do not suffer these effects if the mother is given a local anesthetic.

General anesthesia causes a complete loss of consciousness and sensation throughout all parts of the body, and the patient cannot be aroused until the effects of the anesthetic have worn off. Various injectable anesthetic agents differ in the length of time their effects last and the degree of muscular relaxation they produce. Some are given by injection into the muscles, while others are injected intravenously (into the veins).

Frequently, a short-acting intravenous anesthetic is used to relax the animal sufficiently so that a tube can be put down its throat to deliver a gas anesthetic agent mixed with oxygen. The gas will keep the animal asleep as long as it is administered. A respirator can be attached to the tube delivering the gas to make the animal breathe regularly even if surgery is being done in the chest, or if the animal is failing to breathe on its own for some other reason.

Gas is generally considered to be the safest form of general anesthetic because it acts at the level of the lungs; thus, the liver and kidneys do not have to process any chemicals. Gas anesthesia can also be given with a face mask without any prior intravenously administered drug. This is particularly useful for animals that are high anesthetic risks, such as seniors with kidney or liver disease. For cats that are difficult to handle and for small rodents and birds, gas can be administered into an aquariumlike container into which the animal has been placed. As the pet breathes the gas, it falls asleep. Consciousness is regained rapidly once the gas is no longer present.

Surgery in veterinary hospitals is performed under conditions of sterility rivaling those maintained in human operating rooms. After the patient is adequately anesthetized, it is "prepped" for surgery by shaving the hair from a large area around the surgical site. The area is then scrubbed twice with a disinfecting soap, rinsed well with alcohol or another solvent, and then a long-lasting disinfectant solution is applied. During the operation, the surgeon uses sterilized instruments and wears sterile gloves and usually a cap, a sterile surgical gown, and a mask. To prevent contamination of the surgical wound, the patient will be draped in sterile towels with only the immediate area of the operation exposed. An assistant is usually present to monitor the depth of anesthesia and the patient's general condition during the operation.

There are several ways to close a surgical incision. If the incision is both short and shallow, an adhesive glue can be used to stick the edges of the wound together. Metal staples are used occasionally, but far more common is the use of sutures or stitches. Depending upon the material used, some types of stitches dissolve on their own and others have to be removed ten to fourteen days after the surgery. There can be individual stitches or one long continuous strand, but the latter is not commonly used on dogs and cats, because the animals can inadvertently reopen the incision by chewing off just one knot.

There are usually several layers of stitches closing other layers of tissue beneath the skin. These lower stitches will dissolve, but you might feel some bumpiness beneath the skin during the dissolving process. It is important that the skin stitches be removed at the appropriate time; if they remain in place too long, they will become embedded in the skin, increasing the risk of infection. It will also be harder to see the stitches as the fur regrows, making removal of the stitches more difficult.

It is important that your pet does not lick or scratch the stitches. Inform your veterinarian if the pet is overly interested in the site, or if you notice any licking, redness, or swelling of the area. There is a bitter-tasting cream that can be spread over the stitches to discourage licking—although the occasional patient actually seems to like it!

Sometimes it is necessary to put an "Elizabethan collar" on the pet. This is a large plastic conelike device that attaches to the animal's collar and forms a shield around its head to prevent the pet from licking or biting itself. For a large dog, a plastic pail with the bottom removed can be fitted over its head. It may look odd, but it does work (I have actually received telephone calls from individuals concerned about a neighbor's dog walking around with a pail apparently stuck on its head!).

Home Care

When your pet comes home following an operation, keep it quiet and calm by restricting its activity. If the animal is allowed to be very active, there is a chance that the incision will be irritated, which may cause the pet to lick at it. Do not let your pet eat or drink too much either—the excitement of being home may cause it to vomit. Be sure to follow the veterinarian's feeding instructions.

You may notice some brownish discoloration of the skin or fur around the surgical site. This is the remains of the disinfectant that was applied to the area before the operation, and it will gradually disappear.

If a bandage has been applied, follow the veterinarian's instructions regarding follow-up visits. If moisture gets inside a bandage, infection may set in and some of the skin may die and fall off. Regular bandage changes will ensure that the bandage and the wound stay dry and fresh. If a paw has been bandaged, I always suggest that a small plastic bag be placed over the bandage to keep the site dry when the pet goes outside. Remember to remove the plastic bag when the pet is inside, as the lack of air circulation would cause the limb to become too warm. Even if the bandage seems thick and solid, it is usually porous enough for body warmth to escape.

Do not let your pet lick a bandage or cast, as this will allow moisture into the site and might also move the bandage, preventing it from serving its purpose, and possibly harming other tissues. If you cannot keep the pet from licking or chewing at the area, tell your veterinarian, who can give you a bitter-tasting cream or an Elizabethan collar to use.

If the toes are exposed below a cast or bandage that has been applied to a limb, be sure to check the toes daily for any swelling or change in temperature compared to the other paws. Call your veterinarian if you have any concerns.

Medicating Your Pet

The day may come when your veterinarian hands you a bottle of medication with the instructions: "Give the correct dose to your pet three times daily." Don't panic; you can do it, especially if your pet is accustomed to having its head handled and mouth opened. The same procedure is used to give a tablet to a cat or a dog. First of all, lift the pet onto a slippery high surface, such as a counter or table top, or on top of a freezer or washing machine. This will let the pet know that you have a job to do and that this is not playtime. Also, a slippery surface makes the animal less sure of its footing and generally easier to handle. A large dog should be made to sit on the floor and told to "Stay" while you give it the tablet.

Once the pet is in position, put one hand over its head with your thumb near one hinge of the jaw and the other fingers by the other side of the jaw. Tilt the head up; the more vertical the animal's head, the less the tension on the animal's lower jaw. For a large dog, have your fingers over the dog's muzzle pushing the lips against the teeth; this way, if it decides to close its mouth on your hand, it will be biting its own lips first. With your other hand, hold the tablet between two fingers and use another finger to pry open the lower jaw. Push the tablet as far back in the animal's mouth as you can, and then give it a final poke. Remember to keep the head pointed up. Now close the animal's mouth and blow forcefully into its face—it will reflexively jerk its head back and swallow. You will know that the pet has indeed swallowed the tablet once it licks its nose or lips. If the pill is sticky, you can put a drop of vegetable oil or margarine on it to make it slide easily down the throat. This procedure is illustrated in Figure 4.2.

Giving a pill directly to the animal is the best and quickest way to ensure that the entire dose is received. However, some tablets can be crushed and mixed in with the animal's food (check with your veterinarian first). In this case, add the crushed medication to a small amount of food first, and after you are certain it has been consumed give your pet the rest of its meal. It is sometimes helpful to keep the pet on the hungry side during the time that it is on medication. Crushed tablets can also be mixed with a small amount of treat that the pet likes, such as vanilla ice cream, cheese, softened butter, or peanut butter.

To administer liquid medication, lift the head up halfway towards the ceiling. Leave the mouth closed and pull the lower lip out slightly to form a pouch on one side of its mouth. Insert the tip of the dropper or syringe into this pouch and slowly squirt in the liquid a little at a time. Gently rub the pet's throat to ensure that it is swallowing the medicine. Even if the liquid is pleasant-tasting, a sudden squirt of a large quantity will cause the animal to gag and spray the medicine back

Figure 4.2 **Pilling a dog.**
Left illustration shows positioning of hands to open dog's mouth. Put the pill into the mouth as far back over the tongue as possible. In the middle picture, the dog's mouth is held closed; blowing into the pet's face and/or rubbing the dog's throat (right) causes the dog to swallow and lick its lips.

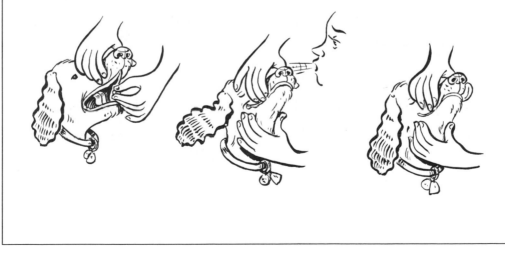

out. If it opens its mouth, squirt the liquid onto the back of the tongue instead of into the pouch.

If you have difficulty administering medicine to a cat because it keeps raising its front paws, try putting a towel around its neck like a bib. This will protect your hand from the cat's claws. You can also wrap the cat's body in a towel with only its head exposed. This is illustrated in Figure 4.3.

If you find yourself unable to administer the medication as directed, ask your veterinarian for assistance. Don't just give up, as this will not benefit the patient!

Sometimes cats must be force-fed canned food or baby food, or given medication in paste form, usually for a hairball treatment or as a nutritional supplement. Put a small portion of the food or paste onto your finger and open the cat's

Figure 4.3 **Pilling a cat**.
The cat can be wrapped in a towel to restrain it while its mouth is opened and the pill is placed over the tongue as far back as possible. The drawing on the right shows how the cat can be held securely under the arm while being pilled.

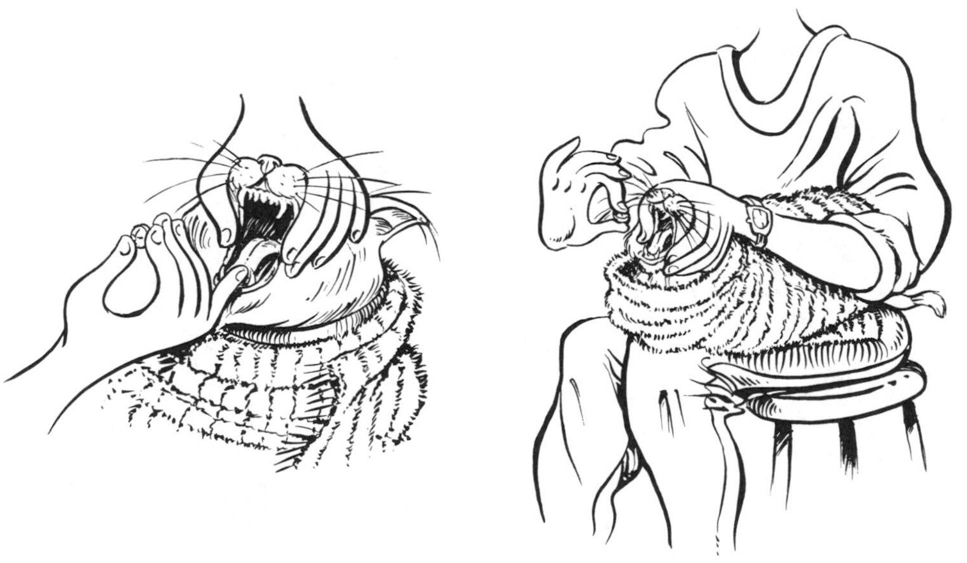

mouth with your other hand. Rub the portion against the roof of the mouth behind the upper front teeth. Close the mouth and the cat should swallow, especially if you gently rub its throat. A client once called me to say she had trouble applying a paste to the roof of her cat's mouth, as the cat was trying to lick it right off her finger! I told her that this was fine—in fact, if your cat likes the taste, you can let it lick the portion directly from your finger or the tube, or you can rub it onto its lips or front paws.

To administer eye drops or ointment, raise the head to a near-vertical position with one hand under the chin. Rest the hand holding the medication container on top of the animal's head so that if the animal moves, your hand moves with it. The fingers of your other hand can usually be slid up the face to gently pull down the lower eyelid. The heel of your upper hand holding the medication is used to gently hold the upper lid open, and one drop of liquid is allowed to fall onto the eyeball. This is illustrated in Figure 4.4. For ointment, squeeze a small amount into the space opened up between the lower lid and the eyeball. After application, gently close the eyes to spread the medication.

If ear medication is to be administered, insert the tip of the dropper into the ear opening. Allow the prescribed amount of medication to fall into the opening and immediately massage the base of the animal's ear. This will cause the medication to flow into the deeper part of the ear; you will hear a "squishing" sound. At this point, even if the pet shakes its head, most of the medicine should remain within the ear canal. Give only the prescribed amount of ear drops;

Figure 4.4 **Applying eye drops to a dog**. In this drawing, one hand, with the bottle of medication, holds the upper eyelid open, while the other hand pulls gently on the lower eyelid.

more is not better and, in fact, can cause outside dirt to stick to the greasy surface. If there is any debris in the ear, it will come up to the surface as the animal moves around during the day and occasionally shakes its head. Remove the debris each time before you insert fresh drops. If you are using a cotton-tipped swab to clean the ear, make sure you can always see where the cotton joins the stick to avoid inserting the stick too far. In dogs and cats there is a 90-degree angle between the vertical ear canal and the horizontal ear canal leading to the eardrum, so you are unlikely to damage the eardrum with a swab. Be certain to gently clean out all the little folds on the inside of the ear flap.

When it is necessary to apply a cream or salve onto your pet, rub in the prescribed amount. Prevent the animal from immediately licking off the medicine by distracting it: feed it, play with it, or take it out for a walk.

It is important to follow precisely the veterinarian's instructions regarding the correct dosage and duration of treatment. The theory that "if one pill works, then two pills will work twice as quickly" is just not true. Nor should you stop giving medication (for example, antibiotics) before the end of the prescribed period, even if the pet seems better. Such practices could seriously hinder the animal's recovery.

If medication is to be given once a day, choose any time convenient to the family, unless you are instructed differently. Be consistent throughout the treatment period. Timing is important because of the length of time required for the drug to dissolve in the stomach, the length of time it stays in the bloodstream, and the speed with which it is absorbed by the tissue. If you are told to give medication "twice a day," give it approximately every twelve hours, not twice at night before bedtime if you forgot to give the medication in the morning. "Three times a day" means approximately every eight hours; that is, early morning, late afternoon, and at bedtime. If you inadvertently miss a dose, don't try to make up for it—resume the prescribed schedule.

When you first administer the medication, watch your pet closely for any adverse or unexpected reactions. No two animals have identical biological systems: the fact that 98 percent of animals tolerate a drug very well does not necessarily mean that yours will. If your pet has developed a problem that began immediately or shortly after a medication was given, do not wait until all the drug is finished before contacting your veterinarian. Common adverse reactions to look for are: skin rash, vomiting, diarrhea, loss of appetite, and staggering. Some medications have side effects your veterinarian should tell you to expect. For instance, anti-inflammatory medication for itching causes increased thirst, urination, and, frequently, an increased appetite. One commonly dispensed antibiotic known as "Tribrissen" will cause cats to drool if they taste the tablet before swallowing it.

Medications that are prescribed for your pet are, in many cases, the very same ones used for human ailments. In fact, the veterinarian may write a prescription to be filled at your local pharmacy. This surprises many families who believe that just because the drug is for an animal, it must be "weaker" or different in some other way. I was once asked by an elderly client whether she was in any danger when she inadvertently took a tablet that was meant for her cat—she said she felt better than she had in years! Luckily for her, one tablet of this medication was not harmful, but in no circumstances should you ever take medication prescribed for your pet. Also, remember to keep all medication out of the reach of small children and pets.

Any unused tablets should be disposed of. Do not build up your own personal pharmacy. Even if your pet, at some future point, develops what appears to be the same condition, you should always consult your veterinarian before giving the same medication. In addition, all drugs have a shelf life and are often of no benefit after the expiry date.

How to Help the Veterinarian Help Your Pet

The job of a veterinarian is very challenging; we deal with animals who cannot tell us "where it hurts." We have to rely on the patient's family to bring the pet to us at the first sign of illness, to provide a complete history and description of the problem, to follow instructions for giving medication, and to provide progress reports. The veterinarian and client work as a team to ensure that the pet receives the best possible health care. Here are some tips to help you and, more importantly, your pet, get the most out of your veterinary visit.

Keeping Appointments

Most veterinarians see patients by appointment, rather than on an "open clinic" basis. An appointment system allows for the most efficient use of the veterinarian's time, which must be divided between surgery, in-hospital treatments, and seeing patients. When you make an appointment, you may be asked to explain the nature of your pet's problem, so that the office can schedule sufficient time for each patient to be properly examined and treated. The goal is to minimize delays and avoid a crowded waiting room, which can cause pets (and their owners) to become nervous. Of course, it is of tremendous assistance to your veterinarian if you are on time for your appointment.

In the Waiting Room

When you are at a veterinary office, you should have complete control of your pet. You should never simply bring a cat to a veterinary hospital in your arms—it might see another animal and escape your control. A cat should be in a carrier; if a carrier is unavailable, put the cat in a sturdy box with small air holes, or a covered laundry basket, or a plastic covered box from a dairy. A cat can also be carried in a pillowcase or wrapped in a towel, with its head exposed. If you are not using any type of carrier, then at least use a leash.

Keep your cat restrained until you are in the examination room with the doctor. I have seen clients arrive at the clinic with their cats in carriers, and immediately let them roam at will in the waiting room! There are too many places for a loose cat to hide, and trying to extract a frightened cat from its hiding place can be dangerous for all concerned. In my office, a frightened cat once leapt from its owner's lap (leaving scratch marks in the process) and ran across the bare arms of the neighboring client (again inflicting injury) before it found a corner in which to hide. Can you imagine the state of this animal by the time I was ready to examine it?

A dog should always be on a leash or in a carrier when brought to a veterinary office. Although some clients feel that their dogs do not need leashes, other clients in the waiting room might not appreciate being visited or sniffed by a strange dog. A loose dog could easily upset a cat that has been sitting quietly in its carrier, or on its owner's lap. Another reason to keep your dog on a leash is to avoid the problem of the loose dog that "labels" every corner of the room with its urine, which only causes additional mayhem!

When you arrive at the animal clinic with your pet, identify yourself and your pet to the receptionist, and briefly explain the purpose of your visit. Do not go into great detail with the receptionist, because you will only have to repeat this information to the doctor.

In the Examining Room

There are several ways to help the doctor and your pet in the examining room. Restrain your pet if you are asked; the pet will be more comfortable and relaxed with familiar hands holding it. If you are unsure of the proper way to hold the amimal, ask the veterinarian. Hold your pet firmly while it is on the examination table; if you step away from the table, your pet could easily jump off (possibly injuring itself) and race around the room looking for a hiding place.

In the examination room, the veterinarian will ask you questions to ascertain the history of the pet and the nature of its illness. Try to answer these questions honestly and in a straightforward manner. Do not hesitate to mention any detail, however trivial, that you feel may or may not be relevant. Let the doctor be the judge of whether or not a symptom is important.

When the doctor is using the stethoscope, do not distract him or her by talking. The stethoscope fills the doctor's ears, so you won't be clearly heard. More importantly, your voice might mask the heart and lung sounds that the doctor is trying to hear. Also, do not pat the animal as this will make it more difficult for the doctor to properly hear the chest sounds.

If you are squeamish about being in the examining room, or do not wish to be present when your pet receives a needle or other treatment, do not be embarrassed to say so. Most veterinarians have a trained assistant available, and it is best for all concerned to avoid the unnecessary risk that you might take ill.

Although most pets are comfortable being held by their owners during an examination or treatment, some will pick up on their owners' anxiety and become very aggressive. Sometimes it is necessary to restrain the animal using heavy protective gloves or a muzzle. At times it must be taken into another room, away from its owner. Don't be upset if the doctor feels this is necessary. Even a very friendly dog or cat can react differently in an animal hospital. Remember that the goal is to give your pet the best possible care with the least chance of anyone, including the pet itself, getting hurt.

Children and the Veterinarian

If young family members accompany you and the pet on a visit to the veterinary office, ask the doctor if they can join you in the examination room. Depending upon the size of the room, the temperament and condition of the pet, and the maturity of the children, there is a good chance that they will be welcome in the room with you. I enjoy discussing the family pet's health with children. When time permits, I invite the children to listen to their pet's heartbeat using the stethoscope, and I explain my examination procedure to them. However, it is difficult to concentrate on the patient if there are a number of youngsters investigating every nook and cranny in the room! So, if you bring children to the veterinary office, keep a close eye on them.

A Second Opinion

There are times when a pet owner wants a second opinion regarding the pet's medical condition. This is quite acceptable; never be embarrassed about wanting the best for your pet. However, it is very important that you tell the second veterinarian that you are seeking a second opinion, and explain the diagnosis and treatment that were suggested by the first veterinarian. If you do not have this information ("A little white pill to be given twice a day" isn't very useful), the second doctor can obtain it from the first one.

It is important that the second doctor be fully informed; if the original treatment or medication was unsuccessful, this doctor can build on the information already available and begin an alternate treatment plan. Besides, in many jurisdictions it is considered unethical for a veterinarian to knowingly see a pet that has been treated by a colleague for the same problem without first contacting that colleague. The second veterinarian should also inform the first doctor of his or her findings and treatment plan.

Take Your Veterinarian's Advice Seriously

A veterinarian tries to treat each case to the best of his or her ability. I know that for certain symptoms I conduct specific tests, prescribe certain medication, and judge the response of the animal. There are many times when it is best to hospitalize the patient or run various laboratory tests and x-rays. However, sometimes even before I have examined the patient, the family will say that they do not want to leave their pet in the hospital. This is unfortunate, because my ability to do what's best for the patient is being compromised.

It's frustrating to deal with a pet owner who seeks my advice and expertise, claiming to have the animal's health as his or her paramount concern, and who then refuses to follow the advice given. I once examined a dog that was desperately in need of dental care; its mouth was terribly infected and many teeth needed immediate extraction. The owner wanted me to clean the teeth but not to extract any of them! I explained that I would never pull teeth needlessly, but that badly infected teeth were a source of infection which would spread throughout the animal's entire body. I advised her that I would not compromise my standard of treatment, and could not allow the dog to continue to suffer. The client was adamant in her refusal to consent to the required treatment. Because she was unwilling to have a toothless dog with a healthy mouth, her pet's mouth and general health continued to deteriorate.

Some clients are too emotional to listen to the veterinarian; they cannot comprehend or accept the fact that their pet is gravely ill. One time, after explaining to a family that their critically ill cat could pass away at any time from acute kidney failure and that it had to be hospitalized for treatment, the owner wanted to know what time the pet could go home the next day! There is an element of denial when one is faced with a crisis. Another client, to whom I had just explained that his pet was fighting for its life, responded by asking me to trim the pet's nails! It is difficult to speak plainly without sounding uncaring; a blunt statement such as "Your pet is probably going to pass away by nightfall" might get the message across but isn't very tactful. The veterinarian, like all health care professionals, must strike a delicate balance between the need to keep the client fully informed and the importance of communicating compassionately and sensitively, especially when conveying bad news.

Often a client will want an immediate diagnosis for the pet's condition. As with the practice of human medicine, this is not always possible, even after a multitude of tests have been conducted. Sometimes the diagnosis of a condition or a disease is not an exact science, but rather a judgment call based on a variety of factors, including symptoms, test results, response to treatment, and so on.

After the Visit

When your pet is being sent home with medication, be sure you understand what the medication is for, and when and how much should be given. If you have any questions, even after you get home, do not hesitate to ask.

If your pet is improving, call and let the doctor know. If the pet is not improving, or not reacting in the way you were told to expect, it is also important to promptly tell the veterinarian. Give the doctor a chance to re-evaluate the situation or perhaps to suggest a second opinion by a specialist. Do not wait until the animal is in much worse condition before returning to the veterinarian, or it may be too late.

Remember that it is always important to give feedback about client service. If you are satisfied with the service you and your pet received, the clinic staff would like to know. On the other hand, if you are dissatisfied, discuss your feelings with the veterinarian or office manager of the clinic. Give them a chance to explain; they may be totally unaware of your feelings. As a client who wants and deserves the best for your pet, you owe it to yourself, your veterinarian, and most importantly, your pet, to keep the lines of communication open.

5

Vaccinations
and Elective Surgery

Vaccinations

Like people, animals can be protected by vaccination against many serious and potentially fatal diseases caused by bacteria and viruses. Vaccines are injected subcutaneously (under the skin), intramuscularly (in the muscle), or by nasal spray. Lifetime protection is maintained by annual "boosters" after an initial series of inoculations. Although a vaccination program should be commenced at an early age, no animal is too old to begin. There are many effective vaccination schedules; your veterinarian will establish one that is best for your pet. Vaccines are always being improved and protection is continuously being developed against new diseases.

Dogs are usually vaccinated against distemper and parvovirus (diseases of the digestive system), hepatitis (a liver condition), and parainfluenza (a respiratory disease). Protection is also available against bordetella (another respiratory disease), leptospirosis (a kidney disease common in rural areas), and coronavirus (another disease of the digestive system).

Cats are regularly protected against panleucopenia or feline distemper (a disease of the digestive system), and rhinotracheitis and calicivirus (two respiratory viruses). Protection is also available against pneumonitis (a respiratory infection), feline infectious peritonitis (a usually fatal intestinal disease), and feline leukemia. Although leukemia primarily strikes cats that go outdoors or that live in multicat households, I recommend the leukemia vaccine to all cat owners who wish the maximum protection for their pets. Annual vaccinations against some respiratory diseases are recommended even for indoor cats that have no contact with other animals, because some of these viruses are transmitted through the air. Every spring and fall I see many patients with respiratory viruses (the cat "flu"), and those with up-to-date vaccinations are much less seriously affected and recover more quickly than unprotected animals. Yearly vaccinations also allow the veterinarian to perform a complete physical examination and identify any developing conditions before they become serious.

All pets should receive yearly protection against rabies, a disease which is described in Chapter 18, "Diseases of the Nervous System," under the heading "The Brain." Vaccination against rabies is a legal requirement in many North American jurisdictions, and affords added peace of mind for a minimal additional cost when given along with other vaccinations. Even cats living indoors in high-rise apartment buildings should be protected against rabies. Bats—a primary carrier of the rabies virus—have been known to fly into apartments through open windows. One morning my assistant found a bat hanging from the ceiling in our clinic; it had entered through a very small space beside a window air conditioner. Bats can enter through any space where you can put your little finger!

The rabies vaccine gives protection for either one or three years, depending upon the product used. In areas where rabies is not a major concern, the three-year protection is adequate, but I always suggest that a rabies booster be given at the same time that the pet receives its annual distemper-combination booster. This way, the owner will not have to remember when the three-year rabies booster is due, and the pet will be protected if it travels to regions where rabies is prevalent.

Young animals, like human babies, need a series of vaccinations before their protection ("antibodies") will last a full year. This is because the temporary protection in the first milk (called "colostrum") provided by the mother counteracts the effects of a vaccination. The amount of protection contained in the milk is highest when the mother's vaccinations are up to date. However, this protection declines and eventually disappears by the time the young animal is fourteen to sixteen weeks old. Since we do not know at any given time the degree of natural protection the young animal has, and the rate at which it is disappearing, we give the first vaccination when the puppy or kitten is six to eight weeks old. We repeat it at one-month intervals until the young animal is four months old; this last inoculation will give immunity for a full year. The rabies vaccination is given at four months of age, and annually thereafter.

No vaccine can guarantee absolute immunity. A vaccine contains disease-causing agents ("antigens") that have been either killed or modified so as no longer to cause disease. The recipient's body recognizes these antigens as foreign and tries to combat them by making its own antibodies, which will last for about a year. If, during that time, the animal is exposed to the real disease-causing agent, the antibodies it has created will destroy the antigens. Factors affecting the level of immunity produced by a vaccine include the degree of stress in the animal's life, its nutritional state, and its age.

Why do some animals get sick even if they have been vaccinated? There are mutations and different strains of viruses in the environment, and vaccines cannot protect against all of them. In my experience, the illnesses caused by these viruses are usually much less severe in vaccinated animals than in unvaccinated ones. Also, there are many different causes of respiratory infections in both dogs and cats, and the vaccines only protect against the more serious causative agents.

Elective Surgery

Operations on animals are performed for two basic reasons: one is to change something about the animal, usually to make it more acceptable as a pet; and the other is to respond to a medical condition or illness that is affecting the animal's health. This discussion will focus on the first category, called "elective surgery."

As with the practice of human medicine, all operations—even elective surgeries—carry a risk. For example, an apparently healthy animal may have an allergic reaction to the anesthetic. Or, an unsuspected bleeding disorder might become apparent during or after surgery. During recovery from the anesthetic, the animal might become excited or agitated and injure itself, or a stitch might open if the animal is overly active too soon after the surgery. However, these risks are relatively minimal, and are far outweighed by the benefits of most surgeries.

Sterilization

As your pet reaches maturity, the question of sterilization will arise. Most veterinarians, myself included, strongly recommend sterilization for all pets that are not going to be bred. Although some people refer to sterilization as having an animal "fixed," the correct terminology is "neutering" for males and "spaying" for females.

I am often asked by clients if their pets will gain weight after being sterilized. There is no proven direct relationship between weight gain and sterilization. However, by the time most pets are sterilized, they have completed their rapid growth phase and tend to be less active, as they are maturing in their behavior. The pet's food requirements will level off and then decrease a little. Naturally, if the pet is fed the same quantity of food as during its growth period, it will begin to gain more weight. If you feel your pet is becoming overweight, decrease its food intake or switch to a calorie-reduced food. It is very important to avoid obesity, which is the most common cause of illness in pets.

I am also frequently asked whether a pet's personality will change after it has been neutered or spayed. Again, there is no proven direct relationship between sterilization and personality change. For example, if a dog is very aggressive, neutering or spaying it will not significantly alter its behavior, since aggression is not a sex-related characteristic. However, most pet owners agree that any behavioral changes that do occur following sterilization are usually for the better, resulting in a more loving animal.

FEMALE ANIMALS

Female animals should be spayed at 5 1/2 to 6 months of age. The pet does not have to come into season or "heat" before the surgery. It should not, however, be spayed while it is in heat, as the increased blood supply to the uterus and ovaries at this time makes surgery more dangerous for the pet.

The most compelling reason to have a female dog (called a "bitch") or cat (called a "queen") spayed, is to prevent the bothersome behavior that occurs when females periodically "come into heat." Bitches must be closely supervised in the presence of unneutered male dogs, as even brief contact can result in mating. A queen in heat will often attract all the unneutered male cats (called "toms") in the neighborhood. They will serenade the queen with loud caterwauling, usually in the middle of the night, and will roam around "spraying" your property with strong-smelling urine. The queen will also make very loud crying noises and may urinate outside of the litter pan.

Aside from the inconvenience to the family of having a pet in heat, there are medical advantages to having it spayed. An unspayed (or "intact") female can develop breast tumors later on in life, whereas statistics show that if a bitch is spayed before it is one year old, there is almost no chance that it will develop breast cancer later. If an unspayed dog does develop breast tumors later on in life, we are faced with deciding whether to complicate and lengthen the surgery by spaying it as well in an effort to prevent a recurrence of the tumors. Although the frequency of breast cancer in female cats is less than in dogs, the risk decreases greatly if the cat is spayed at an early age.

An unspayed cat or dog can also develop a serious medical condition called "pyometra," which is a severe infection of the uterus. The only recourse for an animal with pyometra is an immediate spay, which is a dangerous procedure when the patient is gravely ill. This condition is discussed further in Chapter 15, "Diseases of the Urogenital System," under the heading "Genital System of Female Cats and Dogs."

The spay operation (called an "ovariohysterectomy") is a complete hysterectomy; that is, both ovaries as well as the uterus are removed. We do not perform a tubal ligation as the hormones produced by the ovaries would still allow the female to come into heat, and the dangers of pyometra and of breast tumors would still be present although the animal could not become pregnant.

People who have adopted mature female pets from an animal shelter have no way of determining with certainty whether or not the pet has been spayed. If the surgery has been performed recently, the veterinarian might be able to feel a row of stitches in the muscle wall of the belly. However, this would merely prove that the animal had undergone abdominal surgery of some sort, but not necessarily a spay operation. There are only two ways to determine with certainty whether or not the animal has been spayed: wait and see if she comes into heat; or perform an exploratory abdominal surgery to see if the ovaries and uterus are there. Most people choose the first option.

MALE ANIMALS

A male dog should be neutered at eight to ten months of age, when it has reached maturity; a male cat at seven or eight months of age. The neutering procedure involves the removal of both testicles (called a "castration"). If only a vasectomy were performed, medical problems associated with the male hormones might persist or develop.

There are medical benefits to neutering dogs, such as reducing the risk of prostate infections, eliminating the risk of tumors in the testicles, and reducing the risk of tumors in the anal region. Normally, the dog's testicles will descend into the scrotum shortly after birth, but occasionally one or both will remain within the abdomen. When this happens, the dog is described as a "cryptorchid." The undescended testicle has a greater chance of developing a tumor than one that has descended to the scrotum. In addition, it is almost impossible to know when a tumor is developing in a retained testicle; usually the problem is detected only when the tumor has become so large that it is affecting other organs. For this reason, most veterinarians will recommend neutering cryptorchid dogs, even though the surgery will be complicated by the fact that the testicles must first be located within the abdomen. I once pointed out to a client that her male dog was a cryptorchid. She immediately stated, "Oh, the dog is just like my late husband, who also only had one descended testicle!" I never cease to be amazed at the things some clients will tell their veterinarians.

Another reason to have a male dog neutered is to prevent the behavioral effects of male hormones. If there is a bitch (an unspayed female dog) in the neighborhood, an unneutered male will often pine for her; his keen nose tells him when she is in heat, even though he hasn't seen her. He is apt to go off his food, become lethargic, and even depressed—maybe that's where the term "puppy love" came from! In addition, an unneutered male dog will usually "label" each and every tree or upright structure with a drop or two of urine; this can try one's patience when walking the dog. This behavior is less likely to occur in a dog that has been neutered at a young age.

Neutered male cats generally make better pets than unneutered ones. An unneutered cat will develop visible secondary sex characteristics such as large jowls, thick greasy skin, and coarse brittle fur. They tend not to groom themselves very much. They will frequently "spray" their strong-smelling urine around the house to mark their territory. These traits can be prevented if the cat is neutered at an early age. Neutered cats tend to become more affectionate than they were before the surgery; they lose the tendency to roam and become more interested in the company of people.

In my experience some male clients have been a little reluctant to have their male pets neutered. This may be because the surgery is somehow construed as depriving the animal of its "maleness." Although this concern is understandable, I am not aware of any evidence that a neutered pet has any less sense of self-esteem than an intact male animal. There is no reason to be reluctant to neuter a dog or cat that is not going to be used for breeding.

Declawing

Since cats are capable of scratching the furniture, carpets, and wallpaper, many people choose to have their cats declawed. This procedure, called an "onyxectomy," is the surgical removal of the claws of the front paws, and is performed under a general anesthetic. Depending upon the surgical technique, the paws may or may not be shaved prior to the operation. After each claw is removed, the incision in each toe is usually closed using a dissolvable suture or a surgical skin adhesive. The pet is usually kept in the hospital for a day or two afterwards, so that the veterinarian can monitor the condition of the paws. Although most cats recover quickly and without difficulty, any tenderness in the paws can be controlled with medication.

For about a week after the cat has returned home, its litter pan should be filled with newspaper shredded into strips and covered with a small amount of litter. The cat will recognize its toilet area but its paws won't be irritated by digging through lots of litter. However, if the cat refuses to use the modified litter pan, resume the use of regular litter.

Although the onyxectomy can be performed at any time, veterinarians usually suggest that young cats be declawed when they are being spayed or neutered, rather than at separate times. This is more economical for the owner, and safer and less stressful for the pet, as only one anesthetic and one hospital stay are required.

Some humane societies claim that it is barbaric, unnecessary, and inhumane to declaw cats, and they forbid this procedure on pets they place in homes. I disagree with these views. Modern surgical practices make the declaw procedure a safe and relatively painless one, and render cats more desirable and acceptable as pets than un-declawed ones. There are thousands of homeless cats in shelters, waiting to be adopted by loving families. Surely it is better for these cats to be given a good home—where they might be declawed—than to be destroyed because the shelter cannot find enough adoptive families who are prepared to make a commitment that they will not have the cat declawed.

Some pet owners are hesitant about having their cats declawed. They want to know whether the procedure will be painful, whether it is fair to the cat, and whether the cat's personality will change. The procedure is relatively painless and does not appear to affect the cat's personality in any way. In my experience, after having declawed thousands of cats, not one client has expressed regret at having had the procedure performed. This seems to be a fairly significant endorsement of the declaw procedure.

Once a cat has been declawed, it should not go outside unsupervised. Although it can still use its teeth and hind claws to defend itself, it will be at a disadvantage if it gets into an altercation with another animal. Occasionally, clients will tell me that their declawed cat goes outside, successfully defends its territory, and can even catch mice or rabbits, but I cannot condone letting a declawed cat outside on its own. My declawed cat Alistair was allowed outside on a leash, the end of which was tied to a large brick on the cement patio. This way, if she had to run suddenly, I would hear the brick being dragged along the patio and I would go outside to see what was happening.

The vast majority of declaw surgeries are performed on only the front paws, as these are the ones the cat uses to scratch. The cat's hind claws can be trimmed with a nail clipper (see Chapter 8, "Grooming Your Pet"). Occasionally, I am asked to remove a cat's hind claws as well, because the owner's furniture is made of leather, which scratches easily, or is upholstered with tufted fabric, which snags easily. The cats on which I have declawed all four feet seem to have no more problems recovering from the surgery than those that have been declawed only in the front.

If even a small piece of the growth plate for the claw is not removed during the surgery, a claw may grow back several weeks or months later. This is a rare occurrence but it can happen. Sometimes the regrowing claw will not completely break the surface of the skin, and the cat may have some discomfort when walking on that foot or there may be some discharge from the toe. In such a case, the affected toe is explored surgically and the offending piece of bone is removed. I once had a client who brought in a white cat, claiming that a claw had grown back after we had neutered and declawed it. I examined it and found that *every* claw on both front paws had apparently grown back—a highly unusual occurrence. Just as I was about to advise the client that I would repeat the declaw surgery at no cost, I looked beneath the cat's tail: the scrotum contained two very obvious testicles. Remembering that this cat had supposedly been neutered and declawed, I explained to the client that the testicles *never* grow back and I asked her whether the cat had at any time been unaccounted for since the surgery. She confessed that one day he had slipped out the front door but was found a short time later at the back door. When I told her that this was an "imposter" cat, she insisted that this cat had the same personality as the one that had been operated on. But the presence of the testicles constituted conclusive proof that this cat was definitely not the same cat that had previously been brought to the clinic for surgery!

A declawed cat may still make scratching motions to "label" an object using the scent glands in its paws. This is perfectly acceptable, and is much easier on the object than if the cat still had its claws!

An alternative to declawing is the fitting of soft-edged vinyl claw-shaped covers over the cat's nails. These covers are fairly simple to apply: first, trim the tips of the nails; then fill the vinyl claw about one-third full with special glue, and slip it onto the nail. Hold the paw for at least five minutes to allow the glue to set. This product is not recommended for kittens younger than four months as the vinyl covers are not small enough to fit their claws.

The main disadvantage of vinyl claw covers is that they will come off as the real claws grow, and must be reapplied every four to six weeks. Also, some cats chew off the vinyl covers. I do not recommend this product; I feel that any owner able to apply vinyl claw covers to a cat's claws should be able to achieve the same result by trimming the claws with nail clippers.

Dewclaw Removal

Dogs and cats sometimes have a "thumb" or dewclaw on the inner side of each paw. Although this is fairly common on front legs, dewclaws are sometimes found on the hind legs as well. On cats, hind dewclaws often have several extra nails. Hind dewclaws in dogs can be firmly attached like a regular nail, or they might be dangling loosely in the skin.

There are several reasons to consider removing a dog's dewclaws. First, if the dog is a hunting dog, the dewclaws, particularly on the rear legs, might get caught in the underbrush as the dog runs to retrieve game. A torn dewclaw is quite painful and will usually bleed profusely. In a long-haired dog, it can be difficult to avoid snagging the dewclaws on the comb and brush while grooming the pet.

It is easiest to perform this surgery without an anesthetic on a puppy that is two to four days old. The dewclaw is disinfected and then surgically removed, and the area is cauterized. Often a stitch is used to close the skin. Alternatively, the dewclaws can be removed when the pet is spayed or neutered and/or being declawed.

Ear Cropping

Ear cropping—a controversial elective surgery—is done when the puppy is two to four months old. Historically, a number of dog breeds, including Schnauzers, Boxers, Great Danes, Boston Terriers, and Bouviers, have had their folding ear flap removed to create an erect or "prick" ear. This supposedly makes the dog look ferocious, and exposes less tissue to danger if the dog is used to fight or hunt. Some supporters claim that cropped ears are less prone to developing infections than floppy ears; this is not true.

Most veterinarians are opposed to ear cropping. There is a danger of infection of the surgery site. To make the ears stand erect, they have to be regularly dressed with adhesive tape, which at some point has to be painfully removed. Further, there is no guarantee that the ears will stand properly erect after the procedure is complete. But most significant of all, this surgery requires a general anesthetic, which is very risky in such a young animal. To endanger an innocent puppy's life just so that its head and ears conform to what some dog show judges deem to be acceptable breed standards is, in my opinion, inhumane and barbaric.

As most veterinarians will not perform this unnecessary procedure, it is usually done by unauthorized lay persons—often the breeders themselves—in often unsanitary conditions. I have had ear-cropped puppies brought to my office with a variety of problems: infected incisions; tape digging into the skin; or because the puppy would not leave the bandages alone. Sometimes I have been asked to redress the ears and incorporate wooden tongue depressors into the tape to encourage the ears to stand properly. Although I will treat medical problems such as infections, I will have nothing to do with "cosmetic" problems resulting from ear cropping.

Fortunately, an increasing number of owners are not having their puppies' ears cropped. As a result of persistent lobbying by veterinarians and enlightened breeder groups, some kennel clubs and dog show judges are accepting dogs with uncropped ears in the show ring. I am delighted when I see a puppy with uncropped ears; how wonderfully expressive and natural is its little face!

Tail Docking

Several dog breeds have part of their tails removed (or "docked") shortly after birth, again to conform to breed standards. Among such breeds are Poodles, Old English Sheepdogs, Bouviers, Boxers, Schnauzers, and Cocker Spaniels. This elective procedure is carried out when the puppy is two to four days old. The amount of tail that is removed varies with the breed. For example, Old English Sheepdogs and Bouviers are left with virtually no tail, while Boxers, Schnauzers, and Poodles are left with a short stub. If not enough tail has been left on a Poodle, a skilled groomer can leave an extra long pom-pom on the end to give the impression of a longer tail.

Most veterinarians are not opposed to the tail docking of young animals because it is a fairly simple procedure requiring no anesthetic and presents minimal risk to the animal's life. While puppies of this age will squeal any time they are handled, there is very little further indication of discomfort during the surgery. The nervous system of animals at this age is not sufficiently developed to perceive pain as being different from general discomfort.

Occasionally, I am asked to dock the tail of an adult mixed breed dog, because the owner wants the dog to resemble a purebred. For adult dogs, a general anesthetic is required, more stitches are needed to close the incision, and there is a risk that the pet may damage the surgical site if it is able to lick the area.

Debarking

Debarking involves removing the vocal cords to reduce the noise made by a pet. Although this procedure can be carried out on both cats and dogs, it is much more common in dogs; hence the name "debarking." Sometimes a landlord or a neighbor will obtain a court order requiring that this procedure be performed as a condition for keeping an animal that is a nuisance to others.

The debarking procedure must be performed perfectly; otherwise the vocal cords might grow back and the surgery must be repeated. Post-operative care is also important, since if swelling or hemorrhage were to develop in the throat area, the pet would have difficulty breathing.

If you choose to have your dog debarked, you should understand that even if the operation is successful, the dog will not be totally mute. It will produce a very harsh, hoarse bark; although the volume will be quieter than a regular bark, some families find this sound more unnerving and annoying than the original bark. I once visited a veterinarian who had a Siamese cat that he had debarked himself in a misguided effort to make it quieter. He admitted that he found the cat's new sound almost as annoying as the original "talking" that is typical of a Siamese cat.

In my view, debarking is an unnatural mutilation, since I feel a dog needs to have some means of communicating in an auditory manner. Therefore I will not debark a pet. However, if conscientious training has failed and having an animal debarked is the only way to keep it as a pet, it remains a possible option. I must stress, however, that such a procedure should be used as a last resort, and only by a veterinarian who has considerable experience performing this kind of surgery.

6

Care of Puppies and Kittens

The initial time you spend with a new pet will largely determine the nature of the relationship that will develop. A puppy that is spoiled and "babied" from the start will develop into a very dependent and possibly neurotic pet as it matures. A kitten that is played with in a rough manner from the outset will become a fractious and difficult adult cat.

You will soon discover your new pet is very quick to learn the habits of the household, and you can use this to your advantage. With our own two dogs we established an end-of-the-day routine that I often recommend to clients. When the dogs come in from outside for the last time before bedtime, regardless of the hour, they are given their vitamins in the kitchen. They then run upstairs to the bedroom where they get their dog biscuits after they are on their individual blankets on the floor. They know that receiving their biscuits means it's "lights out" and playtime is over for the day. They settle right down and go to sleep.

Pets often recognize the human routines that affect them and react accordingly. My cat Alistair would wait outside the bathroom while I brushed my teeth at bedtime, and then race to her food bowl, knowing that if everything had been eaten she would get a little more. Brushing my teeth at any other time of the day would not produce this response from her. My dog Blue would not begin eating her supper until I started loading the dishwasher; at that point she knew she would not get even a fingerful of people food, and only then would she be content to eat her dog food. Hope springs eternal in the canine heart! Animals are creatures of habit, and this is probably the single most important factor to apply in establishing a positive and happy relationship with your pet.

Nutrition and Feeding

Never feed your pets exclusively "people" food. In fact, if you can resist the temptation, your pet will be much healthier if it *never* eats table scraps. Cats and dogs need a properly balanced diet suited to their needs. In nature, they eat both meat and fiber (from the intestinal contents of their prey); thus, even dogs should not be on a "meat only" diet. Similarly, dogs and cats should not be given milk once they have been weaned. Mature dogs and cats lose the ability to digest milk and they may experience digestive upsets if they continue to receive it. The best way to provide your pet with a well-balanced diet is by feeding commercial pet food products.

Commercial pet food comes in three qualities. If you carefully examine the label of the lowest quality of canned food, it will say "BEEF flavor" or "CHICKEN flavor," with the word "flavor" in small lettering; a glance at the list of ingredients will confirm that the food is mainly cereal with added flavoring.

The middle quality of pet food generally provides adequate basic nutrition; however, its cereal ingredients may vary from one batch to another, depending upon availability. Your pet may do perfectly well on the food until you begin a new can or bag, and then your pet may start to vomit or have diarrhea. These are indications that your pet might be allergic to, or unable to digest, some of the new ingredients.

The premium foods have very strict quality control standards and the ingredients never vary. The levels of protein, fat, fiber, and moisture are carefully regulated and remain constant from one batch to the next. Not only is the level of protein important, but so is the source. A good-quality protein (from meat) is readily digested and absorbed by the body while poorer-quality protein (from plants) is not as digestible and, thus, may not be available to the body.

As the ideal levels of protein and other nutrients vary with the animal's age, each brand of premium-quality pet food produces different formulas for each life stage: growth formula for young, pregnant, or nursing animals; maintenance formula for adults; calorie-reduced maintenance food for overweight animals; and senior formula for older pets.

Some premium pet foods are not available in the supermarkets, but can be purchased from pet shops and veterinary hospitals. Although premium foods may appear to be more costly than lower-quality foods, you feed less per serving, as these foods are highly concentrated and easily digestible. On a per feeding basis, premium food usually costs about the same as middle-quality food, and is therefore highly recommended.

It is impossible to compare various brands of pet food just from their labels, since the moisture content in each brand differs. However, by calculating the "dry weight analysis," comparisons can be accurately made. The dry weight analysis shows the percentage that each nutrient represents of the total dry matter (that portion of the food that would be left if all of the water were removed) in a particular food.

On the label of every can or package, you will find a "Guaranteed Analysis," which shows, amongst other things, a percentage moisture content. The dry weight is determined by subtracting the moisture percentage from 100. For example, if the moisture content is 75 percent, the dry matter is 25 percent. You can then calculate the dry weight analysis for each nutrient that is listed in the Guaranteed Analysis.

EXAMPLE ONE: A can shows a label guarantee of 10 percent protein, and the moisture (water) is 75 percent. Calculate: 10 percent protein divided by 25 percent (dry matter) = 40 percent protein dry weight analysis.
EXAMPLE TWO: A dry pet food has a label guarantee of 20 percent protein, and a moisture content of 10 percent. Calculate: 20 percent protein divided by 90 percent (dry matter) = 22 percent protein dry weight analysis.

Pet foods are available in cans, packages (semimoist food), and bags or boxes (dry kibble). For cats, I usually recommend a combination of canned and dry food with just a little semimoist food. The canned food provides the cat with extra moisture while the kibble helps keep the teeth clean. For small breeds of dogs I also recommend canned food for palatability and kibble to help keep the teeth clean. Very small breeds may prefer just canned food; however, this lack of chewing hard food often results in dental problems later on in life. Large breeds of dogs usually thrive on an exclusive diet of dry food and plenty of fresh water.

Kibble, which contains about 10 percent moisture, is much more nutritionally concentrated than canned food, which contains an average of 70 to 78 percent water. For this reason dry food will fill up and satisfy an animal more easily than canned food. Therefore, if you want your pet to gain some weight, dry food would be advisable. On the other hand, an overweight animal will tend to lose some weight if it is fed a larger proportion of canned food, as long as the total volume fed remains the same.

I usually suggest that clients avoid the packages of semimoist dog food, particularly for older dogs. This food contains high levels of preservatives (especially salt) to maintain its softness, flavor, and freshness. Too much salt can be deadly for a middle-aged or old dog with a heart condition. For consumer appeal, semimoist food is also laden with food coloring to make it resemble a meat product. Some animals are sensitive to these food additives, and can develop reactions such as hyperactivity or skin irritations.

Young animals are generally weaned right onto moistened canned "growth formula" food, or a weaning formula, when they are around six weeks old. The growth formula has all of the protein, energy, and minerals that the young animal needs to help it grow to its fullest potential. This formula should be used until the pet has completed most of its growing, usually by ten months to a year of age. Growth formula food is also recommended for pregnant and nursing mothers.

The maintenance food formula provides the necessary levels of nutrition for the normal adult. If the pet leads a quiet life without much exercise and/or has a tendency to gain weight, the calorie-reduced formula should be used.

Senior food is fed to larger dogs starting at the age of about eight years. Smaller breeds, which mature more slowly, can be switched to senior food at about ten years. The senior food formula is lower in protein, salt, fat, and minerals to protect the animal's heart and kidneys from potential problems; it is also higher in some of the vitamins and fatty acids needed to maintain the animal's skin and coat in good condition.

It is important to avoid any sudden change in diet. If you are changing from one formula to another, or from one brand to another, mix the two foods together for several days and gradually reduce the quantity of the food you are replacing while increasing the amount of the new food. This will give the animal's body a chance to adjust to the change and lessen the possibility of vomiting or diarrhea.

If you have a dog and a cat in the same household, you will find that, given the opportunity, they will eat each other's food. However, cats and dogs have very different nutritional requirements. In particular, cats need more protein than dogs. Although the occasional nibbling or sampling of each other's food will not immediately harm your cat or dog, long-term exclusive use of the wrong food is definitely not advisable. Dog food is for dogs, cat food is for cats, and people food is for people!

How often should you feed your pet? As a general rule, very young animals are fed three times daily. As they get older, the midday feeding is eliminated when the pet seems less hungry at this time. Most adult dogs are fed once daily; however, there is no harm in feeding twice a day. Some of the larger dogs may even be better off eating two small meals per day, rather than one large one. The important consideration is the total amount of food eaten over the day.

A major problem affecting the health of dogs and cats in our society is obesity caused by overfeeding. Consult with your veterinarian for the recommended food and the proper amount to feed your pet. Although most food labels provide general feeding guides, I have found many of these guides to be overgenerous in the recommended portion sizes. As with people, animals are better off on the slim side than overweight. The subject of obesity is dealt with more fully in Chapter 22, "Risk Factors and Dietary Management of Disease."

There are two ways to feed a pet: free-feeding, and meals. In the former, the daily ration is placed in the animal's food dish once daily and the pet eats when it so wishes. My dog Blue was being fed this way when I adopted her as a one-year-old dog. However, in the middle of the night, when she started crunching loudly on her kibble and then slurped her water, I quickly decided that free-feeding would not work in our household, as I am a light sleeper! It also occurred to me that with free-feeding, if the food bowl always appeared full, one might assume that it had recently been refilled by another family member. If the dog were ill and not eating, it might take several days to realize that this was the real reason the food level did not diminish. I always encourage clients to feed their pets at fixed times. This way, it is easy to assess the animal's state of health by its appetite.

If the hungry pet is fed just before the family sits down for a meal, it is less likely to beg for people food at the table. Maintaining such a feeding schedule also makes housebreaking easier, since puppies usually have a bowel movement shortly after eating.

Table scraps should be given with extreme rarity, if at all. The varying amounts of fat and seasonings in our food frequently cause upset stomachs in animals. If an animal is overweight and is receiving table scraps, I always suggest that, for one day, all the tidbits destined for the dog be placed on a plate; at the end of the day you can actually see how much food the dog would have consumed! Animals can easily get into the habit of begging for food from the table and not eating their own food until a handout of people food is received. Taken to the extreme, the pet will quickly learn that if it refuses its own food, the amount of tasty table food it receives will increase. It won't take the pet long to have the family trained to give it the food it prefers, even though most types of people food are not healthy for animals.

The owner of a tiny five-month-old Maltese puppy once complained to me that the dog would not eat its food, and had to be hand-fed table food. She asked me when the dog would start to eat dog food and I told her that it was probably too late to change the dog's eating habits, as it had already developed a taste for people food and would not likely accept dog food. Every time I saw the dog over the next few months, the owner repeated her complaint that the dog was not eating enough. However, every time I weighed the dog, its weight kept increasing. Fairly soon, its weight exceeded the breed standard for a Maltese, all because it was fed an inappropriate diet of people food, which was far too high in calories. It is interesting, and perhaps fairly telling, to note that the owner herself was rather large and presumably enjoyed people food as much as her pet!

Clients often ask about treats they can offer their pets. Although they are not necessary if an animal is fed a proper diet, many families like to use treats as positive reinforcement when training their pets. Commercial dog biscuits are enjoyed by most dogs; the chewing action may help to keep the dog's teeth clean. Often, however, large dogs take a bite or two and swallow the rest of the biscuit whole, so the idea of feeding biscuits to "brush" the dog's teeth should not be overestimated. Flavored vitamins and other natural, chemical- and additive-free pet treats, which are usually available at your veterinarian's office, can also be used as treats. Other commercial treats should be considered as equivalent to "junk food." While these treats may not cause immediate harm, they contain a lot of salt and other additives that make them appealing to the pet, but over the long run might prove unhealthy.

As stated earlier, people food is not recommended for animals, and can in fact be dangerous. For example, chocolate is poisonous to dogs and cats and can cause cardiac problems, muscle tremors, seizures, and coma, sometimes terminating in death. For a more complete discussion of household items that are harmful to your pet, see Chapter 3, "Protecting Your Pet From Harm." There are some foods, however, that can be offered to your pet as healthy treats. It is all right to let your cat lick a small amount of milk left over from your bowl of morning cereal, or a tiny amount of ice cream (not chocolate!). Such small quantities should not result in digestive upsets. I am told by some clients that their cats enjoy pieces of broccoli or even olives! Many cats like frozen green beans or peas that are nice and crunchy. A dog can be offered various fruits; my dog loves bananas, apples, and grapes. Some of my patients enjoy orange segments, although cats seem to avoid citrus smells. Whenever "Lance," a large Golden Retriever, comes in to board at my office, he arrives with a supply of apples and each day he anxiously waits as an apple is peeled, cored, and cut into pieces for him to have before his dinner.

I am vehemently opposed to giving real bones to dogs. As the pet gnaws on a bone, tiny splinters get broken off and swallowed. Stomach acid softens these bone chips and as they pass into the intestine they stick together and reform into a larger mass. The dog will become very uncomfortable and be unable to pass this solid mass of bone. On several occasions I have had to anesthetize a large dog, such as a German Shepherd, to try to dislodge this type of obstruction from its rectum. It is unbelievable how solid such a bony mass can be and how difficult it is to break apart.

Small soft bones, such as chicken bones, can also be dangerous for an animal to eat; these bones can get stuck in the throat or even pierce the esophagus, stomach, or intestine at any level. If a client absolutely insists on giving a bone to his or her dog, I stipulate that a large beef knuckle bone be offered (raw, not cooked, as cooking will soften the bone), and at the first sign of splintering, the bone should be taken away. But I repeat, the preferable rule is: no bones for your pet!

Items such as plastic or nylon bones or specially prepared beef hooves last much longer and are much safer than real animal bones. Rawhide "bones" are also enjoyed by most dogs, but should be offered infrequently. My big dog will devour a large rawhide bone in half a day—and usually have diarrhea afterwards! Your pet should be supervised when playing with chew toys. On several occasions, clients have told me that a piece of rawhide bone became wedged in their dogs' throats and the owners have had to do a "Heimlich maneuver" to expel the obstruction. Even cat play toys should be checked regularly for any loose buttons or bells that might be swallowed. When threads start to unravel from a toy, it is time to invest in a new one.

When Nature Calls

Cats

For our animals to be acceptable as pets their toilet habits must conform to certain norms. Teaching an animal to eliminate in the proper place is known as "housetraining." For cats this is generally not a problem. Most kittens are trained by their mothers to use the litter pan. When you introduce a new kitten into your household, immediately put it in the litter pan. From there it will hop out and explore its new surroundings. If, by chance, the kitten relieves itself somewhere other than the litter pan, wait until it has eaten a meal, and then try again. Move its front feet to make digging motions in the litter. If this doesn't work, taking some of its stool and placing it in the pan should do the trick.

There are several types of litter pans available at pet supply stores. The basic litter pan is a plastic dish about 15 to 20 centimetres (6–8 in.) deep; it should be filled with 8 to 10 centimetres (3–4 in.) of litter. Some people prefer to use covered litter pans; the tray is fitted with a tall plastic lid with an opening in one side to allow the cat access to the litter. In this type of pan the cat will be less likely to spread the litter while digging and scratching, and the odor from the litter does not permeate the room as much as from an open pan. Some covered litter pans even have air filters or fans built into the top.

Basic cat litter is composed of small crushed pieces of clay rock. As some brands are rather dusty, I usually fill the litter pan outdoors. You can add odor-eliminating substances to the litter, such as baking soda or commercial litter-deodorizing products. Some brands of litter have been pretreated with deodorizing substances, such as chlorophyll, to freshen the aroma.

Other materials are also used as cat litter. One type is composed of small pellets of recycled newspaper; its advantages are that it is dust-free, and it absorbs most of the liquid waste and most of the odor. This type of litter can also be used for small rodents. Another type of litter is "clumping sand." When moisture (urine) hits this material, a small firm ball of sand forms, which can be easily removed. The manufacturers of this product claim that you never have to empty the litter pan, as the waste products, both liquid and solid, can be removed daily. This product supposedly can safely be flushed down the toilet, which greatly simplifies disposal. Many cat owners agree that this is an excellent product, although some of the sand may be tracked about the house by the cat after it has used the pan.

Regardless of which type of litter you are using, solid matter (feces) and very wet litter should be removed from the pan daily. It is important to empty and change the entire litter pan at least once a week, or more frequently in a multicat household. Wash the pan with a mild detergent and thoroughly rinse and dry it before refilling. In my experience, cats usually go immediately to a clean litter pan and "christen" it anew with urine or feces, even if they had just used the pan before it was cleaned!

Your kitten may avoid using the litter pan for a variety of reasons: if the litter is scented, it might not seem like natural dirt to the kitten; if you are using a covered litter pan, the kitten might be afraid to enter through the small opening, especially if it has a noisy fan; or if the litter pan is located near a loud machine such as a furnace or central vacuum cleaning unit, the kitten might associate the frightening noises with the litter pan.

I have read accounts of cats learning to eliminate into the toilet bowl. Some books on cat behavior instruct the reader how to teach a cat to perform this task. A client once told me that her cat started eliminating into the toilet without any instruction! Another client told me that her cat liked to flush the toilet, presumably to watch the water go around and then disappear. Maybe we should get these two cats together!

Dogs

A crate or kennel is a great help in housebreaking a puppy because a dog instinctively tries to keep its nesting area (the crate) clean. Be sure to buy a crate that is the correct size: large enough for the adult dog to stand, sit, and stretch out, but not so large that the puppy will have room to romp around in it. You do not want enough room for the puppy to sleep at one end and eliminate at the other. If necessary, block off part of the crate area with cardboard.

If the puppy is kept in the crate at night and when you are not at home, it will try not to eliminate until you take it outdoors or to the desired toilet area. You must remember to be realistic in judging the puppy's capabilities for keeping its kennel clean; don't expect a two-month-old puppy to hold its urine for twelve hours! However, you will find that using a crate will speed up the housebreaking process. It will also ensure that the dog stays out of mischief when you are away from home or sleeping.

Get the puppy used to the crate gradually. At first, place it in the crate for a few minutes while you sit down beside the crate and talk to the puppy in a happy voice. Keep praising the dog when it is inside, lengthening the periods it is left in the crate. Any complaining the puppy might do at first is not created by the crate, but by the new controls set by this unfamiliar environment. Do not let it out of the crate when it is whining or complaining—this will only reward bad behavior. Wait until the dog has been quiet for about five minutes, then release it, but without an emotional "welcome," which again would be an inappropriate reward. As a general rule, you should take the puppy outside every time it is released from its crate. Carry the dog so that it does not have an "accident" on the way.

If you make the crate comfortable with a towel or blanket, preferably one with your scent on it, and perhaps a treat when you are leaving, the dog will learn to readily go into its little "house" when it wants to nap; it will feel secure and happy there. By giving all meals and treats inside the crate, the dog will quickly learn to enter on its own. Reward the dog with praise whenever it goes into the crate. Remember that the crate must be an enjoyable place and must never be used for punishment.

The crate should be kept where your dog can still be with you, and be a part of the family activities, even if only as an observer. Do not put it in the basement or some other remote part of the house. The kitchen or family room is a good place; you can even move the crate around with you. At night, the crate should go in your bedroom. Not only does this provide comforting company, but your own sleeping sounds will encourage the puppy to slumber on.

Housebreaking a puppy is usually a little more involved than litter-training a kitten. The most important rule in successful housetraining is to prevent the dog from making mistakes, rather than to correct mistakes that have already been made. Generally, the puppy will have to relieve itself after it wakes up, after active play, and after eating. Some people train their pet to eliminate on newspaper when it is young and then later they train it to go outdoors, but this is not necessary; you can start right away training your puppy to eliminate outside.

The first step is to establish a regular feeding schedule. After your puppy has finished eating, or after it wakes up from a nap, take it outside to the spot you have designated for its toilet activities. Praise the dog when it eliminates there. Take the puppy back inside and play with it for a while, then return it to its crate for a nap. Every hour or so, take the puppy outside to its special spot and wait a few minutes. If the puppy does not relieve itself, return it to the crate immediately.

Each time there is success, praise the dog and leave it out of its crate for a while under close supervision. If you catch the puppy starting to sniff the ground and turn in circles, or just starting to squat, immediately take it to where you wish it to eliminate and praise it when it does. It is worth repeating that the goal is to prevent mistakes and reward good behavior.

Before placing the puppy in its crate, be certain it has had sufficient exercise and attention. Some puppies may be content with a short walk, but many are not tired out until they have had fifteen to thirty minutes of vigorous exercise. As a general rule, if the puppy has had sufficient exercise and has eliminated, the number of hours it can be confined to its crate can be calculated by taking the puppy's age in months and adding one. This means that a two-month-old puppy should have two to three hours of control, a three-month-old puppy up to four hours, and a four-month-old up to five hours. Of course, there will be some individual variation.

If the puppy has to be left alone for longer periods than it is capable of remaining clean, a small room rather than a crate should be used for confinement. Select a room where there is little mischief for the puppy to get into. Have the crate, food, and water in one section, and place newspaper on the floor in another section, just in case.

If absolutely necessary, an adult dog can control urination for up to thirteen hours, depending on activity, air temperature, the amount of water consumed, and other factors. Some people place newspaper in a corner, or in the basement, just in case the dog gets caught "short" when no one is at home.

A basic housebreaking principle I always stress is that praise works better than punishment. A slight reprimand will work only if the puppy is actually caught in the act of soiling; if you discover a mess on the floor, scolding the puppy after the fact is totally useless. Some misguided owners rub their puppies' noses in feces several hours after the mistake has occurred—this is entirely ineffective because the dog cannot connect the act of defecating with the "punishment" it is receiving. The animal will simply learn that its nose will be rubbed in stool when the owner returns home, without understanding why. This behavior on your part may also give the dog the message that eating feces is appropriate! Another point to remember: do not let the dog see you cleaning up its mess, as this may be construed by some pets as a reward.

Crate training is considered the quickest and surest way to housetrain the average puppy. Occasionally, however, you will find a dog that does not care if it messes in its crate, or anywhere else for that matter. One training technique is to place a lead on this type of puppy and tie it to your belt. As you go about the house, the attached puppy goes with you. If it attempts to mess, you are right there to issue a stern verbal correction. Be sure to make eye contact with the dog. Immediately take it to its toilet area to finish the job. This is one sure way of getting the idea across rather quickly.

It is a good idea to avoid playing with your puppy, or taking it for a walk, until after it has relieved itself in the designated spot. Some dogs delay eliminating simply because they have learned that as soon as they eliminate, the owner brings them back home; in effect, the dog feels it is being punished for having relieved itself!

One further thing to remember: keep the dog's designated toilet area clean by removing the deposits every day or two. Otherwise a point may be reached where the dog does not want to use this area any more, or another problem known as "coprophagia" (the eating of feces) might develop. Although this activity occurs most frequently in puppies and tends to decrease after the dog is one year old, there is great individual variation. Many dogs outgrow it, others partake only in the winter when the stools are frozen, some indulge occasionally, and others never kick the habit. If your puppy persists in eating its own stool, a product called "ForBid" can be added to its food. This is supposed to impart a taste to the stool that will discourage the dog from continuing this behavior.

Be a responsible pet owner when walking your dog. Pick up any stool the dog eliminates on public or private property. This is more than just the right thing to do—in many jurisdictions, it is the law and hefty fines are levied against those who do not comply. Always carry several plastic bags in your pocket when you go out; it won't take you long to determine which size bag to use. The easiest way to pick up your dog's stool is to put your hand into the plastic bag as if it were a mitten, bend down and pick up the stool through the bag. With your other hand take the free edge of the plastic and, after inverting the bag, tie it closed.

A young male dog will urinate by squatting, just like a female dog. As it gets older it will learn to lift a leg and urinate on vertical objects that have been "labeled" by other dogs. Some males never acquire the habit of lifting a leg to urinate. This is fine—there is nothing wrong with squatting. Conversely, some female dogs occasionally lift a leg—this, too, is not a cause for concern.

Handling the Young Pet

A kitten or puppy should become accustomed to having various parts of its body handled. It should get used to having its mouth opened to ensure that the pet won't panic if medicine has to be given orally at some point, or if a foreign object has to be removed from its mouth. Handling the head at an early age will make it easier for a groomer to give the pet a proper haircut, if necessary. You should examine the pet's ears regularly for early detection of infection or other ear problems. Regular handling will also make it easier to apply medication into the ears should the need ever arise.

The first time I examined a particular four-month-old Shih Tzu, he resisted my checking his ears and I instructed the owners to work on this. Unfortunately, they had already resigned themselves to the fact that this puppy had an aggressive streak and was going to rule the household. Sure enough, when the dog subsequently developed an ear infection, the family found itself totally unable to treat it, and stated that they would have the dog euthanized if the problem worsened. How sad, and how easily prevented this situation could have been, had the owners taken the time to accustom the dog to being properly handled.

I also suggest that pet owners make a point of handling their young animals' feet. This will make it easier to wipe dirt or moisture off the feet should the need arise, and will also facilitate trimming the pet's nails as necessary. An animal that is used to having its paws handled should not be upset by the sound of the nail clippers or the slight pressure on its toes; only if the nails are cut too short will it feel discomfort. A very large Golden Retriever was once brought to my office to have its nails trimmed. It did not like this procedure and the only way my assistant could restrain it was to straddle the dog's back and hold its head up while I held the leg I was working on. This worked for a short while until the dog simply decided to get up and walk away with my assistant still on its back!

A young animal should also be brushed and combed regularly to maintain its coat. Begin by brushing your pet for a few minutes every day, then reward it with a tasty treat.

Even if you plan to have your dog professionally groomed every few months, you will probably want to bathe it in between groomings. The ideal time to learn the correct technique is when the dog is small and easy to handle (for details on bathing see Chapter 8, "Grooming Your Pet"). I started bathing Aimée, my very large dog, in the kitchen sink shortly after I got her; now she enjoys baths and will calmly stand in the bathtub, especially when she is getting a gentle back massage.

Taking a young puppy to a professional groomer for a hair trim will make it easier for a proper grooming to be done once the fur has grown long enough to require it. This first minor trim will get the puppy used to being handled by a stranger. It will also introduce the puppy to the sound of electric clippers, the feel of scissors and nail trimmers, and the experience of the bathing and drying processes. Don't wait until the animal's fur is long and tangled before making the first grooming appointment. By this time the dog will be so attached to its family that it will resent being handled by others, especially if that handling involves the removal of large tangles.

It is also very important to get the young pet used to traveling in a car. Some dogs suffer from motion sickness, so begin with short trips around the block before mealtime. Most dogs quickly learn to enjoy the ride, while sitting quietly in the back seat. There is more on car traveling in Chapter 11, "Vacation Time."

Teething

Puppies and kittens begin to cut teeth while they are nursing. By the time they are five or six weeks old they have several sharp teeth; no doubt this motivates the mother to start weaning her offspring. Over the following weeks, a second set of teeth push through the gum line to permanently replace the baby teeth. The young animal usually swallows the baby teeth as they come out, and they pass through the digestive tract without problem. The last adult teeth to erupt are the fangs or canine teeth. The baby fangs are curved, sharp, and very tapered; by six months of age these are fully replaced by adult canine teeth, which are wider and straighter.

In some small dog breeds, particularly Shih Tzus, teething will take much longer than six months. Occasionally—again, in the smaller breeds—some of the baby teeth may not come out after the adult teeth have erupted. Veterinarians usually recommend extraction of these extra teeth as they can alter the bite of the entire mouth and can allow food particles to become trapped between the double teeth. This extraction can be done with a brief general anesthetic by itself, or any time the animal is under anesthetic for another surgery.

When a puppy is teething, it will have a voracious need to chew on anything it can find. Offer it various chew toys to focus its attention appropriately. See also the discussion of canine behavior problems in Chapter 7, "Establishing Good Behavior."

During the teething process, it is not uncommon for the pet to go off its food for a day or two, due to the discomfort caused by a loose tooth. Bleeding, caused by a baby tooth wiggling in its socket, might occasionally occur while the pet is eating. Do not be alarmed if you see a little bit of blood—it is all part of the normal process of growing up.

Sleeping Arrangements

Where is your new pet going to sleep? I try to discourage clients from having their dogs sleep in bed with them. If the dog develops a flea problem, your bed would also be infested. If the dog develops medical problems (vomiting or diarrhea or urination during the night), your bed would not be a pleasant place to find out about it!

There are also nonmedical reasons against sleeping with pets. A small puppy that is allowed to sleep on your bed may grow up into a large dog that takes up more of the bed than another person. If someone special comes into your life with whom you would prefer to share your bed, the dog may become jealous and resentful if it is suddenly required to sleep elsewhere. Years ago, one of my clients told me that her Dalmatian would hop up onto the bed with her and would not allow her husband into bed! Dogs should sleep on the floor, not on the owner's bed. Although some will disagree with this view, I feel it is important that pets realize that the household furniture is for the use of people. You can purchase a comfortable bed for your dog at any pet shop if you would prefer that it not sleep on the floor. Or, you can place a thick blanket or a bath mat on the floor beside your bed, as I do; your dog will be very cozy there.

Most cats will jump up onto the bed to curl up against you and sleep. Most people do not mind this, although some complain, with a twinkle in their eyes, that the cat wakes them up early in the morning purring in their ears! If you do not want your cat to sleep with you, shut your bedroom door or confine the cat to another part of the house at bedtime. This is also a good idea if you tend to get out of bed during the night and want to avoid disturbing the cat's sleep or accidentally tripping over it in the dark. Again, set the ground rules early on, and the cat will easily accept them.

Home Alone

It is important to get your new pet, especially a puppy, used to being left alone. I once had clients with a Toy Poodle that was very spoiled by the housebound wife. The dog was used to having someone always at home; in fact, the dog spent most of its time on the woman's lap. Whenever the couple had to go out, the dog was brought to my office for a few hours of "doggy day-care," because it would bark incessantly if left in their apartment.

A crate that is being used for housetraining can also be put into service when you are going out for short periods of time. Before leaving, ensure that the dog has had a fair amount of exercise so that it will be sleepy during your absence. Place the puppy in the crate, reassure it calmly that you will be back soon, and leave. Do not make your departure an emotional one, or the dog will pick up on your anxiety! People who make a production of saying goodbye to their dog often unconsciously adopt a whining tone of voice that imitates the stress whine used by anxious, nervous dogs. It is best to simply say goodbye calmly and leave. The animal will feel less abandoned if you play the radio or television for a little while prior to your departure, leave it on while you are away, and don't shut it off until a while after you return home. If you turn it on just as you go, the dog will associate the sound of the radio with your leaving, instead of as a source of company and comfort. Once the dog is housetrained, you no longer need to use a crate, but you should restrict the animal to one or two rooms where it cannot do any damage.

Some dogs bark when left alone. This can be a difficult habit to stop once it is acquired. Remember that praise is more effective than punishment; the idea is to leave the puppy for progressively longer periods of time and listen outside the front door. If it stays quiet, return and praise it.

A lonely dog may sometimes act out its frustrations by engaging in unacceptable behavior, such as chewing, barking, or howling. If you return home to find that your dog has misbehaved, do not punish it after the fact. As with housetraining, remember that all reprimands and corrections must be administered while the dog is actually engaging in the bad behavior, so that it connects the behavior with the punishment. If the dog associates your return home with punishment (because of something it did hours previously and has since forgotten), it may fret as the hour of your return home approaches, and may misbehave even more!

Some destructive behavior might be due to hunger pangs. Most families feed their adult dogs only once a day, in the evening. Left alone all day with an empty stomach, a dog might develop the urge to nibble. A light meal early in the morning could make things easier for both of you.

When you return home, avoid an enthusiastic greeting. Wild "hellos" can get a dog so keyed up for your return that it turns to destructive behavior if you are delayed. Just greet the dog cheerfully and save the active play for a little later.

Some young dogs will dribble some urine—a sign of submission—when they are excited at your return home. If this happens, do not reprimand the animal. Remain calm, prevent it from becoming overly excited, and boost its confidence by introducing it to a variety of new and nonthreatening experiences. Don't make a fuss over the puppy. Simply lift it up and immediately take it outdoors and praise it if it urinates there. Usually the young dog will outgrow this behavior.

7

Establishing Good Behavior

It is very important to begin teaching your new pet the rules of acceptable behavior right away. As your pet matures it will constantly "try" you to see what it can get away with. It is better to start off stern; you can always relax the rules later, but it is very difficult to go from being lenient to strict once an animal has acquired inappropriate behavior.

The first step in establishing good behavior in your pet is for you to demonstrate self-confidence and control. Animals quickly sense anxiety and fear in people; if you are afraid of your pet, the animal will sense this and build on it. This is particularly true in the case of dogs because they are "pack" animals. There must always be a "leader of the pack"; if you are not the leader, the dog will very quickly and happily assume the role! I recall a mild-mannered family that adopted a large dog. Unfortunately, they were afraid of it and kept it locked in the kitchen most of the day. It was never taken outside on a leash because they could not control it and would not discipline it. By the time I saw it at the age of one year, the damage had been done—the dog was completely uncontrollable. This family should have had help in training the dog right from the outset. Sadly, the dog was euthanized a couple of years later.

Basic Behavior Training for Dogs and Cats

It is important to realize that what is acceptable as "cute" from a young animal may turn into a serious behavioral problem later on. With this in mind, kittens or puppies should never be allowed to chew on your fingers or toes. React strongly with a stern "No" and then remove the target as much as possible: sit on your hands or try to cover your feet. The tone of your voice is important: speak sternly and assertively (never scream); if you are laughing or using an encouraging tone, the pet will quickly interpret this as positive reinforcement, and will grow up to believe that biting is acceptable.

Similarly, it is inappropriate behavior for a dog to jump up on people. Many experts recommend hitting the dog's chest with your knee when this happens, while others suggest squeezing its paws when it jumps up and saying "No." Better yet, you should prevent the dog from jumping in the first place by teaching it to sit. When you or a visitor comes through the door, command the dog to "sit"; then kneel down and give it the hug it wants so much.

Be consistent in what behavior is acceptable. Your pet cannot differentiate between the old shoe you gave it to chew as a puppy or kitten, and your expensive new dress shoes. Avoid confusion and temptation by removing all footwear from the pet's reach.

When your pet breaks the rules, it must be corrected. To be effective, the reprimand must be administered at the time of the wrongdoing or immediately thereafter. It is pointless and sometimes counterproductive to correct the animal after the event. Here is an example. When I walk my dog (on a leash, of course), another dog being walked on the other side of the street without a leash will sometimes run towards us. When its owner finally catches up to it, he or she will severely reprimand it. The dog does not realize that it is being punished for having run across the street. From the dog's point of view, it is being punished for having let its owner catch up to it, since this is what occurred immediately before the reprimand. With this in mind, the dog will probably try even harder to evade its owner's attempts to catch it next time. Similarly, *never* call your dog or cat over to you for a reprimand—it will stop coming. Instead, calmly go to the scene of the inappropriate activity and scold the pet there. If you charge frantically towards it, it will become frightened and run away. By the time you do catch it, it won't remember the reason it was being chased, and the lesson will be lost.

What is an effective form of reprimand? It must be sufficiently startling and unpleasant to deter the animal from repeating the behavior, but must not be overly forceful, either physically or verbally; otherwise you will scare and alienate your pet, and it will learn to be as aggressive as you. Reprimand does not mean pain; rather, use intimidation. For example, grabbing a dog or cat by the scruff of the neck, giving it a shake or a slight smack on the rump and an eye-to-eye stare while sternly saying "No!" is effective. Another effective technique is to command a dog to sit, and just stare at it for several moments.

Another way to correct a pet's undesirable behavior is to temporarily isolate it. Social deprivation is a strong deterrent for a young animal. When you have caught it engaging in some inappropriate behavior, start with a firm "No," then put it in a small empty room such as a laundry room or bathroom for fifteen minutes or so.

Immediate action must be taken if your pet hisses or growls at you while you are disciplining it. Do not back off or it will learn that it can intimidate you. When a kitten hisses, swats, or bites, simply take hold of it, shake it slightly, and say "No!" loudly and firmly. Mean it, because this is a battle of wills and you must be stronger. If it immediately tries again, give it a smack on the rump and say "No!" again. Similarly, if your puppy growls aggressively in response to a reprimand, hold its face firmly and stare it in the eye, saying "No." Remember that dogs are pack animals and you must establish yourself as the leader of the pack.

Whenever possible, follow a reprimand with a demonstration of the proper behavior. For example, if you scold your pet for begging at the table, wait a few minutes, then take it to its dish and give it a treat. If it is in a place where it is not allowed to be, reprimand it, wait a few minutes, then take it to an acceptable place and give it a treat.

You should wait several minutes between a reprimand and a reward because it is important that your pet not associate a reward with an unacceptable habit. For example, if you correct your cat's habit of clawing the couch with a firm "No," and take it immediately to its scratching post for a treat, the cat will associate scratching the couch with receiving a treat. It has learned that the unacceptable behavior brings a reward! Let the correction sink in before moving on; five minutes or so is usually long enough. This way it will learn to associate the reward with good behavior and the reprimand with bad behavior.

There is no getting around the fact that puppies and kittens like to chew—this is part of the normal teething process. You can reduce your pet's temptation to chew on specific things by removing the items in question, removing the pet from the items, or by coating the items with tabasco sauce or a mixture of cayenne pepper and petroleum jelly. After you have stopped your pet from chewing something inappropriate, give it something it *can* chew, such as a rawhide stick.

Electrical wires, if chewed by your pet, can be dangerous. Hanging cords can be irresistible but harmful to a playful kitten or puppy; an iron or lamp could be pulled over, injuring the pet. One way to discourage your pet from playing with wires is to take a piece of unused cord and attach it to something harmless such as a tinfoil plate or a light paperback book. Balance it precariously on the edge of a table or shelf. When your pet starts to play with the cord, the object will fall down and startle it. Alternatively, smear tabasco sauce on the cord—your pet will definitely not like the taste!

Since you cannot always supervise your pet, try to remove temptation as much as possible. If your kitten likes to unroll the toilet tissue, close the bathroom door. If the kitten is a plant chewer, place plants out of its reach. If you do not want your pet sleeping on the furniture, cover the furniture with something unpleasant, like plastic or tinfoil.

Dealing with Feline Behavior

Cats have an instinctive need to scratch, to sharpen their claws, and to mark territory with the scent glands on their feet. If you choose not to have your cat declawed, its scratching can cause considerable damage to furniture, wallpaper, and carpets, unless you train it from the outset to use a scratching post. Construct or buy a scratching post that is tall enough for an adult cat to stretch out, and sturdy enough to withstand its strength. The post should be covered with a rough fabric, such as the back of a carpet remnant. To the top of the post, attach an enticement such as a dangling toy containing catnip. Show the kitten how to use the scratching post by moving its paws in a scratching motion against the rough surface. Talk softly and praise the kitten; give it a tasty reward after it uses the scratching post. This positive reinforcement, coupled with the negative response of being squirted by a water pistol when it scratches other items, should teach it to scratch only the post.

Some cats love to chew houseplants and dig in the soil. If you cannot remove the plants from the cat's reach, make the plants undesirable. Take white vinegar, lemon juice, or lime juice, and place just a few small drops on your cat's gums. This will not harm the cat, but it should find the taste disgusting. Then make up a mixture consisting of whatever you used on its gums, plus a very small amount of commercial cat repellent. Spray the plants with this mixture (it will not harm most household plants). If the cat approaches the plants, the smell and taste should remind it of its previous unpleasant experience, and the cat repellent should be a further deterrent. Incidentally, never spray cat repellent directly on or at your cat; you could seriously harm it.

To prevent your cat from digging in your potted plants, wrap tinfoil around the base of the plants and over the soil, and put a heavy stone on the tin foil to keep it in place. If this does not work, try cutting a piece of chicken wire to fit the soil surface around your plant and cover it with a layer of earth. When the cat starts to dig, its feet will get caught and it won't be amused.

To discourage your cat from climbing, place pieces of two-sided sticky tape in places where you do not want the cat to climb. The cat will not like the sensation of the tape sticking to its feet. This also works to discourage scratching.

The treatment of elimination problems in cats can be very complex. Often, success is achieved only after considerable discussion with a veterinarian. Try to determine whether the cause is physical, environmental, or psychological. The physical causes of a cat soiling in the house include: unneutered male cats marking their territory; female cats in heat; medication that can cause abnormal urination; and kidney or bladder problems. Feces being deposited outside the litter pan might be caused by intestinal infections, parasitism, or food intolerance. For this reason it is recommended that a cat which is soiling inappropriately should have a complete physical examination, including a urinalysis. In several cases I have discovered that the patients had diabetes. I have come to conclude that, when a previously well-trained and hygienic cat suddenly begins urinating outside the litter pan, the cat is usually trying to alert the family that it has a medical problem requiring immediate attention.

If your veterinarian has ruled out a medical cause for the problem, the cause is likely psychological. This type of condition is relatively infrequent, but more difficult to treat than the physical causes. Cats do show emotional behavior patterns, and sometimes urinate or defecate inappropriately when upset or anxious. I have had clients report that their cats suddenly became super-fastidious and would not use the same litter pan for both stool and urine functions, or would shun the litter pan if it was not clean enough (by their standards, not yours). There is nothing wrong with having two litter pans next to each other.

Recent changes to a cat's environment could cause it to soil in inappropriate places. Examples of such changes include: moving into a new home (especially if the previous residents had animals); obtaining a new piece of furniture or new rugs; using a different type of litter, a different litter pan, or changing its location.

If the cat tends to have accidents in one area of the house, restrict its access to the area, or put a second litter pan there. If the cat uses it, then gradually move it towards a more desirable location. An alternative approach is to totally change the cat's perception of this inappropriate area by placing its food and water bowls there. This should work well, since cats generally do not want to relieve themselves where they eat.

The introduction of another animal into the household is a frequent cause of elimination problems. If there is rivalry and stress in a multicat household, having only one litter pan may result in one or more cats soiling out of the pan. A client once reported to me that one of her two cats started urinating in her running shoes. I suggested putting down another litter pan and she reported that while neither cat used the new pan, there was no further soiling. Cat psychology can be a real mystery!

Here are a few tips to remember when trying to encourage your cat to resume the use of its litter pan. Use plain clay litter with no perfume or chlorophyll additives. Change the litter daily, or twice a day if necessary. Offer your cat more than one litter pan, and in different locations. Do not steam clean your rugs as this makes the urine odor permeate the rug even more, and will attract the cat back to the same spot. Use white vinegar to clean urine stains on carpets (color test a small area first) and then put moth ball crystals into the carpet (if you have young children, this is not recommended as moth balls are toxic). Do not use ammonia-based cleaning compounds as urine is also ammonia-based. Do not punish the cat. If you catch it in the act, pick it up and put it in its litter pan.

Leash Training

Indoor cats can get used to going outside on a leash, attached to a collar or harness. A harness consists of two straps that are buckled around the animal's body, one across the chest in front of the front legs, and a second behind the front legs; these straps are joined by another that runs along the pet's spine, and to which the leash is attached. At first the cat will probably struggle and fuss, but it will soon learn that the leash means access to a fascinating world of sights and smells: grass to nibble on, insects to play with, and so on. But never leave a leashed cat unattended. It could become entangled, or not be able to escape or defend itself from a loose dog.

Your young puppy should also be introduced to the collar or harness and leash at an early age. A dog harness, which has the same design as a cat harness, is very useful for small dogs, such as Maltese or Pekingese, as it does not put pressure on the throat if the dog pulls. Any small animal with a collapsing windpipe, or one that coughs easily, would be less distressed with a harness than with a collar. Also, as a harness does not put pressure on the neck, it reduces the chance of injury to an animal with a disk or spine problem.

There is a variety of collars available for pet use. A fixed flat collar that is buckled around the neck can be used for regular exercise. The collar should be fitted so that you can easily fit a finger between it and the pet's neck. For training purposes, a "choke collar" is more effective. This metal chain has a large loop at each end; hold one of these loops and let the rest of the collar fall through it. Now pull one end so that the collar forms the letter "P." Face the dog and slip the loop over the head of the dog. The links leading away from the loose ring must pass across the top of the dog's neck, not lead down under the chin. When a leash is attached to the loose ring at the end of the stem of the "P," the collar will tighten when the dog pulls away from you and loosen when the pressure is released. This is illustrated in Figure 7.1. Coupled with the proper voice commands, the dog should learn that if it does not pull, it will not be choked by the collar.

If a regular choker is not effective, some trainers recommend a spiked collar. This is a wide metal collar made up of individual links that have blunt metal spikes projecting towards the dog's neck; when the dog pulls, these spikes exert pressure against the animal's skin. This type of collar gives excellent results in large, solidly muscled dogs when the regular choker is not getting the dog's attention during a training session. A spiked collar should only be used after proper instruction from a trainer.

Training collars should be used only during training sessions. If it is worn all the time, the dog will end up with "broken fur" on its neck due to the constant pressure and rubbing. The dog could also end up with an injury if the collar were to get caught on something.

Recently, the "head halter" has rivaled the training collar in popularity. The halter resembles a muzzle, in that there is a strap over the dog's nose; but, unlike the muzzle, the halter still allows the dog to open its mouth, although pulling on the lead will cause the mouth to close. The concept of the head halter is simple. Mother dogs discipline puppies by grabbing them by the scruff of the neck; older

Figure 7.1 **Using a choke collar**.
The first and second drawings show how to form the choker by dropping a section of chain through one of the end loops. The "P" shape is then formed and slipped over the dog's head. In the final frame, the leash has been attached to the choke collar. The loop of the leash is secure on the walker's right hand, with extra slack taken up with the left hand.

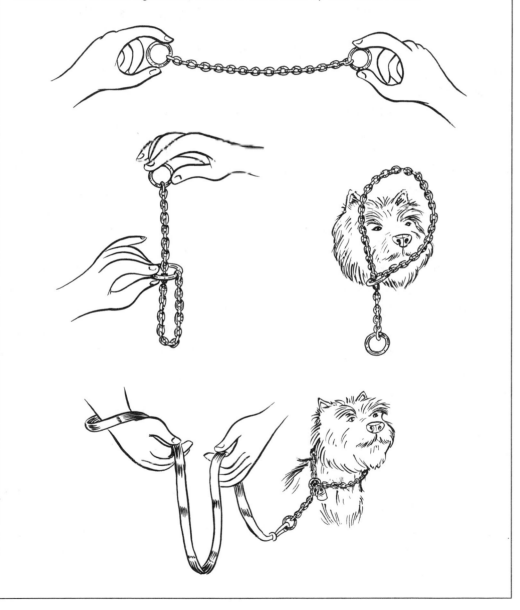

dogs in a pack will often nip at each other's muzzles to demonstrate dominance. The head halter has neck and muzzle straps that exert pressure in these areas, thus impressing upon the dog that someone is in control. Excellent results have been reported in preventing large dogs from lunging by using a head halter. Also, since a halter allows you to gently draw the dog's face up to your own, you have the dog's undivided attention and regular obedience training can proceed at an accelerated pace.

Leashes are most commonly made of leather, heavy rope, linked metal, or nylon fabric. I generally recommend a leather leash because it is strong yet gentle on the hands if your dog should pull.

Often, when the leash and collar are first put on, the puppy will either refuse to move or it will go backwards. To avoid this situation, let the puppy wear the collar around the house for a day or two. Then attach the leash, and allow the pet to drag the leash wherever it goes. When this no longer bothers the dog, take the end of the leash and allow the dog to lead you around the house. Slowly, over the next day or so, try to direct the dog's movements with the leash by exerting pressure. In this way the dog should learn the relationship between itself, the leash, and you.

The correct way to hold the leash is to put your entire right hand through the loop and then grab hold of the straight part of the leash with your left hand. This gives extra security; if the dog pulls very strongly, there is little chance that the leash will be pulled out of your grasp. If the dog is pulling and you want to keep it close to you, grasp the leash closer to the dog (with the loop still around your wrist) and hold it securely at the appropriate distance until you decide to give the dog a little more freedom.

Retractable leashes have also become popular. A retractable leash allows you to control how far the dog can stray from your side. If the dog is interested in sniffing something at a distance, you can let the leash unwind, and lock it at a set distance. When the dog returns, the leash will coil up again inside the handle. Be certain you know how to operate this leash and that you have an accurate idea of the amount of freedom available to the dog. Occasionally when I have been out walking my dog, a dog on the other side of the street has had so much extended leash that it was able to run halfway across the street towards us. What is the point of having a dog on a leash if it has the freedom to run onto the roadway and risk being injured?

Obedience Training for Dogs

Although both dogs and cats can be taught *not* to do certain things, such as sleeping on the furniture or entering certain rooms, dogs can, in addition, be trained to "do" things on command: sit, stay, heel, and so on. This is known as obedience training and is very rarely done with cats.

Begin obedience training by teaching the dog simple commands while on the leash. The dog should always be on your left side; this is the normal "heel" position, meaning that the dog walks by your left heel. During a training session, work in an area where there are minimal distractions. When you stop walking, the dog should immediately sit. This can be taught by simultaneously pulling up on the leash and pressing your hand gently on the dog's rump, while you firmly say "Sit." Praise the dog when it has obeyed.

"Down" is another easy command for the dog to learn. Firmly say "Down," while pulling the leash (and the dog's neck) to the ground. With repeated practice, the dog will learn to lie down when you point to the floor and give the "Down" command. With the assistance of books and instructional videos, you can also teach your dog other commands such as "Stay" and "Come."

Use simple one-word commands, and be consistent. For example, avoid the command "Sit down!" if the dog is learning "Sit" and "Down" as two distinct movements. The tone of your voice is very important. Never ask your dog to do something in a questioning tone of voice. Give your commands assertively and authoritatively, with confidence.

Many trainers suggest giving a food reward to speed up the dog's learning process. Try keeping dog biscuits in your pocket and use them sparingly as positive reinforcement when your commands are obeyed.

It is an excellent idea to take your dog to obedience classes, which are often given by professional trainers through the local humane society, school boards, or veterinary offices. Some trainers offer private sessions to assist in difficult cases. Some will take your dog for several weeks and return it to you "completely trained." While this may sound appealing, there is a risk that, since you have not been involved in the training, the dog might not accept your authority.

Contrary to popular belief, obedience schools do *not* train dogs; they train the *owners* to train their dogs. Nor is the purpose of obedience training to teach the dog "tricks"; rather, the emphasis is on control and instilling good behavior.

At an obedience course, one person, usually an adult or older child, is the principal "handler," working with the dog in class and at home. Other family members work with the dog only after it has thoroughly learned each command. The lessons progress according to an organized plan, in which students receive clear, precise instructions on what to do. Questions are encouraged, and instructors provide individual attention for students who are having problems. If a particular training method fails for a given dog, the instructor will demonstrate alternate techniques. Even if your dog does not master every command to perfection, the course will have provided you with the basic techniques so that you can continue working with the dog on your own.

Obedience training lets your dog channel its energy in a positive way, and makes it feel intelligent and satisfied when it pleases you by obeying your commands. This also reaffirms your position as "leader" of the pack. In addition, if your dog attends obedience classes with other dogs, it is learning how to control itself when other dogs are near. It must learn to pay attention to *you* and overcome its natural inclination to play with the other "pupils." I recall one of the very impressive exercises that my dog Aimée and I were taught in obedience class. About half the dogs and their owners lined up along one side of the room, while the rest of the dogs and owners walked by them. If these dogs responded to the presence of the sitting dogs, they were given a correction (a tug on the choke collar coupled with a firm "No"). The value of this type of training becomes very apparent when you are out for a walk and you can actually pass another dog in the street without having your pet pull you madly towards the other animal.

Guard Dogs

Guard dogs require very specialized training. Unfortunately, some people buy puppies of the large working breeds (such as German Shepherds and Dobermans) and proudly praise every sign of aggression, without training the dog to recognize when such behavior is permissible and when it is unacceptable. The result is a canine time-bomb waiting to explode! Guard dogs must have excellent, balanced temperaments, and be trained to be aggressive only on command. At other times, they will seek a friendly pat as eagerly as any other dog. A properly trained guard dog will stand guard, but never attack unless provoked or given the appropriate command, and will stand back immediately if the aggressor backs down or the handler commands it to stop.

When all Else Fails

For those unfortunate pets with severe behavior problems, a veterinary psychologist should be consulted. Your veterinarian can refer you to one in your area. It is very sad when a beautiful pet is given away or euthanized due to its behavior, because, in my experience, every dog and cat has the capacity to be well behaved. The blame for poor behavior in pets almost invariably belongs to its owners.

8

Grooming Your Pet

Grooming refers to the process of keeping your pet neat and clean. This involves brushing and combing the fur, bathing, trimming its nails, and cleaning its ears and eyes. Depending upon the type of coat and the breed, shaving or cutting the fur might also be required from time to time.

Grooming is more than just a matter of appearance and aesthetics; it is an important part of your pet's hygiene and health care—it reduces the amount of shedding by removing dead fur; prevents tangles and matted fur; and spreads the natural skin oil onto the fur. In cats, hairball problems (vomiting swallowed fur) are minimized by regular grooming. In addition, the grooming process provides an excellent opportunity to inspect the pet's skin and notice any problems such as flaky skin, sores, lumps or bumps, hair loss, and so on.

Several types of brushes are available for cats and dogs. "Pin brushes" have soft bristles with rounded tips, similar to brushes for people, while the more traditional "slicker brush" consists of short pieces of wire protruding from a plastic rectangle. Use a slicker brush gently; you can hurt the animal if you apply too much pressure against the skin. For pets with very short fur, such as Rex cats, Boxers, or Dobermans, a special glove, similar to a car chamois, should be rubbed gently over the animal's coat to remove dead fur and shine the coat.

A metal comb will help to keep the fur of long-haired pets from tangling.

Coping with Tangles and Mats

It is important to keep your pet's fur free of tangles. A small tangle starts the formation of a larger mat, which grows increasingly tighter against the skin, resulting in irritation and sores, and causing discomfort. Parasites such as fleas can easily escape detection beneath a mat. In warm weather, your pet will suffer from the heat that will be trapped beneath the mats.

After you have finished brushing a long-haired pet, run the comb through to ensure that there are no mats or tangles at skin level. Don't forget to check for tangles on the stomach and under the legs. Some of my long-haired patients appear at first glance to have no tangles or mats. However, a close examination discloses large mats of fur beneath the surface; this indicates that the owner has been combing only the ends of the hair.

A tangle-splitter can be used to cut apart a mat. It resembles a straight-edged razor with a 90-degree angle between the handle and the blade, which has a rounded tip to protect the skin. Another tangle-splitting tool resembles a metal comb with a sharp cutting edge on each tooth. A sharp pair of scissors can also be used by opening the scissors and using one blade to split the mat. Push the open blade through a small section of the mat near its base, then use a sawing motion to move the blade through the mat away from the skin. A mat split this way in a few places can be combed or brushed out.

Always use extreme caution when removing mats from a pet's fur. An animal's skin is very thin and can be cut easily. Even if there is no bleeding, a gash in the skin should be checked by a veterinarian to determine whether it needs to be repaired.

Proper Brushing Technique

Gradually accustom a young pet to being brushed by doing a little bit each day. Work slowly, speak reassuringly, praise good behavior, and follow the brushing session with a pleasant play period or a tasty treat; your pet should quickly learn to like being brushed!

If your dog or cat strongly resists being brushed, but enjoys having its belly rubbed, hide the brush behind your back while you gently rub the pet's belly until it falls asleep. While it sleeps, continue to rub its belly with one hand, and start brushing gently with the brush in your other hand. You will be surprised at how much brushing you can accomplish this way while the pet sleeps!

It is not necessary to brush the entire pet at each brushing session, especially if you have a large dog. Try working on one-quarter of the pet's body at a time.

Proper Bathing Technique

"Bathing" is the term which refers to washing your pet, but in reality the washing process is more of a shower than a bath. Most dogs and many cats will accept being bathed if they have been introduced to the process at an early age. Some cats, I am told, even jump into the bathtub with family members! Most dog breeds should be bathed no more than once every six to eight weeks, as more frequent bathing may cause dry skin. Some skin conditions are treated with more frequent medicated baths; this should be done only on the instructions of a veterinarian.

Decide where you will bathe your pet: kitchen sink, laundry tub, bathtub, backyard wading pool if warm water is available and weather permits, and so on. It is best to use a hand-held shower nozzle or a short hose. Have all of your supplies at hand so that your pet won't have an opportunity to race through the house in the middle of the process while you get something you forgot. You will need shampoo (types of shampoo are discussed below), a supply of towels, a brush, and possibly a hand-held hair dryer. If you are bathing your cat, remember to clip its nails before proceeding!

It is important to remove all mats and tangles before bathing the animal because they will become more difficult to remove once they are wet. Place a rubber mat at the bottom of the sink or tub to give the pet a secure footing, and put the pet in the tub. Hold its head with one hand and allow a gentle stream of warm (never hot) water to flow onto the pet's muzzle. Use a little bit of shampoo to wash around the animal's mouth. Next, wash the top of the head and raise it to allow the water to run off the pet's back. Keep water and shampoo out of the pet's ears and eyes. Use a cotton ball to plug the ears or hold a finger over the ear opening. A drop of mineral oil can be placed into each eye before bathing to provide a protective film in case any shampoo enters the eyes. Continue to shampoo the rest of the body and rinse very well.

Once the rinsing is complete and the water has been turned off, gently squeeze the water out of the pet's coat with your hands, especially from the tail, ears, and feathering on the legs; this will speed up the drying process. You can get a dog to shake itself by blowing gently into one of its ears. Gently towel dry the body. A blow dryer can then be used to continue the process, but do not blow hot air directly into the eyes, and don't hold the dryer too close to the body or too long in one spot, or you may burn the skin. Brush and comb the coat while it is drying, to prevent mats from forming. If it is winter, make sure the house is warm and keep the pet inside until it is completely dry.

Types of Shampoos

There are many types of pet shampoos available from veterinary offices, supermarkets, and pet stores. Remember that animal skin is not like human skin; it is thinner, has no sweat glands, and has a different surface acidity. For this reason, human shampoos are not recommended for use on animals. Shampoos can be categorized into three groups: general cleansers; antiparasitic products (to control fleas, for example); and therapeutic shampoos to treat skin problems. Some shampoos have keratolytic properties to loosen and lift off dry flakes from the skin surface. Emollient products restore natural oils to the fur, while hypoallergenic shampoos are very mild cleansers that do not leave a residue and are recommended for pets with sensitive skin or allergies. Special rinses and conditioners are also available for pets with skin and coat problems. "Dry" shampoos can be used during cold weather or if your pet gets exceedingly dirty while traveling and there are no proper bathing facilities. Aerosol foam shampoos create suds without water and can be easily removed with a towel. Ask your veterinarian to recommend a suitable shampoo for your pet, and be sure to use it as directed.

Flaky skin on your pet may be due to dry air in the house. Most pets enjoy sleeping near a warm place, such as a heat vent, but the constant flow of hot air can dry out the skin. A light spray of a coat conditioner containing protein or mink oil, brushed into the coat and massaged into the skin, will help eliminate flaking. Flaky skin can also result from harsh shampoos and inadequate rinsing, or lack of fat in the diet, which can be corrected by feeding a nutritional supplement containing fatty acids. Discuss this with your veterinarian.

Bathing to Remove Tar and Skunk Odor

Two conditions that require special bathing products are the removal of tar and the removal of skunk odor. When a pet walks on an asphalt surface in very hot weather, the tar may be so soft that it clings to the pet. Do not use harsh chemicals to remove it. Remember the adage that "like removes like"; rub mineral oil, another petroleum derivative, on the fur to remove the tar, and then bathe the pet with a gentle cleansing shampoo.

If your pet has had an altercation with a skunk, it will need to be bathed to eliminate the odor. Although most people can recognize the scent of a skunk from a distance, the smell at close proximity is even more pungent. One day I examined a cat that the family thought had been in a fire or got into some toxic liquid. Its coat was very sticky and it smelled like burnt rubber. In fact, this cat had been sprayed at close range by a skunk.

If the skunk sprayed into the pet's eyes, they will be very irritated and inflamed. Rinse the eyes with cool water, and bring your pet to the veterinarian right away.

Your veterinarian may have a shampoo specifically designed to remove skunk odor from your pet. However, in my experience the following home treatment works just as well. First, liberally sprinkle baking soda on the animal's coat and brush it well. Then rinse the pet with vinegar, avoiding the eyes and ears. Follow this with a regular bath, and put a little vanilla extract in the final rinse. The traditional remedy of bathing the pet in tomato juice or milk may also be effective, but usually several baths will be necessary. In fact, regardless of the treatment used, the pet will still give off a mild skunk scent when it gets wet, but this will gradually disappear.

Special Grooming Concerns

Even if your pet receives regular professional grooming, there are certain parts of the body that require attention more frequently.

Dried discharge should be removed from the corners of the eyes with a warm damp cloth. If these discharges are not removed regularly, they can cause skin irritations.

Although some veterinarians recommend that you leave your dog's ear hair alone as long as there is no problem, I am of the opposite opinion: remove the hair regularly to prevent problems from developing. Definitely pluck the hair from inside your dog's ears if there is any odor or buildup of waxy debris. You can use your fingers or a small pair of tweezers (with extreme caution to avoid pinching the skin) to pull out the hair. Ear-cleaning powder can also be used to make it easier to grip the greasy hairs and facilitate their removal. If there is no infection or broken skin, the ears can now be wiped with ear-cleaning solution, a little hydrogen peroxide, or rubbing alcohol—this will help prevent the buildup of wax and the development of infection.

If your pet has long hair, you should regularly trim the fur around its rectum. This will prevent the accumulation of stool on the fur, causing obstipation and skin irritations, which are explained in Chapter 14, "Diseases of the Digestive System," under the heading "The Intestines." The fur near the dog's genitals can also be carefully trimmed to maintain cleanliness and prevent skin irritations caused by a buildup of discharge.

Care of the Feet and Nails

Pay attention to the pet's feet. If mats form in the fur between the pads of the paws, the pet will experience discomfort and even lameness when it walks. In addition, the skin becomes irritated when moisture is trapped beneath the mats. Cut away the mats with a small pair of blunt-end, curved scissors. Professional groomers use a narrow blade on electric clippers to remove these mats.

It is important to keep your pet's nails well trimmed; you may do it yourself or have the veterinarian do it. For private use, I recommend the "guillotine" style pet nail clippers, rather than the scissor-type clippers. Hold the clippers with the fixed handle against the palm of your hand. As you squeeze your fingers against the movable handle, the blade will slide across the opening and cut the nail. By holding the clippers this way, you will have an added measure of safety, as the blade guard will cause the blade to leave the nail a little longer than you planned, reducing the risk of cutting the nail too short and causing bleeding. This is illustrated in Figure 8.1.

To trim a cat's nails, hold the paw with one hand and gently press down near the base of the toe to extend the nail, as depicted in the insert of Figure 8.1. Trim only the clear hook at the tip of the nail; avoid the pink part, as this contains the blood vessel and, when cut, will bleed. Not all the nails must be trimmed in one session. I found that if I started working on my cat as she was waking up, I could trim the nails of one paw before she started to fuss. A few days later, I would work on the other paw. Eventually she learned that the process was not painful, and I could trim all the nails at once.

Be sure to trim *all* of your cat's nails. Cats can have several extra toes and extra nails, some of which get no wear when the cat walks around. There is a tendency for these extra nails to become ingrown if they do not get trimmed regularly.

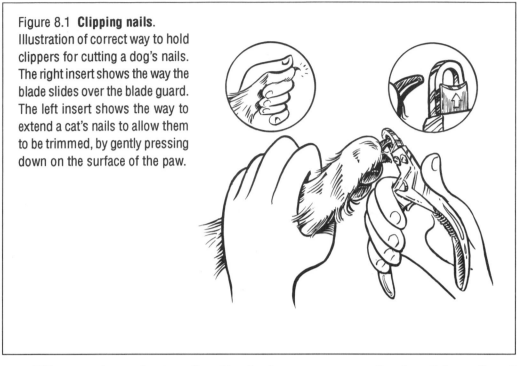

Figure 8.1 **Clipping nails**.
Illustration of correct way to hold clippers for cutting a dog's nails. The right insert shows the way the blade slides over the blade guard. The left insert shows the way to extend a cat's nails to allow them to be trimmed, by gently pressing down on the surface of the paw.

When cutting a dog's nails, slip the instrument over the tip of the nail and trim a short piece. Avoid removing too much. If the nail is white, avoid the wide pink part containing a nerve and a blood vessel, as this will bleed if cut. If the nail is a dark color, trim only a very small part from the tip. When the nail has been trimmed, you will see a black circle in the center of the cut surface; this is the end of the blood vessel. This is the place to stop; if you cut any farther, the nail will bleed.

Repeated trimming of small amounts from a long nail every few weeks will cause the blood vessel to retract. Thus, it is better to trim a very long nail just a little bit every two to four weeks, rather than cutting it to the desired length all at once.

If the nail has been trimmed too short and is bleeding, do not panic—your pet won't bleed to death! Just pack dry cornstarch on the bleeding surface with your finger and hold it there for a minute or two; the bleeding will stop. Pet shops also sell a coagulant powder that will painlessly stop the bleeding. Veterinarians often use silver nitrate sticks to cauterize and disinfect a bleeding nail; this is very effective and easy to use but may sting a little when first applied to the nail.

If you examine the feet of certain breeds of dogs, such as Great Danes and Dobermans, you will notice that their nails grow outward from the front of the paw and then angle down to the ground. The nails may appear to be long, but actually they are barely touching the ground and do not need trimming unless they extend below the foot pads.

The frequency with which a dog's nails require trimming depends upon the amount of wear and tear on the nails. If the dog is regularly exercised on a concrete or asphalt surface, the nails will be worn down on their own. In contrast, the nails on a dog that always walks on a grassy or carpeted surface will require more frequent trimming. If the paws make "clicking" sounds when the dog is walking, the nails probably need trimming.

Do not forget to trim the dewclaws or "thumbs" if your dog has them on any of its paws. These nails get no wear as they do not touch the ground, and if they are covered with fur, they are easily forgotten and become ingrown, which is a very painful condition requiring veterinary attention.

Professional Grooming

Dogs that have a continuously growing coat, such as Poodles, Schnauzers, Cocker Spaniels, and many mixed breeds, require regular haircuts. Long-haired dogs such as Collies, Afghans, and Sheepdogs require regular brushing and trimming. Most dogs should become accustomed to the clippers and scissors at an early age. You might attempt to groom your dog yourself, but most families use the services of a professional groomer. Many veterinary clinics offer grooming services.

Some cats will tolerate brushing by a very patient groomer, but many are tranquilized to avoid undue stress. It is very important to accustom long-haired cats, such as Himalayans or Persians, to being brushed at an early age. Some of my long-haired feline patients who have not been taught to tolerate regular brushing must be brought to my clinic several times a year (in a horribly tangled and matted state) for a complete shave!

Discuss the various options for shaping the pet's coat with the groomer. Consider whether you want bangs over the dog's eyes, a beard or mustache, closely shaven paws, a trimmed or bushy tail, and so on. If the dog's coat is badly tangled, the groomer may have to shave off the mats, and this will restrict the styling options.

Some families want their pet shaved short all over to make the coat easy to care for, and to reduce the amount of shedding. However, when the hair grows back it will be thicker than before. Although you might think that a shaved pet will be cooler in warm weather than a long-haired pet, a shaved pet runs the risk of being sunburned. A long coat does not make the animal overly warm in hot weather; the air trapped between the layers of hair serves as insulation from the heat. Think of the nomads in the desert; they wear several layers of long clothing to protect themselves from the heat.

I find it humorous when families buy a purebred Poodle and want it trimmed like a Schnauzer, or a Cocker Spaniel that they want to look like a Poodle, and so on. But all of my furry little friends leave the facility looking much cleaner and neater than when they arrived!

9

Breeding Your Pet

Professional Breeders

People often feel that professional breeders raise purebred dogs and cats as a way of earning large amounts of money. From what I have seen, this is far from the truth. Breeding animals is a labor-intensive and often money-losing undertaking—more a labor of love than a business. The breeder must purchase the initial breeding stock, the physical structures and supplies to house and care for the animals, and the food. If one has only a female, a stud fee is usually charged by the owner of the male, who may also have "pick of the litter," which is the right to choose any one of the young at no cost. Sometimes animals must be transported to distant places to breed with specific individuals, and this costs money. Veterinary fees can quickly mount up: pre-breeding examinations and laboratory tests to determine the best time for mating; assistance during mating or even artificial insemination; help during a difficult delivery; a cesarean section if necessary; treatment for uterine or mammary gland infections; care for weak newborns; vaccinations for puppies and kittens before they go to their new homes; and so on. Although animals have been reproducing on their own for centuries, things do not always go smoothly and sometimes veterinary intervention is required.

Breeders strive to produce the perfect, ideal specimen of their chosen breed. Reputable breeders belong to clubs that meet to discuss breed standards and ways of improving the appearance and characteristics of their particular breeds. The physical conformation of each animal is constantly evaluated against the breed standard.

Each animal in a litter is rated by the breeder as being either "show quality" or "pet quality." The sale price is higher for show-quality than for pet-quality animals. Since pet-quality animals are considered to be inferior to the breed standard, the purchaser usually must sign a "nonbreeding" agreement and possibly an agreement to have the pet spayed or neutered.

Show-quality animals will usually be sold with an agreement to enter the animal on the show circuit. A handler, either the purchaser, the breeder, or another professional, will enter the animal in various shows where it will win points to reflect its ranking by the judges. After ten points have been reached, the animal is awarded a championship. This animal is then considered to be more valuable as a breeding animal, since its offspring have a good chance of approaching the ideal breed standard.

I enjoy listening to and learning from breeders, who are usually very informed about a wide range of subjects relating to animal health. For example, a breeder of West Highland White Terriers felt that her dogs were very sensitive to the vaccination against leptospirosis and she warned purchasers of her puppies not to have this vaccine given to them. Although it is difficult to accept that one breed of terrier would have more of a reaction than other breeds, I have seen this breeder's animals react a little more strongly than other dogs to this particular vaccine, and so I have come to agree with her. Other veterinarians have scoffed at this breeder's warning, and their patients have had fairly severe reactions, some to the point of requiring additional treatment. On the other hand, a breeder once asked me to perform a cesarean section on her dog that was in labor. She felt that her particular breed was very fragile and could not maintain prolonged labor without endangering the lives of the mother or the offspring. I was persuaded to perform the surgery, basically because I knew the breeder had attended more whelpings (deliveries) of this breed than I had. In retrospect, I feel that the surgery was probably not necessary, and that the breeder should have been more patient and let nature take its course.

Many breeders routinely give one dose of deworming medicine to all their young offspring. However, the medication used may not be effective against all types of parasites, and a purchaser may have a false sense of security that every parasite has been eliminated from the pet. Therefore, many veterinarians suggest that a fecal sample from the new pets be examined for parasites. This procedure ensures that medication is given only to those animals that need it. If parasites are found, a specific deworming schedule can be designed to best benefit the animal.

The law in all North American jurisdictions restricts the practice of veterinary medicine to licensed veterinarians. However, it is fairly common knowledge among veterinarians that some breeders perform minor surgical procedures, such as the removal of dewclaws or the docking of tails in puppies that are just a day or two old. These are not complicated procedures and do not require anesthetic. However, some skill is required to adequately close the surgical site, to control bleeding, and to prevent infection. If complications were to arise, it could be difficult for a veterinarian to repair the damage.

Prebreeding Care

Most breeders of cats or dogs will not breed their females on the first heat. Also, not breeding on the first heat following pregnancy allows the mother's body to recuperate after giving birth and nursing a litter.

Every animal that is to be used in a breeding program, both male and female, should be carefully examined by a veterinarian to make sure that it is healthy. A fecal test should be performed to ensure that the female has no internal parasites, which could be passed to the young. The female's vaccinations must be up-to-date, since temporary protection for the young against disease will be passed in the first milk ("colostrum") after birth.

Many breeders of purebred cats require a negative Feline Leukemia Virus (FeLV) test for animals used in breeding to help keep the deadly virus out of the cattery. Vaccination against FeLV and Feline Infectious Peritonitis (FIP) is suggested for all breeding cats.

Dog breeders should require a negative brucellosis test for both male and female dogs prior to breeding. Brucellosis is a bacterial disease that can cause recurring fevers, weakness, lethargy, loss of appetite, and loss of weight. Females may have vaginal discharge and males may have infection and painful swelling of the testicles. Brucellosis can be spread through sexual activity between animals and can result in reproductive failure and sterility.

A sperm count can be performed to ensure that the male is capable of breeding. This would be especially important if money and effort were being spent to ship the stud dog to another city. In addition, the specific stage of the female's reproductive cycle can be determined.

Breeding Cycles

Cats

There is some seasonal influence on the sexual maturation of the cat. Although female cats generally come into heat at about six months of age, some can come into heat as early as four months if spring is approaching. For some reason unknown to me, cats also tend to go into heat around Christmas. I usually receive frantic calls on Boxing Day from one or two cat owners who think that their pets have been injured or are in pain due to their noise and unusual posture. Close questioning reveals that the cat is just displaying the normal symptoms of being in heat. Talk about the Christmas spirit!

When a female cat is in heat, she will tend to roll around on her back and make odd crying noises. Stroking her back will cause her to extend her hind legs and crouch with her front legs. Her tail will also be extended up and forward over her back towards her head. Sometimes she will tread with her back legs as her back is being stroked. Some female cats in heat will urinate in unusual places around the home.

Male cats become sexually mature at about six months of age, although again, some cats are more precocious in their development than others. If a male cat becomes aware of a female cat in heat nearby, he will tend to spray urine in his environment to warn other male cats that this is his territory, and to "advertise" his presence to the female cat.

The courtship and mating of two cats is a vocal and usually somewhat violent affair. Both the male and the female cat will caterwaul. This sound is a combination of shrieking, hissing, and sirenlike wailing, with some breeds (the Siamese is a striking example) sounding like a baby crying. Most of us have had at least several nights' sleep disturbed by the caterwauling of cats outside our homes! If this noisy courtship is successful, the male will grab the female by the scruff of the neck and mating will proceed.

Cats do not ovulate until they are stimulated by the act of mating, even if the mating attempts are by a neutered male (some recently neutered males retain the mating instinct until their hormone levels fade). After ovulating, the heat period will be over for about two months. If there is no other cat in the vicinity, and the female does not ovulate, she may come into heat every two weeks or so, and each heat period will last four or five days.

Dogs

Female dogs (bitches) have their first heat at about six months of age, although this may be delayed several months in very small breeds as well as giant breeds. They come into heat again every six months thereafter, although there is some individual variation. The first sign that a bitch is coming into heat is when the lips of the vagina begin to swell. Although male dogs may be attracted at this point, the bitch will not be receptive to mating attempts. After several days of vaginal swelling, there will be some bloody discharge. After about a week, the discharge will become pale, almost straw-colored. During this time the female is most fertile and most receptive to mating. This final stage takes about a week, with the heat season lasting about three weeks in total, although there is a fair amount of variability in the length of each part of the cycle.

Some bitches have only a small amount of vaginal discharge, especially during their first heat, while others produce a much larger quantity. Many small dogs with minimal discharge lick themselves clean. There are some canine hygienic products that the dog can wear to prevent it from soiling its surroundings; these might also serve as "canine chastity belts" to discourage mating. Some enterprising clients put an old pair of underwear briefs on the dog to hold a sanitary napkin in place.

There are some chlorophyll tablets on the market that supposedly reduce the odor produced by a female dog in heat. This might help to keep male dogs away from her; however, they are not birth control pills and will not prevent mating if a particularly persistent male dog still finds her irresistible.

Male dogs are capable of mating at ten to twelve months of age, although some dogs become sexually mature as early as six to eight months. During mating, the male will mount the female. The penis of the male contains a "bulb" which will swell up and be held within the female's vagina. When the male dismounts, he may remain attached to the female and turn around so that the dogs are tail to tail. This is called a "tie," and signifies a good breeding with an excellent chance of a fertile mating. During a tie, which lasts up to fifteen or twenty minutes, the animals cannot be separated without causing severe injury to both animals.

If a bitch is bred close to the time of ovulation, there is an excellent chance that the mating will succeed. The veterinarian may suggest taking vaginal swabs to predict the ovulation time. Some cells are removed from the vagina with a cotton-tipped swab and examined under the microscope. The exact stage of the cycle can be determined, and the time of ovulation will be predicted, based upon the type of cells seen. If swabs are not taken, I recommend breeding on the seventh, ninth, and eleventh days after the first appearance of blood.

If a bitch in heat has been accidentally "caught" by a male dog, pregnancy can usually be prevented with a "mismate shot." This injection of hormone will prevent the fertilized egg from implanting in the uterus. Mismate injections have the greatest chance of success when given within twelve hours of mating. This injection will also double the length of the current heat and it can be given only once during any one heat. Some veterinarians may use other mismate chemicals in tablet form, but I have had the greatest success with the injectable hormone.

Each litter a bitch produces is totally independent and unaffected by the preceding litters. Thus, if a purebred animal mated with a mongrel, this would have no effect on subsequent pregnancies. The female animal will not be "spoiled" for future mating by having had a mixed litter.

Feline and Canine Pregnancy and Delivery

"Gestation" is the medical term for pregnancy, and "parturition" refers to the birth of the young, although the terms "whelping" and "queening" refer specifically to the delivery of puppies and kittens, respectively. The average litter size for cats is between two and four kittens. Dogs usually have between one and four puppies, but the large breeds can produce up to eight or ten puppies in a litter.

After being in heat, a female dog can have a false pregnancy, gaining weight and even producing milk. She will "mother" inanimate objects, make a nest, and act as if she were preparing to bring a family into the world. I enjoyed a cartoon in a veterinary journal showing the veterinarian answering his telephone in the middle of the night. The client on the other end of the line was saying, "Doc, you know the false pregnancy you said my dog was having? Well, she just had her four 'false' puppies!" This illustrates that a definitive diagnosis of a false pregnancy is impossible to make, just as a diagnosis of early pregnancy can be difficult to make.

Gestation in dogs and cats lasts about sixty to sixty-three days. There are no blood or urine tests to determine whether the animal is pregnant. About twenty-one to twenty-eight days after mating, a veterinarian can feel the abdomen to determine if the pet is pregnant. Beyond this time frame, the developing young are usually tucked up behind the rib cage, beyond the reach of probing fingers. X-rays to confirm pregnancy and to evaluate the size and number of young can be taken after about forty-two days. At this stage an x-ray is very safe and will not affect the developing babies.

Experienced dog breeders can often tell that an animal is pregnant by seeing a mucoid vaginal discharge early in pregnancy, and by checking if the dog's nipples have become larger and pinker. Some pregnant dogs seem to experience nausea and vomiting in the mornings, similar to morning sickness in human expectant mothers. Breeders often notice a mellowing in the personality and activity of pregnant animals.

Acquaint the expectant bitch with the whelping box several weeks before the delivery date. This box should be a solid enclosure with a door or cut-away area on one side to allow the mother easy passage into and out of the area, but it should keep the puppies contained. Similarly, the pregnant cat should be introduced to the queening box or area in which you would like her to deliver her kittens. Select a box, drawer, or closet where the mother can go in and out, but where the kittens are confined from wandering off. If no specific area has been set aside, the new mother will deliver her young in an area of her choosing; she may then proceed to move her family all over the house seeking a safe place to settle down with them.

Cover the bottom of the area with lots of newspapers and old soft towels. As the time of delivery approaches, the bitch or queen will spend more and more time in the box, fussing around in it and rearranging the towels and papers, making sure it is to her liking. You can put an electric heating pad on the bottom of the whelping box, underneath a few layers of towels. Since puppies and kittens cannot maintain their own body temperature during the first two weeks of life, the temperature of the whelping box should be maintained at about 33°C (93°F). Make certain that there is room for the mother and young to move away from the heating pad if they find it too warm. Keep testing the heating pad by feeling it through the towels to make sure that it is not too warm.

There are several signs that you can use to predict when an animal is about to go into labor. The body temperature drops sharply, usually to less than 37°C (98°F) from the normal temperature of 38.5° to 39°C (101°–102°F). Most pets go off their food twelve to twenty-four hours before giving birth. Usually their nipples will become a brighter pink and milk can be easily squeezed from them within a day of delivering. If you want to know whether labor is imminent, the veterinarian can examine the vagina to see if the cervix or opening of the uterus is dilated. Once it has dilated, labor will begin shortly.

When an animal goes into labor, you will see the abdominal muscles contracting. There should be delivery of a kitten or puppy within thirty minutes of heavy labor; if not, contact your veterinarian or emergency clinic. Prolonged labor without the delivery of a baby can exhaust the mother, and this can endanger both her life and the lives of the babies. One or more young may be malformed or too large to pass through the vagina, or a baby might be dead and not stimulate the necessary uterine contractions. If the mother is becoming exhausted from labor, or if she is becoming "toxic" (developing a fever, vomiting, becoming very weak, and going into shock) because she is carrying a dead baby, a veterinarian can determine whether labor should be chemically assisted, or whether a "cesarean section" operation must be performed to deliver the litter through an incision in the mother's abdomen.

Most anesthetic agents administered to the mother will affect the babies within the uterus; they will be very depressed when born and might have difficulty beginning to breathe on their own. Also, if the mother takes a long time to recover from the anesthetic, she will not be able to adequately nurse and care for her new litter. For these reasons, a strong sedative and local anesthetic are commonly used for a cesarean section. As each baby is removed from the opened uterus, it is handed to an assistant, who will cut the umbilical cord, remove any membranes from its head, and stimulate it to breathe by rubbing it briskly and clearing fluid from its mouth. After the entire litter is delivered, the mother can be spayed before the abdomen is closed, if she is not going to be bred again.

The reason necessitating the cesarean section will determine the prognosis of the operation. If labor was not prolonged and the young are strong, both the mother and her new family should recover well. On two separate occasions in my veterinary practice, the owners did not bring their very ill dogs to me until thirty-six hours after whelping. In both cases, I performed a cesarean operation as a dead puppy was still in the uterus. In one case the mother died less than a day after the surgery from complications including severe infection and kidney failure. In the second case, the mother was in critical condition for forty-eight hours but then made a full recovery.

One other sad case involved a seven-year-old Beagle that was pregnant for the first time. She showed no signs of going into labor at the appropriate time and chemicals were ineffective in inducing labor. An emergency cesarean section was performed and I discovered that she was carrying seven very large puppies, each of them dead. After the operation, the mother's condition became critical as she developed generalized infection, kidney failure, and severe alterations in the chemical balance in her bloodstream. Her recovery took over a week. Although most animals do not have difficulty in delivering their young, it is important to keep in close contact with your veterinarian, who can advise you if labor is progressing as it should.

Even during normal labor and delivery, there are occasions when you will have to lend a hand. If a kitten or puppy appears to be stuck at the vaginal opening, *gently* take hold of the exposed part of the baby and rotate it in a corkscrew type of motion as you pull it down between the mother's legs. However, if it does not move fairly easily or if it makes the mother very uncomfortable, contact your veterinarian.

Once a baby has been delivered, the mother will usually lick it to stimulate breathing and to clean it. If the baby does not seem to be breathing, pick it up and clean off any membranes from its head. Cradle it between the palms of your two hands held together in front of you, with its head pointed down and away from you. Extend your arms out in front of you and then move your arms rapidly downward; remember to keep the newborn's head cradled away from you. This motion should drive any fluid out of its chest into its nose and mouth, which can be wiped with a tissue. Stimulate the baby to breathe by vigorously rubbing its body, and by blowing air towards its face. This procedure is illustrated in Figure 9.1.

The mother will usually bite through the umbilical cord. If she does not, tie two pieces of thread around the umbilical cord about five centimeters (2 in.) from the baby, and cut the cord between the two threads. A drop of iodine on the baby's end of the cord will prevent infection. The umbilical cord will dry up and fall off the newborn in two to three days.

It is important to account for each afterbirth or set of fetal membranes during delivery, since any retained afterbirths will lead to a severe infection. The mother should eat at least one afterbirth, which contains hormones that stimulate milk production and bring out the "maternal behavior" necessary to successfully rear her new family. Ingesting too many afterbirths may upset her stomach.

Figure 9.1 **Resuscitation of a newborn puppy**.
The puppy is held cradled between the palms, while the arms are swung down from a horizontal position. In the third drawing, a facial tissue is used to wipe mucus and fluid from the puppy's mouth and nose. The puppy can also be stimulated to breathe by gently rubbing its chest.

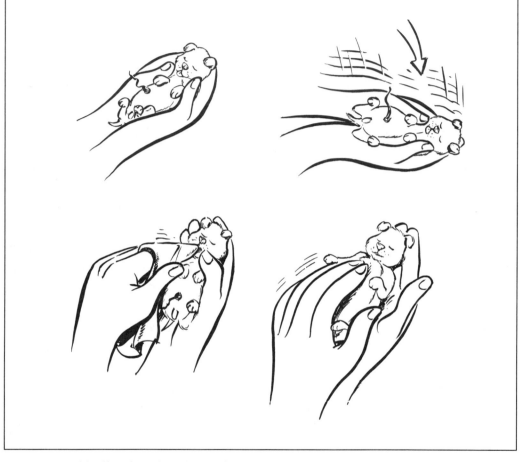

A good indication that the entire litter has been born is when the new mother settles down with them, cleaning them and making certain that they are nursing properly. She may want a little bit of food and water at this point.

As with humans, some animals are born prematurely. If the babies are born more than a few days premature, it is unlikely that they will survive.

"Colostrum" is the milk that is produced by the mammary glands during the first few days following birth. This milk is different from that which is produced during the rest of the nursing period, in that it is especially rich in minerals and vitamins and, even more importantly, it contains very high levels of antibodies that will protect the newborn from various diseases during the first few weeks of life.

There usually is a "runt" in every litter that is smaller and frailer than its littermates. Very often, however, this individual catches up with and even surpasses its littermates in size by the time they are six to twelve months old. If there is a particularly weak baby, or one that does not seem to be nursing adequately, place it on one of the posterior nipples, since these glands are the most productive. You can squeeze a little milk from the gland onto the nipple to encourage the baby to suckle.

"Mastitis," or infection of the mammary glands, can develop during the nursing period. Usually the mother will have a fever and go off her food. The affected mammary glands are hot, swollen, discolored, and hurt the animal when touched. If milk is squeezed from the nipple of an infected gland, it is usually discolored and lumpy. Treatment consists of antibiotic tablets for at least a week, and the application of warm moist packs to affected glands three or four times daily. In cases of severe infection it may be advisable to squeeze out the milk by hand. In any case, the nursing young must be removed from the mother and fed a formula diet to prevent serious illness from swallowing the infected milk.

I always recommend that the mother be examined by a veterinarian within twelve hours of the birth of the last baby. During this examination, the doctor will check for any remaining young that were not delivered and for any retained afterbirths. The mother's temperature should be taken to make certain no infection has set in during the delivery process. A small quantity of milk should be expressed from each nipple to check that an adequate production of milk is underway. I usually give the mother an injection of long-lasting antibiotic to guard against infection of the uterus or mammary glands. I also give an injection of a hormone called "oxytocin" which will increase the pet's maternal behavior, as well as stimulate milk production and cause contraction of the uterus to expel any remains of the birth process. Without this injection, some animals will continue to have a messy vaginal discharge for several weeks. I also give an injection of calcium gluconate to prevent the development of eclampsia, or milk fever.

Eclampsia occurs when a nursing mother has lost so much calcium through its milk that it becomes seriously ill. The signs of eclampsia are panting, nervousness, restlessness, and a very high temperature (up to 41.5°C [107°F]). This is followed by weakness and collapse with an inability to rise, and muscle-twitching progressing to tremors and convulsions. Untreated, eclampsia is fatal; however, early diagnosis and treatment with intravenous calcium gluconate solution will result in a rapid visible improvement. Eclampsia usually develops within the first week or two of nursing. It can be prevented by feeding the animal a premium well-balanced diet developed for growth and lactation throughout the pregnancy and nursing periods, which will ensure that sufficient protein and minerals are ingested to meet the needs of the mother and the new family. Depending upon the size of the litter, the mother will require up to three times her normal amount of food by the third week of nursing. Calcium supplementation is sometimes recommended, either through powder or tablets, or through milk products such as sliced processed cheese, cottage cheese, or vanilla ice cream. Once eclampsia occurs, the litter must be immediately weaned and raised by hand.

Care of Newborn Kittens and Puppies

Kittens and puppies are born with their eyes and ears closed. Their ears generally open by the age of fourteen to seventeen days, and their eyes open by the time they are ten to fourteen days old. Any discharge from the eyes, especially before they are fully open, indicates an infection. The veterinarian may decide to open the lids surgically, and the infection can be treated with antibiotics.

Normally, the mother cat teaches her kittens to use the litter pan by about four to five weeks of age. In the case of a kitten being raised by hand (see "Hand-Raising Newborns" in this section), you will have to litter-train it. Put it in the litter pan at the appropriate age and move its front paws in a scratching motion; it should catch on quickly.

Within two to four days after being born, puppies should have their tails docked, if desired, to conform to the standard for breeds such as Poodle, Cocker Spaniel, Doberman, Old English Sheepdog, and so on. At the same time, it is a good idea to remove any dewclaws from the puppies' legs. Dewclaws that have not been removed can easily get caught and torn in underbrush if the dog goes through fields or forested areas. These minor operations are performed without anesthesia.

Normally, kittens and puppies begin to eat growth formula food at about four to six weeks of age, although they may still nurse occasionally. Milk will continue to be produced as long as nursing is occurring. When nursing has ceased, the mammary glands will swell up for a few days until the pressure stops further milk production; the swelling will then slowly subside. During these few days the mother will naturally be a little uncomfortable, but if the milk is removed, production will continue and the process of "drying up" will be prolonged. However, if the glands feel very hot or lumpy, either during the nursing period or after the young have been weaned, or if the mother seems feverish or goes off her food, she should be checked by a veterinarian in case the mammary glands have become infected.

Normal weight gain for puppies is an increase of 1 to 1.5 grams (0.05 oz.) for each 500 grams (1 lb.) of anticipated adult weight per day. A puppy should double its weight in eight to ten days. The anticipated adult body weight can also be related to age in this way: 10 percent at one month; 20 percent at two months; 33 percent at three months; 50 percent at four months; and 100 percent at ten months.

Hand-Raising Newborns

Large breeds of dogs often have eight or ten puppies in a litter. When the mother dog is so blessed, supplemental feedings of the puppies will be necessary since most females have only eight nipples. To prevent the mother's body from becoming overly burdened, only about half the litter should be allowed to nurse at a time, and the others should be bottle-fed.

In addition to supplementation of feedings, there are other times that a newborn puppy or kitten might have to be completely raised by the owner. The most obvious situation would be when the young are orphaned by the loss of their mother during the birth process. Although not a frequent occurrence, this tragic situation can happen.

Sometimes, particularly with a first pregnancy, a very nervous mother will reject the entire litter. Maternal behavior can sometimes be stimulated by a hormone injection. Often, if someone in the family to whom the new mother is particularly close quietly reassures and pats her while she is in the nesting area, her offspring will have a chance to nurse. After a day or two, the mother might take over full responsibility on her own.

If the mother develops milk fever or infected mammary glands, the young should not be allowed to nurse. They might be able to stay with the mother for warmth and comfort, and she might be allowed to clean them, but they must be supervised to prevent nursing.

Often the mother will reject one of her litter. Usually this is the runt, or the smallest and weakest animal, that may be suffering from "fading puppy/kitten syndrome" which is discussed in the following section. If you notice one puppy or kitten always away from the mother, you can try to place it on a posterior nipple. If the newborn is too weak to nurse, you must decide whether to attempt to hand-raise it, which requires a commitment of at least two weeks of careful attention to many details, and which may not succeed.

Commercial artificial formulas for kittens and puppies, as well as pet nursers, are available at some veterinary offices and pet food stores. Use a kitchen scale to weigh the newborn, monitor its weight gain, and determine the correct amount of formula to feed, which increases with the animal's weight. A nursing bottle for animals is better than an eyedropper, which could easily make the formula go down the animal's windpipe and choke it. If the animal is extremely weak and will not nurse even from the bottle, it should be fed with a stomach tube. Your veterinarian will show you how to do this. Hand-raised animals should be fed at least every six to eight hours.

After feeding, hold the puppy or kitten upright and gently rub its abdomen to encourage it to burp. A newborn is dependent on its mother (or foster mother) for its elimination needs until it is eighteen days old; the mother must stimulate it to urinate and have a bowel movement by licking its genito-anal area. If the animal is being hand-raised, gently rub its genito-anal area with a moistened cotton swab after every feeding to stimulate its toilet functions.

Maintenance of a proper environment is one of the most important factors in hand-raising newborns. The normal body temperature of a newborn is between 34.5° and 36.5°C (94° and 97°F) during the first two weeks of life. But, since shivering reflexes do not develop until after the first week of life, the baby's body temperature may become much lower if it is neglected by the mother or if it is orphaned and supplementary heat is not provided. Thus, during the first three days of life, the temperature around the young should constantly be between 29° to 32.5°C (85° to 90°F). At the end of one week the temperature can be reduced to 27°C (80°F), and then to 24°C (75°F) when the young animals are four weeks old.

With an inadequate intake of nutrients, abnormal physical condition, or maternal neglect, the newborn's body temperature will fall, and cold skin may result in the mother rejecting it further. Rectal temperatures below 35°C (95°F) are accompanied by ineffectual nursing. Affected young cry in a plaintive manner and will die in a matter of hours if not treated by being slowly warmed. The radiant heat of the human body can be used by placing the newborn in an inside coat pocket. The warming process should take one to three hours, depending upon the degree of chilling. A sugar solution given orally will counteract dehydration and low blood sugar during this warming process. Quick energy can be supplied by sugar water consisting of five grams (1 tsp.) of sugar to thirty milliliters (1 oz.) of water fed very cautiously by stomach tube or dropperful every half hour. An animal that has been rejected by the mother because of cold skin temperature will usually be accepted by her once the skin temperature is within normal range.

Fading Newborns

Of all puppies born alive, 28 percent die within the first week of life and another 10 percent die during the second week. Most of these deaths are due to "fading puppy syndrome," signs of which include excessive crying, an inadequately filled stomach, failure to gain weight, and reduced body temperature. The puppy could appear normal at birth and may even seem to be nursing initially, but shortly it will be ignored by the mother.

Fading puppy syndrome is believed to be due to a combination of poor nutrition, ineffective transfer of high levels of antibodies in the mother's first milk (colostrum), and probably an infectious component as well. Puppies that do not take enough milk will become dehydrated, and will have decreased heart and lung functions. If body temperature falls due to lack of energy intake, puppies will lose their drive to suck, which further compounds the problem. Aggressive treatment at the earliest sign of a problem is the only way to save these puppies; even so, with some puppies, treatment is futile. In these cases, a congenital liver, kidney, or heart defect, or severe infection, may have been present that is incompatible with life.

Similar problems can occur in kittens, where the term is "fading kitten syndrome" or "kitten mortality complex." I have had personal experience attempting to hand-raise a newborn kitten. The mother cat developed severely infected mammary glands when the litter was three days old and her three kittens had to be hand-raised by the family. One kitten died that day, one seemed to be nursing adequately, and one was very weak and would not nurse. Since the family was away from home for twelve hours a day and the weak kitten's condition was too critical for it to be left for that length of time, the family asked whether I would try to raise it for them, and I accepted the challenge. I kept the kitten with me at work during the day and at home at night, and fed her by stomach tube every four to six hours, including once during the night. Some days she seemed a bit stronger and would crawl a little on her own, but other times she would not accept the formula and cried a lot. Finally, on the ninth morning, she seemed very cool to the touch, and she passed away a few hours later in my hands. I learned that one becomes extremely attached to such a tiny helpless creature that depends on you for all of its needs, and its passing was very sad for all of us who had been so dedicated to caring for her.

Another client adopted a pregnant stray cat that delivered four kittens without difficulty. The owner reported that one by one each kitten would suddenly seem weak and die in spite of her efforts at hand-raising them. She was devastated that none of the kittens survived. I tried to reassure her that she gave them all the help she could, but many times it seems that nature has its own way of preventing weak animals from surviving.

It is important to take a deceased puppy or kitten to a veterinarian so that an autopsy can be performed. If the cause of death is an infection, this may help save the remaining littermates and the mother by allowing proper treatment.

10

The Senior Years

When does your pet become a "senior citizen"? Generally, the last 25 percent of an average pet's life is considered to be its senior years. Since most cats live sixteen to eighteen years, the senior years would start around twelve to fourteen years of age. In contrast, a dog's lifespan is related to its size. Small- to medium-sized dogs can live up to twenty years, whereas large or giant breeds are considered very old at the age of eight or nine years. According to the *Guinness Book of World Records* (1993 edition), the oldest known dog was twenty-nine years, five months old, when it died in Australia in 1939. The oldest known cat passed away in England in 1957 at the age of thirty-four years. I have personally treated several cats that had reached the age of twenty-four years.

One of the most difficult situations to deal with in my veterinary practice concerns elderly people with senior pets. These clients often identify with their pets' increasing age-related health problems. They are especially appreciative of our efforts to alleviate the health problems of their longtime animal friends. However, when the time comes that nothing more can be done for the pet, it is terribly devastating for all concerned. I have had senior citizens tell me that they have nothing further to live for once their pet dies.

Many natural changes occur in the older pet, and it is important to know what can be done to keep the pet in comfortable good health as long as possible.

Care of the Skin and Fur

One of the first changes that will give a dog a "senior" look is a graying of the hairs around the eyes and muzzle. This can happen as early as five or six years of age. There may be a change in the number and shape of dark freckles or pigment spots on the pet's lips or gums. The skin may darken in some areas, lose its elasticity and become flaky, and the fur may become dry and brittle. To counteract some of these changes in the skin and fur, diets formulated for seniors are supplemented with zinc and fatty acids.

It is important to groom the older pet regularly. Proper brushing will eliminate mats, remove the dead fur, stimulate oil production in the skin, and spread it over the fur. Also, the nails can become very brittle and need to be kept well trimmed. A vicious cycle can easily develop; inactivity allows the nails to grow long and sharp, which makes it uncomfortable for the pet to walk, leading to further inactivity. Untrimmed nails can also grow into the pad of the paw, causing unnecessary pain.

Lumps and Bumps

Lumps and bumps may be noticed on an older pet's skin. Skin growths, though not usually malignant, should be examined by the veterinarian and removed if necessary. Some dogs will develop numerous cysts over the body; as these are removed, additional ones may develop. It is important to check that cysts or warts do not become infected if the pet chews at them or if they get nicked during grooming.

Older animals can develop a benign fatty tumor, called a "lipoma," beneath the skin. Lipomas feel soft and can be highly variable in size, occurring more frequently in overweight animals. The veterinarian may consider taking a biopsy from it or removing it, depending upon its location and size. Any tissue that is removed should be submitted for a biopsy to determine the chances of regrowth or spreading.

Tooth Loss

Tooth loss is common in older animals, particularly in small breeds of dogs. Teeth that fall out are usually swallowed, and the family is often unaware of the loss. If many teeth are missing from your pet's mouth, changes in diet may be required. However, I have known virtually toothless cats and dogs that still enjoyed chomping on dry food!

Arthritis and Muscle-Wasting

Stiffness and arthritis frequently afflict senior pets. Although any joint can be affected, it is usually the hips that bother the animal the most. The pet may be reluctant to get up, and move stiffly after a long period of rest. It may have difficulty maintaining its footing, particularly on slippery floors. In this case, put "slipper sox" (socks with grippers on the soles) on an old dog's paws—it may look silly but it will help by providing traction. In addition, arthritis, coupled with poor vision, can make it difficult for the pet to jump up onto its favorite piece of furniture. Help the pet on and off the furniture, instead of letting it jump by itself and possibly getting injured. Move the cat's food and litter to the level of the house where it spends most of its time so that it does not have to navigate a flight of stairs. A padded bed, away from cold weather, dampness, and drafts, will help ease the pet's discomfort. Dry the pet off when it comes in from outside on wet cold days. Anti-arthritic medication prescribed by your veterinarian can make the pet more comfortable. The effects of arthritis are compounded in overweight animals; keep your pet's weight under control to reduce the stress on its joints.

Older cats and dogs often experience a wasting of muscles in the hips, hind legs, and on top of the head, making the bones more prominent. The pet's back may begin to sway and its muscles may tremble after only moderate exertion. Muscles will gradually diminish in size, especially if kidney disease allows proteins, the building blocks of muscle, to leave the body. Reduced activity will also lead to a general loss of muscle tone. The use of anabolic steroids will improve appetite and increase vitality, as well as keep protein in the body and help maintain muscle tone.

Obesity

Obesity is a serious risk to a senior pet's health. The reduced physical activity, combined with a slowing of the body's metabolism, increases the tendency for weight gain. Obesity—unhealthy in any pet—is especially harmful to the senior's joints, heart, and other organs.

Changes in the Senses

A senior pet may develop a bluish-gray translucent haziness or clouding of the lens in the center of each eye. This untreatable condition results from a compaction and hardening of the lens fibers, called "nuclear sclerosis." Dogs and cats with nuclear sclerosis may have better vision in dim light than in bright light, as the lens of the eye cannot adapt to too much light.

A cataract is a partial or complete opacity in the lens, and can develop in one or both eyes, impairing vision and eventually causing blindness. Surgery can be performed to remove a cataract.

Senior dogs and cats can suddenly develop a balance problem of the inner ear called "geriatric vestibular disease" which is very upsetting for the family and the pet. I can vouch for this, as it happened to my dog Blue. The animal will hold its head at an angle, stumble sharply to one side when it tries to walk, and be very uncoordinated. Its eyes may exhibit rapid fluttering movements. This is a benign condition that will gradually pass without treatment within three or four days, as the pet learns to compensate for its altered space perception. As the above symptoms could be caused by other illnesses, a pet exhibiting balance problems should be examined by a veterinarian.

The sense of hearing usually deteriorates in senior animals. A useful test to evaluate your pet's hearing is to call it by name when it is asleep. There is no treatment for hearing impairment in pets. But remember, this will cause the senior pet to sleep more soundly—be careful not to startle it awake.

Loss of Bladder Control

Older dogs may have urinary incontinence. This refers to a perfectly housebroken dog leaving small puddles of urine in the house. The animal is unaware that this has happened (and will usually be very embarrassed when it discovers the accident). Frequently, the sleeping dog will leave a small puddle of urine where it is lying. One time, I was scratching my dog Blue on the head. When I reached her "ticklish" spot behind her ear, her hind leg came up in a reflexive move to scratch as well. While her hind leg was moving, I noticed a small amount of urine trickling from her genital area; she was totally unaware that this was happening.

Urinary incontinence in female dogs may be due to a loss of muscle tone in the bladder wall. Treatment with a female hormone (diethylstilboestrol) is usually effective. These tiny tablets are given once daily for a week or two, and then on a reducing dosage. Usually the dog will need the tablets for the rest of its life, although the family might try stopping the medication after several months while watching for a recurrence of the problem, in which case the medication should be resumed. One time I had a patient who needed a tablet every eight days; if it did not receive one, on the ninth day, like clockwork, it would be incontinent again! Another drug that can be used is the antihistamine, ephedrine. Your veterinarian will decide which is best for your particular case.

Although male dogs can become incontinent, dribbling urine when walking is a sign of prostate disease, not a bladder control problem. See Chapter 15, "Diseases of the Urogenital System," under the heading "Diseases of the Prostate Gland."

Digestive System Problems

The digestive system of an older animal may undergo some changes. Foods that were offered as a treat to the younger animal, and which were tolerated with ease, may now cause stomach upsets, particularly if they are high in fat content. A good plan is to keep the pet on the food that is best for it, and that it likes; avoid any sudden dietary changes.

Constipation is a problem that is frequently seen in older cats, and sometimes in senior dogs as well. The formation of drier, harder stools, as well as the stretching of the large intestine due to loss of muscle tone, contribute to this problem. Hairballs in cats may also complicate constipation. Once the veterinarian has removed the stool from the pet, fluids are given to combat any dehydration that might be contributing to the problem. Oral medication is often prescribed to help stimulate intestinal movement and reduce the possibility of a recurrence. A prescriptive diet with increased fiber content is helpful in maintaining proper bowel function.

The Senior Diet

Diseases of internal organs such as the heart, lungs, kidneys, and liver occur more frequently in older animals than in younger ones. These organs work with gradually decreasing efficiency as aging progresses. If an older pet is fed a diet formulated for young animals, the high levels of nutrients such as protein, phosphorous, and salt may harm the body over time. Therefore, it is recommended that older pets be fed a diet specially formulated for senior animals.

Good nutrition cannot guarantee perfect health or reverse the aging process, but it can, along with proper exercise and rest, improve the quality of life and forestall the onset of disease. Proper nutrition is one important factor that can increase longevity in many species. A discussion of diet and old age can be found in Chapter 22, "Risk Factors and Dietary Management of Disease."

Behavioral Changes

Any change in an aging pet's personality is usually for the better, although if it has always been a grouch, time may only intensify its grumpiness. In my experience, most pets mellow out as they mature. Nevertheless, if an aging pet is ill and in pain, it may become irritable.

With advancing age, pets become less and less physically active, just like people. They sleep for long periods, although this may not be noticeable in a cat that has always been sedentary! Do not be concerned by this slowing down process—it is normal. While it is important to keep the animal active, this should be done with moderation. Several short periods of exercise should be substituted for the long walk or jog that the dog enjoyed in its youth. Avoid excessive exercise, which may be dangerous, especially for animals with chronic heart or lung disease.

The Geriatric Screen

The best way to assess the general condition of an older animal before problems become apparent is to conduct a geriatric screen. The idea is to be proactive and uncover problems at the earliest stage when they will be easiest to treat, even if the pet seems perfectly well. A geriatric screen usually includes chest and abdominal x-rays (to check the heart size and condition of the lungs and abdominal organs); an ECG (to study heart function); various blood tests (to monitor the functioning of the liver, kidneys, and other organs); and a urine test (to evaluate kidney function). From the geriatric screen, recommendations can be made for medication or diet changes which should forestall the development of diseases. Periodic follow-up tests will monitor the pet's progress.

The family should watch for any changes in the older pet's behavior. For example, is the pet drinking more water than usual without a valid reason, such as hot weather? If so, this could indicate a possible urinary infection, diabetes, or kidney disease. All behavioral changes should be reported to the veterinarian, who will investigate the possible cause.

11

Vacation Time

When you go on vacation, arrangements must be made for the care of your pets. Most people choose to either travel with their pets, leave them at home in the care of a pet sitter, or put them into a boarding facility. Your destination, the health and personality of your pet, finances, and personal preference should all be considered before making a decision on vacation pet care.

Traveling with Your Pet

Before traveling with your pet to another jurisdiction, ascertain from the appropriate authorities the documentation required. Even within one country, the regulations might vary: for example, in Canada, a health certificate is required for a pet to visit Vancouver Island in British Columbia, or to enter the province of Newfoundland. Most countries require a health certificate issued by a veterinarian less than one week before traveling, and proof that a rabies vaccination was given more than a month but less than one year before the trip.

Make sure, as well, that your pet will be allowed back into your country of origin. Some areas (for example, the British Isles and the state of Hawaii) require a six-month quarantine of all animals that enter, including animals from their jurisdiction that have been out of the area. As rabies does not exist in those regions, every precaution is taken to prevent the disease from entering. I have had clients whose animals have gone through the quarantine period (one cat on three separate occasions) with no apparent adverse result. The family was allowed to visit and to take it outside for brief periods. Still, this quarantine period is probably stressful for a family pet.

Depending on the distance to be traveled, there are important precautions to take. Since changes in water or diet can trigger digestive upsets such as diarrhea or vomiting, you should bring plenty of water from home as well as your pet's regular brand of food, which may not be available at your destination. Remember to pack any medication the pet is taking, as well as its dishes and some toys. Pack a first-aid kit containing bandaging material (gauze, cotton, adhesive tape), antiseptic powder or cream (for minor cuts or skin irritations), tweezers (for removing ticks), and scissors.

If your trip includes an overnight stop, plan ahead: check hotels, motels, parks, and campgrounds to ensure that pets are allowed. Even if you are relying on a guidebook which states that pets are welcome, telephone ahead for confirmation, as guidebooks quickly become outdated. *Touring with Towser*, a book produced by the Gaines dog food company, lists lodgings in North America that welcome dogs.

When staying at a hotel, try not to leave the pet unattended in your room, as it might get into all sorts of dangerous mischief, or be excessively noisy, making it a very unwelcome guest indeed. The potential for theft also exists if the pet is left alone. If, however, you must go out without your pet, place a "Do Not Disturb" sign on the door, and advise the motel staff that the pet is alone.

Most inns require pet owners to sign a form accepting responsibility for any damage caused by their pets. Do not allow your pet to sleep on beds, chairs, or bedspreads. If this is not possible, take along a lint brush to remove pet hair from the furniture. Keep the animal under control at all times. Make certain that your dog does not become a nuisance to others and always clean up after it. If you groom your pet, do not flush combings down the toilet as this may clog the plumbing.

Once you have arrived at your vacation destination, supervise the pet when you let it out of the carrier. Show a cat where its food and litter are placed. Walk your dog on a leash until it becomes acquainted with the property. Eventually, you may want to remove the leash, but keep in mind that an unsupervised dog running loose could invade another dog's territory and get into a nasty fight, or tangle with area wildlife, including skunks and porcupines, or chase livestock on neighboring farms. This experience might trigger hunting instincts that were dormant up to now, or the dog might enjoy its first taste of freedom so much that it will try to escape every chance it gets.

If you are staying near water, protect your dog from potential dangers. If it drinks dirty water, it may have skin reactions or stomach problems. Small dogs can get wedged under a dock. Slippery rocks around a lake pose a safety hazard for a dog, even an experienced swimmer. My large dog Aimée almost fell into a cold lake while watching me launch a canoe!

If you are taking a dog on a boat for the first time, put a "doggy lifejacket" on it (these are available at boating supply shops) and restrain it on a leash. Make the dog sit and stay, and do not let it hang over the edge, where it could get caught in the propeller, or jump or fall out.

Car Travel

Some families take their cats and dogs with them on car trips. Animals usually fare well on motor trips if they have been accustomed from an early age to this form of travel. A young pet should be taken on rides of gradually increasing duration over a period of several weeks. Take your puppy to a park and play with it there; it will connect the car travel with fun activities and look forward to these rides.

Some dogs suffer from car sickness and will vomit when traveling. You can prevent this by withholding food and water for several hours before getting into the vehicle. Some of my clients claim that motion sickness can also be prevented by hanging two antistatic straps from the car's back bumper. If these suggestions do not work, ask your veterinarian to prescribe medicine to settle the dog's stomach. Bring lots of paper towels in the car in case the dog gets sick, as well as plastic bags in which to seal the garbage. Most puppies will eventually outgrow car sickness.

Keep your pet under control when in a moving vehicle. A loose pet can distract the driver by getting under the pedals or jumping onto the driver's lap or headrest. A frightened animal may hide under the dashboard or seat and be very difficult to extract at trip's end. An unrestrained pet could also escape from the vehicle as passengers are getting in or out. Although dogs and cats usually settle down in the back seat or on a passenger's lap, I recommend that, for safety's sake, pets be kept in a carrier. Make sure the carrier is securely placed so the animal is not subjected to excessive jolting. The pet should always be with you in the car; *never* put it in a camper, trailer, trunk, or the back of a pickup truck.

If your pet is not confined to a carrier, it should be kept on a leash—even on short trips—to prevent a sudden escape if the door or window is opened. Never let a dog, however well trained, off the leash in an unfamiliar area. As an added precaution, attach an identification tag to the pet's collar with your name and the telephone number of a person who can reach you. It is also wise to bring a recent photo of your pet with you, just in case the animal does get lost.

Never allow a dog or cat to ride with its head hanging out of the window. Many problems are caused by foreign objects flying into ears and eyes as the car speeds down the highway. The pet can also become excited by something it spots along the roadway (another animal, for example), and jump right out—with disastrous results.

You should never leave a dog or cat in a parked car. Even with the windows partially open, and even in weather that is not particularly hot, the temperature can soar in minutes, transforming the vehicle into an oven. You may think the car is in the shade, but shade moves with the sun. If you absolutely must leave a pet in a parked car for a very short time, lock all the doors, leave the windows open a small amount, and check the animal frequently.

Air Travel

When traveling with your pet by airplane, contact the airline well in advance to check regulations and services and to make a reservation. A direct midweek flight, or one with minimal stops, is usually best. Make certain the aircraft has a cargo hold that can accommodate live animals. Most airlines require animals to be at the airport several hours before takeoff; if the weather is very hot or cold, make sure that the cage will not be left outside on the tarmac for an unreasonable length of time. During the summer months, early morning and late evening flights are best so the animal will not be loaded or unloaded in the blazing sun.

Properly crated pets are allowed on the major airlines in the baggage compartment. Ideally, the pet should travel as "excess baggage" on the same flight that you are taking. The required carrier, made of high-impact plastic with a wire entry door, should be large enough to allow the animal to comfortably stand up, lie down, and turn around in. Carriers may be purchased at pet stores or directly from the airline. For hygienic reasons, airlines do not usually rent carriers. Put your name, address, telephone number, and destination on the carrier, as well as a "Live Animal" label, with arrows indicating the upright position. Fasten all pertinent paperwork—health certificate, proof of vaccinations—in an envelope on the outside of the carrier, and keep a copy of these records with you and another copy at home.

Don't let the pet eat or drink six to eight hours before departure, and don't put food or water in the crate. Exceptions can be made for medical reasons or in very hot weather, but check with your veterinarian first. Animals can go a long time without food or water—about twelve hours for smaller animals and up to twenty-four hours for larger ones. If the flight is long or there is a stopover, pack some dry food and a sturdy dish in a mesh or cloth bag, and fasten it to the carrier, together with feeding instructions. A plastic watering bottle can also be enclosed so that the airplane crew can offer the pet a drink through the closed door—they are not permitted to open the carrier.

Some airlines will allow tiny dogs in the passenger compartment (usually one per flight) if confined in a crate small enough to fit under a passenger seat. One of my clients regularly traveled by airplane with her small Chihuahua in her purse; however, when x-ray procedures were introduced for security measures, she was no longer able to sneak the dog on-board!

Never allow your pet to be off-leash in an airport or other large public place. This may seem to be common sense and not worth mentioning, but I actually witnessed a man taking his Siamese cat out of its carrier and allowing it to wander freely around the departure lounge! The man did not seem to be aware of the number of places his cat could hide if it suddenly became frightened or upset.

If you are not traveling on the same flight as your pet, expect difficulties to arise. One of my clients sent his Boxer bitch from Toronto to Chicago to have her bred; for several hours the airline could not locate her! To diminish the risk of such problems, select airlines that are recommended by your veterinarian or by breeders in your area, and try to schedule the most direct route possible.

Animals traveling by air are subjected to many strange and frightening experiences: being caged, carted around by strangers, and spending time in noisy, unfamiliar places. If your pet tends to get easily agitated and nervous, ask your veterinarian about the possibility of giving it a tranquilizer before the trip. If medication is given, keep a note of the name of the drug, the dosage given, and the expected duration of its effect. The airline may request these details, and it will assist a veterinarian at your destination in the event that the pet needs to be seen shortly after arrival.

One final consideration: airlines assume limited liability when shipping animals, so you may wish to obtain additional insurance coverage to minimize the risk of financial loss arising from accidental injury or the death of your pet.

Buses and Trains

Other forms of public transportation, namely buses and trains, are difficult to use when traveling with a pet. Most buses will not accept pets. If you are traveling by train in Canada, pets—except for guide dogs—must travel in a separate baggage car. However, not all trains have baggage cars and therefore your choice is limited. Railway employees will not normally feed or give water to animals but, unlike the plane, passengers do have access to their pets. Let the train staff know that your pet is being transported and you may be permitted into the baggage car. Obtain all of the details from your chosen carrier well in advance of your trip.

Leaving Your Pet at Home

Many families feel that it is easier for all concerned to leave pets at home during vacation. Elderly or nervous animals, or those that are blind, deaf, or ill, are generally happier at home, even in their owners' absence. If they are boarded in a kennel, the new environment, filled with noises and excitement, might stress and frighten them. If you have several animals, the cost of boarding may exceed that of a live-in sitter. If you are worried about the security of your home as well as the comfort of your pets, a live-in sitter will alleviate both concerns.

Home visits are another option that may suffice for animals that mostly sleep and do not engage in destructive behavior when left alone. Remember, apart from two or three visits a day, the pet will be alone. You must weigh your concern for its comfort against the loneliness it might experience.

Rather than impose on relatives and friends, many pet owners prefer to retain the services of professional "pet sitters," and I have generally received very positive feedback from clients who have used such services. These fully bonded and insured persons either stay in the client's home, or make frequent visits to care for the animals. It is best to personally interview the staff who will be caring for your pets, and supervise their first encounter. Watch the type of rapport that develops between the sitter and the pets, and decide whether you feel confident that your pets will be properly cared for. If you are engaging a visiting pet sitter, rather than a "live-in" sitter, ask how long each visit will be. If some of this time is spent watering plants, collecting mail, checking through the house, paying or forwarding bills, and so on, how much time will be devoted to your pet?

Although a cat can be left alone for up to three days with plenty of food and water available, problems could develop: its water bowl could spill or it could become ill. It is much better to have someone come to your home once or twice a day to feed the cat and change the litter. Depending upon a dog's routine, it will usually be content if it is fed on schedule and taken out two or three times a day. Give the caretaker the name and telephone number of your veterinarian as well as a means of contacting you, if at all possible. It is a good idea to tell your veterinarian the name of your pet's caretaker. You should also sign a consent form in advance of your trip, authorizing your veterinarian to perform emergency measures for your pet. Consider making arrangements for the veterinary office to extend credit as might be necessary to treat your pet in your absence.

Give the pet sitter written detailed instructions regarding feeding, exercise, grooming, likes and dislikes, and any special needs your pet may have. Discuss the action to be taken if the pet becomes ill or is injured during your absence. Include a copy of the pet's veterinary records and vaccination certificate together with information about the veterinary hospital, such as location, hours, and the name of your preferred veterinarian if it is a multidoctor clinic.

Provide the sitter with a current picture of your pet, to assist in locating it if it escapes. Some animal control agencies will not release an animal to anyone other than the owner without a "power of attorney for care," granting the pet sitter authority to take possession of the animal during your absence. You can write up a permission letter of your own, or ask local agencies if there is a ready-made form available. Advise the sitter of the circumstances under which you are to be contacted (for example, for *any* problems or only for emergencies), and leave a copy of your itinerary with addresses and phone numbers. Establish a contingency plan to be followed if your return home is delayed.

Professional Boarding Facilities

If you are not taking your pet with you, and prefer not to leave it at home with a pet sitter, you can board it at a kennel. Kennel-boarding is particularly suitable for young, rambunctious pets that enjoy plenty of activity around them; pets that require monitoring due to special needs; animals with behavioral problems; and animals that get distressed when left alone.

In addition to asking the usual questions about a boarding kennel, such as location, cost, and hours for dropping off and retrieving pets, you should ask to inspect the facilities. Ask the kennel operator the following questions:

1. What is the staff-animal ratio? (This will give some indication of the amount of human contact each pet receives.)
2. Can your pet's regular food be fed?
3. Are dogs allowed outside in individual runs, or are they taken for walks?
4. Are the dog runs protected from the elements?
5. Is the inside environment temperature-controlled?
6. Are the cats housed individually or communally?
7. Are the cat facilities in close proximity to the dogs?
8. Are older pets kept apart from young, noisy ones?
9. Does the kennel require proof that all animals entering the facility have been vaccinated against communicable diseases?
10. What measures are taken to protect animals from acquiring worms or external parasites from other boarders?
11. What steps are taken if an animal becomes ill, and who will pay any veterinary fees incurred?

The responses you receive should help you determine whether the "comfort level" of the kennel satisfies you and meets the needs of your pet.

I recall an occasion where a client brought her elderly Siamese cat to me after picking it up at a boarding kennel. It had been kept at the facility for six days. The cat was emaciated, extremely dehydrated, and very weak; it was obvious that the poor animal hadn't eaten or drunk anything for days. The kennel attendants told her that they had been unable to entice the cat to eat. In my experience, some cats, especially Siamese, appear to lose the will to live in very stressful situations, and this is probably what happened in this case. The kennel staff should have taken the cat to a veterinary hospital for proper care. Tragically, the cat passed away despite two days of intensive efforts to revive it.

One way to ensure that your pet will be adequately cared for during your absence is to board it in a veterinary hospital. At a veterinary facility, your pet's welfare will be closely monitored: if for some reason it is not eating or drinking adequately, or if it becomes ill and needs medication, appropriate steps can be taken immediately. Animal hospitals in most jurisdictions are regularly inspected to ensure that a high standard of cleanliness is rigorously adhered to. If you are considering boarding your pet at a veterinary clinic, make sure that the kennel area for boarding is separate from the ward for ill or recuperating patients; you do not want your healthy pet boarded in the same area as sick animals.

At my clinic, we have a number of "regulars" who board with us quite frequently; it's amazing how quickly they adjust to the routine. One particular dog immediately heads for the kennel area and sits in front of his usual compartment, demanding entry! On the odd occasion that another dog is occupying that compartment, the boarder becomes visibly upset until we move the other dog.

Although it is natural to feel some anxiety about leaving your pet behind when going on vacation, remember that the vast majority of pets survive these situations without incident. If your pet has been at a kennel, it may smell a little funkier and be a little thinner or fatter when you pick it up than when you left it, but it almost certainly will be frantically glad to see you again, unless it falls into that rare class of pet that "sulks" for a while!

12

Changes in the Household

We live in a mobile society, and our lives are full of change. Pets are also affected by their owners' changes of residence, and by the addition or loss of family members, both animal and human.

Moving Your Residence

The process of changing one's residence is very disruptive and stressful for all concerned, including animals. Some pets become visibly confused and upset as their familiar environment is reduced to a collection of boxes. At first, a cat may have great fun playing in the cardboard packing boxes. But as the packing progresses, it might start to hide as it feels increasingly insecure. Dogs, too, can sense oncoming change, and usually demonstrate this by becoming more attached to the family, and not wanting to be left alone.

Plan ahead to make sure that your pet is out of the way during the actual move. Consider leaving the pet with a friend or neighbor, or putting it into a boarding facility for several days. It would be tragic if your pet were to escape through the open doors during the move, or if a mover were to trip over your pet and injure it.

Once you have moved and unpacked the major items, introduce your pet to its new home. Use the same procedure with a cat as was used when you brought it home for the first time. Set the cat down near its litter pan, and let it find its own way to its food and water bowls, and then to the rest of the house. A cat will usually begin by walking around the edges of the rooms; it may take quite a while before it ventures out into the center of the rooms. The familiarization process will not be very lengthy if the furniture in your new residence is the same as in your former home.

If your cat is used to going outside, do not be in a hurry to let it out of its new house. It might easily get lost or be attacked by other animals in the neighborhood. Supervise your cat during its first few excursions outside. Make certain it has an identification tag on its collar, and give your veterinary hospital your new address and telephone number to update their records.

One day, a dog wearing a tag from my clinic was brought in as a stray. We tried to contact the owner, but the information in our files was out of date. We kept the dog for ten days and then took it to the humane society for adoption. Several months later, the owner appeared at my clinic with a new puppy that she said she had adopted to replace her lost dog. You can well imagine her disappointment when I told her that her lost dog had been found but we were unable to locate her. Make certain to include your veterinarian on your list of people to notify of an address change.

The Arrival of a New Baby

Although expectant parents frequently express concern that their pets will be upset with the arrival of a baby, problems rarely arise. However, it is probably fair to say that, regardless of how much you love your pets, they will no longer come first in your heart and home once your first child arrives. A few proactive steps can help ease your pet's adjustment to life with a new baby.

Make any necessary changes in the household rules as soon as you learn of the upcoming blessed event. For example, if you are no longer going to let the pet on the furniture or in bed with you, change the rule now to prevent it from associating the change with the baby's arrival and feeling resentment towards the newcomer. Train your pet not to jump onto your lap unless invited; you do not want an added guest when you are feeding the baby!

Pets are generally interested in household changes, so try not to exclude them from the baby's room. Let your pet familiarize itself with the new furniture. Initial introductions can begin while the mother and infant are still in the hospital. The father can bring home blankets or other objects that carry the baby's scent, and let the dog or cat sniff but not play with them.

Once the baby has come home, periodically lavish the pet with attention to prevent it from becoming resentful and jealous of the baby. It will soon learn that when you are with the baby, it must wait to receive attention.

Many new parents make the mistake of keeping pets far away from infants, and this may cause resentment. Give your pet an opportunity to be part of the family and to get to know this strange new creature; it is quite permissible to let a cat or dog give a baby a good (albeit supervised) sniff! A particularly rambunctious dog can be controlled with a leash if necessary.

While some people go overboard separating the baby from the pet, others expect too much, thinking that the animal will instinctively want to "protect" the child. Animals have no instinctive inclination to "protect" human infants. Never leave an animal, however well behaved, alone with a baby. You can never predict what your child will do to provoke a bite.

Bear in mind that an infant's mouth will have the aroma of milk after feeding. Cats are naturally attracted to this scent and may want to lick the baby's face and mouth. Cats also like to curl up in the crook of a person's (or baby's) neck. Old wives' tales about cats suffocating babies stem from this instinctive attraction to milk and soft warm bodies.

Sometimes problems develop when the child begins to crawl. Supervise your child at all times when it is with the pet, and do not let the child play too roughly with it. The initial play periods should be brief. The pet should have a quiet place to escape to when it has "had enough." In addition, a child should *never* touch an animal's food bowl when it is eating.

It is exciting to observe the bonding that develops between an infant and a kitten or puppy as they grow up together. Ultimately the child will benefit by learning to be compassionate, kind, and considerate of all living creatures.

Other Changes in the Family Unit

Pets usually accept new adult members into the family unit without difficulty. However, I have heard horror stories—which, thankfully, are quite rare—of animals that were so attached to their owners that they would not accept another person. There have been incidents of cats viciously stalking or attacking people, or of dogs not allowing a newcomer into the owner's bed or onto other furniture. One way of encouraging a pet to accept a new family member is to give the newcomer the sole responsibility of feeding the pet. If possible, arrange for the pet to be left alone with the newcomer for a few days. It will quickly bond with the person.

Sometimes, however, one is faced with the decision of whether to try to retrain the pet or to find it another home. If the pet does not adapt to a new home (for example, if it refuses to eat, or becomes vicious or destructive), it might, unfortunately, have to be euthanized. Gladly, such situations are extremely rare.

Another significant change in a pet's world occurs if a member of the household who used to be home most of the day begins working full-time. This should not present a problem if your pet has been accustomed at an early age to being left alone for varying lengths of time, as was discussed in Chapter 6, "Care of Puppies and Kittens." If possible, gradually increase the length of your absences, so that when you begin working full-time, the pet will be used to being home alone for the whole day. Ensure that it has had sufficient exercise before you leave in the morning.

One client told me that her family's dog would only come upstairs to the bedroom once all the family members were home. When a family member began to work shifts, the dog would wait for him all night by the front door. The adjustment to this work schedule was as difficult for the dog as for the person!

Some pets show behavioral changes when family members to whom they are attached die or move away. The pet may act depressed and withdrawn. The mere passage of time will usually restore the pet to its previous character. A client once told me that her dog became extremely subdued when a family member was in the hospital. After several weeks, the dog perked up somewhat after visiting the person in the hospital, although it did not recover fully until the family member was back home.

It is important to plan for the care of your pet in the event that you are hospitalized or otherwise unable to care for it. Interim pet care arrangements are discussed in Chapter 11, "Vacation Time." If you have concerns that you may be permanently unable to care for your pet, other more final steps must be taken. These are discussed in Chapter 23, "Saying Goodbye to Your Pet." I had one client who left his dog with a close friend while he traveled around the world for a year. Before he left, he took out pet insurance to cover any major health care expenses that might be incurred on behalf of the pet. This is an excellent idea.

We are living in an age where family breakdown and disputes over "pet custody" are not uncommon. I have had situations where a person has boarded a pet at my clinic, and the person's estranged spouse has come to pick it up, claiming to have authority to do so. My staff are trained to release an animal only to the person who checked it in, or to someone who has written authorization from that person to retrieve the pet. If you have concerns that your pet may be abducted, advise your veterinary office, groomer, and boarding facility of the situation to ensure that the pet will be released only to you.

Addition and Loss of Pets

Although individual personality differences exist, most young animals accept each other after some initial posturing. A mature pet will generally accept a very young animal more rapidly than it will accept another adult pet. Some animals are friendly to all newcomers; others will tolerate no other pets in the household.

It can be difficult to integrate a new pet into a household that already has an animal. This must be handled with foresight and sensitivity. Do not simply put two animals "nose to nose" and then stand back—the fur will most definitely fly! It is better to let them discover each other in their own time and on their own terms. One of my clients held her two cats near each other so they could fight, thinking that this would allow them to quickly work out their differences. She was injured by the fighting cats that, to this day, still do not like each other!

A newcomer may be perceived by the resident pet as a threat to its position in the family "pack." To avoid issues of territorial dominance, introduce the animals to each other on neutral ground, such as a neighbor's yard. Be sure there are no distractions such as unusual or frightening noises, and that there is no food to fight over.

Avoid overwhelming a new puppy when introducing it to existing pets. Introduce it to its new human and animal family members one at a time. When you arrive home with the puppy, make a big fuss over the other dogs, playing with them for a few minutes, especially if that is your usual practice. Do not let them see the new puppy until you have finished your routine. When you introduce the puppy to the other dogs, stay with them. You may hear growling, or see posturing, but chances are that the puppy will want very much to be accepted and will show signs of submission, such as rolling onto its back or crawling towards the adult animals.

If possible, when introducing a new dog or cat to a household that already has a pet, have an outside person bring the newcomer into the house. This way the new animal will not have the owner's scent on it, and will not be likely to arouse the resident animal's animosity. The resident pet might assume that the person who brought the new pet will eventually leave with it; the resident animal will not immediately suspect that the newcomer is there to stay!

When a new adult dog is introduced into a household with a resident dog, the common aggression that may occur between the animals is not "jealousy." Rather, it is called "sibling rivalry" (even though the dogs are not littermates), and indicates competition for social position. It occurs when the dogs are of near or equal dominance, and the fights are generally stimulated by competition for the owner's attention or for food, toys, or a favorite sleeping area. Often, the owner's presence makes the submissive dog feel more confident and willing to challenge the position of the dominant (usually the resident) dog. When a fight erupts, the owner's natural impulse is to punish the resident dog, believing it to have been the aggressor. This lowers the social status of the resident and raises that of the submissive animal. The dogs are not able to establish a stable dominance hierarchy, so the fighting continues.

To deal with sibling rivalry, the owner must determine which of the dogs is more dominant. From the time the problem is recognized, it is essential that the owner reinforce the dominance hierarchy by always dealing with the more dominant dog first: give it treats first; offer it affection first; exercise it first, and so on. Although this blatant show of partiality may seem cruel by human standards, dogs do not expect to live as equals, and both the dominant and submissive dog will be happier and more secure with a stable hierarchy.

A client who regularly introduces stray cats into her multicat household uses a very large wire pen to house the newcomer in view of the other cats for a week or so. This gives the resident animals a chance to sniff at the new cat, and possibly hiss at it, while the new cat is protected from injury. The residents get used to the idea of having the new animal around and will accept it when it is released from the enclosure. This period of partial isolation also helps to prevent the spread of diseases.

Many families maintain an assortment of pets—dogs, cats, gerbils, birds, and other animals. It does take some planning to achieve household harmony, but the enjoyment of seeing a dog grooming a kitten makes it worthwhile. The secret to a peaceful co-existence is to raise mixed species together from a young age. This allows the animals to form lasting attachments before the hunting instinct develops (at about twelve weeks of age in dogs and cats). When introducing a small caged pet to your household, be sure not to leave it unattended until your cat or dog has had a chance to adjust to its presence, and you are absolutely satisfied that the larger animal is trustworthy. A small animal's movements can quickly activate a larger animal's prey-catching instinct.

Give pets time to get used to one another's signals. For example, dogs must learn that rabbits or cats that lie still and allow themselves to be sniffed are being friendly, not provocative.

In a multipet or multispecies household, a private space for each animal is essential—even if it is only under a sofa. A simple cardboard box on a shelf or counter will provide security for a cat that needs some time away from a dog.

Cats that are upset with the introduction of other cats to the household can develop elimination problems. The cat that wants to be "top" in the pecking order is not likely to stop exhibiting its displeasure as long as the second cat is around. You can try spending more time playing with the offender, but in some cases the only solution is to find a new home for one of the cats.

Elimination problems can even occur with dogs. Occasionally, a dog will forsake housetraining as an attention-getting maneuver when its domain is invaded by a newcomer. Bolster the older dog's morale and give it a lot more attention for a while. Once the dog feels secure again, it should resume its normal habits.

The animals in your expanded household will probably learn to like each other, even if they don't become best buddies. However, like people, there are some animals that will simply never become friends. They may tolerate each other or they may simply steer clear of each other totally. But the day may come when you arrive home to find your pets lying together on the floor or on the furniture, even though in your presence they appear to dislike one another!

When a pet leaves the household, the remaining animals can be affected in various ways. Although it has never been conclusively proven that animals have the capacity to grieve, some pets exhibit signs of depression and lethargy. Others actually appear to acquire a renewed vitality and sociability, as if they enjoy being the only animal in the household.

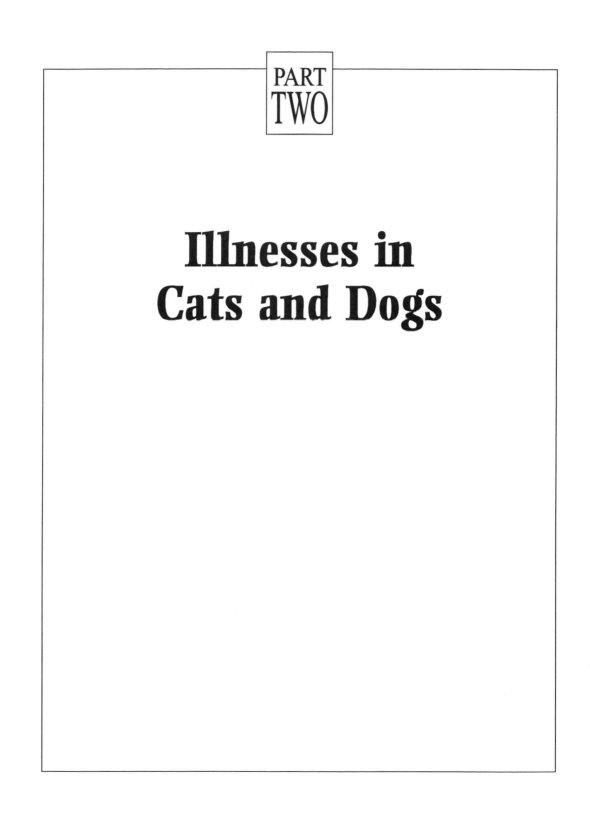

PART
TWO

Illnesses in Cats and Dogs

13

Respiratory and Cardiovascular System Diseases

The functioning of the heart, circulatory system, and respiratory system are very closely related, and it is, therefore, appropriate to review these systems together.

Respiratory System

Upper Respiratory System

The upper respiratory system includes the nose and air passageways down to, but not including, the lungs. Cats are susceptible to **rhinotracheitis**, **calicivirus disease**, and **pneumonitis**, which are upper respiratory viral diseases producing symptoms similar to those of the human cold: coughing, sneezing, and runny nose and eyes. Very young animals can become lethargic due to high fevers, and cease to eat or drink. Respiratory diseases are very contagious among cats, with an incubation period of up to seven to ten days. In addition to causing respiratory symptoms, calicivirus also causes blisters on the tongue and affected cats may stop eating. Rhinotracheitis, caused by feline herpes virus I, results in profuse nasal discharge and a consequent loss of appetite, since cats rely heavily on their keen sense of smell to identify their food. This virus also causes thick discharge from the eyes.

Another cause of feline respiratory disease is chlamydia infection, which results in pneumonitis with severe coughing, as well as sneezing and persistent eye discharge.

As we cannot treat viruses directly, the treatment for upper respiratory disease is mainly supportive. If the animal is reluctant to eat, it can be force-fed highly palatable and/or concentrated food. Sometimes I will recommend offering sardines, which would be easy for the cat to smell even with a stuffy nose. Put the cat in the bathroom if someone is taking a hot shower or bath; the steam should help unplug the nasal passages and enable the cat to breathe more comfortably. Eye symptoms can be treated with drops or ointment. Antibiotics are usually given to prevent bacteria from setting up a secondary infection in the damaged lining of the respiratory system. Left untreated, this illness can be fatal. If the patient receives proper treatment, recovery usually takes several days, although it can take longer if the cat has a high fever, no appetite, or blisters on its tongue. Even after the symptoms have ceased, some cats become carriers of the disease and transmit it to other cats. They may also have relapses under stressful conditions, or when the weather changes in the spring and the fall.

A vaccination is available against the major components of upper respiratory disease in cats.

A similar upper respiratory disease in dogs is **tracheobronchitis**, commonly known as **kennel cough**. This highly contagious disease causes bouts of hacking coughs, followed by swallowing when the throat is finally cleared. The sudden onset of this gaglike coughing sounds as if the dog has something stuck in its throat. The veterinarian's examination will determine if such is the case, or if the problem is tracheobronchitis.

Kennel cough usually improves quickly with antibiotics. Occasionally, a cough suppressant will be used, especially if the dog is unable to get its rest. Although kennel cough is not a serious condition in itself, if it is left untreated it can develop into pneumonia. A coughing dog will also serve as a source of infection for other dogs.

Protection against one major cause of kennel cough, parainfluenza virus, is usually included in the dog's annual vaccinations. A vaccine is also available against the bacteria known as "Bordetella bronchoseptica," another cause of respiratory infection. Some kennels and veterinary hospitals require all dogs admitted for boarding to be protected against bordetella.

Dogs can develop **tonsillitis**, which causes difficulty swallowing, poor appetite, and gagging sounds while the dog makes frequent attempts to clear its throat. Antibiotics should ensure a rapid recovery. If the dog has frequently recurring severe tonsillitis, the veterinarian might recommend surgery to remove the dog's tonsils (sound familiar?).

A **collapsing trachea** or windpipe is a structural problem in the dog's throat causing a hacking cough during exercise or extreme excitement. The trachea is composed of firm round rings of cartilage. If a section of the trachea is weak, it will collapse and trigger a cough reflex when air is moving rapidly through it. A collapsing trachea is depicted in Figure 13.1. This condition, which is not life-

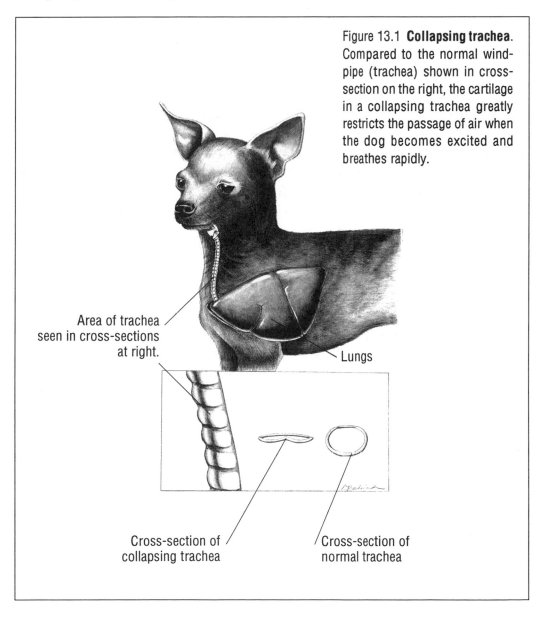

Figure 13.1 **Collapsing trachea**. Compared to the normal windpipe (trachea) shown in cross-section on the right, the cartilage in a collapsing trachea greatly restricts the passage of air when the dog becomes excited and breathes rapidly.

Area of trachea seen in cross-sections at right.

Lungs

Cross-section of collapsing trachea

Cross-section of normal trachea

threatening, occurs most frequently in young dogs of small breeds, such as Poodles, Pomeranians, and Maltese. A veterinarian can diagnose the existence of a collapsing trachea from the family's description of the symptoms, as well as being able to cause the cough reflex by pressing on the windpipe.

Surgery to correct this disorder is generally not successful. Usually the family has to put up with this bothersome condition, although if care is taken to keep periods of excitement to a minimum, the coughing bouts will be infrequent. Ease the pressure on the dog's windpipe by using a harness instead of a choke chain or tight collar. The frequency of coughing seems to diminish as some dogs get older.

A persistent nasal discharge in dogs or cats is often a symptom of **rhinitis**, an inflammation of the nasal passages. Usually, this is just part of an upper respiratory/kennel cough infection, and it is treated successfully with antibiotics. However, if the symptoms persist, other causes, such as a small grass awn lodged in the nose or sinuses, must be suspected. An endoscopic examination, in which a long, flexible tube with a lens attachment for viewing is inserted up the nostrils, will usually pinpoint the offending object, and with its removal, the symptoms should quickly disappear. If no foreign object is found, cultures are taken from deep within the nose to identify rare bacteria and fungi that might be growing in the sinuses. Hunting dogs, for example, could pick up a small foreign object or a rare bacterial or fungal infection while sniffing the trail of their prey.

If a fungus is discovered in the nasal passages, the treatment is very difficult and frequently unsuccessful. The only available drugs can be very toxic to the patient. In addition, it is difficult to penetrate the medication deep into the sinuses where the infection is growing. Surgery is performed to remove the affected bones, and medication is then repeatedly applied to the problem site. I have assisted in the ultimately unsuccessful treatment of several dogs with a fungus growing in the sinuses.

Lower Respiratory System

One disease of the lower respiratory system, or lungs, is **pneumonia**, which can occur in dogs and cats. Pneumonia can be caused by various viruses, bacteria, and more rarely, fungus, attacking the lung tissue. The animal will have difficulty breathing, and take rapid, shallow breaths. There may be coughing, sneezing, and a heavy nasal discharge. Frequently, these symptoms are accompanied by lethargy and a fever. A diagnosis of pneumonia can be confirmed with chest x-rays.

The illness is treated with a course of antibiotics. In severe cases, treatment includes medication, either in tablet or aerosol form, to open the air passageways in the lungs.

Another lower respiratory disease, that usually strikes young to middle-aged cats, is **asthma**. Symptoms range from loud breathing (even when the animal is at rest with its mouth closed), to wheezing and shortness of breath during exercise. In very severe cases the cat may be reluctant to rest with its head down, and may sit instead with its head raised, to make its breathing a little easier. Asthma in cats may be caused by an allergic reaction to something in the environment, or it might be an autoimmune disease, whereby the cat's immune system attacks its own respiratory tissue.

Diagnostic procedures for asthma include chest x-rays and possibly an electrocardiogram. However, a definitive diagnosis can be made only by a lung biopsy and an examination of lung fluid, which can be done with an endoscope.

Although feline asthma cannot be cured, it can be controlled and hopefully put into remission for long periods of time. Anti-inflammatory medication is usually given either by tablet or long-lasting injection to ease breathing. Often the dosage of medication will be gradually reduced to see if the patient can get along without it for certain seasons. Some cats will be fine without treatment for several months or longer, while other patients need medication on a daily or alternate-day basis.

Dogs can develop **bronchitis**, an inflammation of the bronchi or air passages in the lung. If these passageways become infected, a bacterial or viral bronchitis results. In these cases, antibiotics are usually beneficial. If the air passages have been damaged, a bronchodilator drug might be given to help unclog the airways.

Allergies in dogs can cause the bronchi to become obstructed or partially closed. In these cases anti-inflammatory drugs are usually helpful. The severity of allergic bronchitis in dogs and asthma in cats can vary with the seasons.

A very serious condition of the respiratory system in animals is the development of a **diaphragmatic hernia**, which is a tear in the muscular wall separating the chest from the abdomen. This allows some of the abdominal organs, usually the stomach and liver, to enter the chest. Although this condition often results from trauma, such as when an animal is struck by a car, some animals are born with an incomplete diaphragm.

An animal with a diaphragmatic hernia caused by trauma will immediately experience difficulty breathing. When the condition is present at birth, respiratory distress occurs after the animal has eaten, at which time the distended stomach interferes with lung function and breathing. However, a small congenital diaphragmatic hernia can remain undiagnosed for several months. This condition causes the partial vacuum, which is necessary for the lungs to function, to extend into the abdomen. When the abdomen is opened during surgery, the vacuum is lost and the animal can no longer breathe. The opening in the diaphragm must be located and sealed, and a vacuum must be re-established in the chest, while the patient's breathing is assisted with a ventilator. This unexpectedly happened once while I was performing a spay operation. The lesson to be learned is that no surgical procedure is entirely "routine" or free of risk, although problems of this nature are rare.

A traumatic diaphragmatic hernia can be diagnosed from clinical symptoms and from x-rays. Surgery is the only effective means of repair, and this is a dangerous operation due to the animal's respiratory difficulty.

Dogs and cats can develop **tumors** in any part of the respiratory system. Tumors in the nose or sinuses can cause a visible swelling of the nose. Tumors in the lung cause breathing problems, coughing, and shortness of breath. Tumors can also occur around the heart, causing heart failure. While x-rays are useful in diagnosing chest tumors, surgery might be the only way to actually determine whether or not the tumor is operable.

Cardiovascular System

Heart Disease

The heart and circulatory system have numerous functions, including the transport of oxygen and nutrients to the tissues, the transport of carbon dioxide and other waste products to the lungs and kidneys, the distribution of substances such as hormones, and temperature regulation. Consequently, many other organs are affected when cardiac function is impaired, even before signs of heart failure become apparent.

Dogs and cats can be born with some structural abnormality in the heart or major arteries leading from it. These defects account for about 10 percent of all canine heart problems, and a lower percentage in cats. The conditions can usually be detected during a thorough physical examination, which is one of the many reasons why I recommend that young pets be examined by a veterinarian.

Congenital heart murmurs, in which the heart valves do not close properly, will usually not cause symptoms at an early age. However, as the animal gets older, it might have stunted growth and respiratory difficulty, especially following exercise. Left untreated, an animal with a congenital heart defect would not be expected to live a long or active life.

Various types of x-rays of the heart will highlight the exact nature of the problem in a young patient. Surgery can usually be performed to correct the congenital defect.

A condition which accounts for the vast majority of heart disease in cats affects the heart muscle itself and is called **feline cardiomyopathy**. Basically, cardiomyopathy is an enlarged and misshapen heart. Although cats of any age can develop this disease, young cats are most commonly afflicted. Early in the disease, the cat may have only a decreased appetite and appear a little listless. Eventually, its breathing will become fast, shallow, and labored. The normally pink color of the gums and tongue will turn bluish, particularly after exercise. Cats, unlike dogs, rarely cough as a result of heart disease; coughing in cats is more likely an indication of asthma or some other respiratory infection.

A cat with cardiomyopathy may produce an **embolus** or **blood clot**. After a clot forms in the pumping chamber of the heart, it may break away into the aorta, the largest artery in the body. The clot is trapped where the aorta divides into two much smaller branches leading into each hind leg, stopping or greatly reducing the flow of blood to those legs. The hind legs will feel much colder than the rest of the body; they will have no sensation and the cat will not be able to use them when walking. These symptoms can develop very suddenly. A client once let her cat out the back door and it was fine. A few minutes later it arrived at the front door paralysed in the hind end; it had suffered an embolus from cardiomyopathy.

A veterinarian may be suspicious that a cat is developing cardiomyopathy by hearing a heart murmur or by learning of the cat's shortness of breath or other vague respiratory symptoms. Cardiomyopathy can be confirmed through an electrocardiogram, chest x-rays, and blood tests. Before a blood clot has formed, treatment is aimed at preventing clotting through the use of a low dose of aspirin. As well, the workload on the heart is decreased through the use of diuretics that lower the cat's blood pressure, while other drugs are used to actually strengthen the heartbeat. A low-salt diet will aid the circulation by preventing the accumulation of fluid in the body. This special diet and medication, which may have to be modified from time to time, will have to be continued for the life of the cat.

Once a blood clot has formed, surgery might be performed to remove it, and then medication and a low-salt diet will be prescribed. However, there are usually many more clots still in the heart; if a blockage is removed, it would likely soon be replaced by another one.

The underlying causes of the changes in the heart that lead to cardiomyopathy are not fully understood, and research into this condition is continuing. Recently it was discovered that cats not receiving sufficient quantities of taurine (an amino acid) in their diets were at risk of developing this disease, and chances of recovery improved if extra amounts of taurine were given. As a result, most good-quality cat foods and vitamins now are supplemented with taurine.

A cat afflicted with feline cardiomyopathy is not generally expected to live to a ripe old age, although medication and close supervision of its condition can prolong its life.

Dogs are also affected with heart disease, although usually treatment is more rewarding than with cats. In the dog, symptoms of heart disease can be shortness of breath, lack of stamina, fainting, and coughing even while at rest. While listening to the dog's chest, a veterinarian may detect a heart murmur, caused when the valves in the animal's heart are not closing efficiently and some blood is flowing back against the direction of circulation. Canine heart conditions can be confirmed through chest x-rays, electrocardiograms, and blood tests.

Heart disease in dogs will usually lead to **congestive heart failure**, which is an inability of the heart to adequately pump blood. The disease is graded according to its severity, with Grade I being a very minor heart condition with a slight cough and a barely audible heart murmur, and Grade IV being a very ill animal with a loud constant heart murmur and poor circulation.

To illustrate what happens in the early stage of heart disease, picture the blood as railway trains, entering and exiting a railway station (the heart). If the switching mechanism is not working efficiently, and more trains enter the station than leave, there will be a buildup of trains in the station and eventually some trains will leave the track. Similarly, when the heart is not pumping efficiently, as the blood passes slowly through the chest, fluid leaves the blood vessels and accumulates in the chest. This causes the animal to cough; cardiac cough is an early symptom of heart failure in the dog. Chest x-rays will show changes in the size and shape of the heart as well as fluid in the lungs. An electrocardiogram is essential to make an accurate assessment of heart disease.

This early stage of heart failure is treated with diuretics or water pills, used to decrease fluid buildup in the body, and particularly in the chest, to alleviate the heart condition. The dog will urinate the excess fluid, much the same way that people with high blood pressure react to the same type of drug. Usually, after a few days on medication, the frequency of urination will normalize as the body gets used to the drug. At this point the dog must also begin a salt-free diet. Salt causes water to be retained in the body, and this will be counterproductive to the effect of the diuretic. All treats, including dog biscuits, must be as low in salt as possible. Avoid dried beef products, which are very high in salt content.

Over time, the dog's heart will slowly deteriorate. Other medications will be added to actually strengthen the heartbeat. A pacemaker to maintain a regular heartbeat can be implanted by a specialist, although this is not done as commonly as in human medicine.

Another cause of heart problems in dogs and occasionally in cats, is **heartworms**. This subject is discussed in Chapter 20, "Parasites."

It is important to realize that, while heart disease can usually be controlled with medication for varying lengths of time, the dog's heart condition will not be cured. Therefore, have the dog evaluated by the veterinarian at regular intervals, report any observed changes in the dog's condition, and faithfully administer the prescribed medicine. Dogs with heart conditions can live rather full lives; however, close liaison between the family, the pet, and the veterinarian is essential.

The Lymphatic System

An important part of the circulatory system is the lymphatic system, a network of tiny vessels that filter fluid picked up in the body and return it to the bloodstream. This fluid (lymph) seeps through all body tissues, eventually collecting in a series of ducts and ending up in the lymph nodes, spleen, tonsils, and other lymphatic tissue. Dogs and cats have at least one hundred lymph nodes acting as barriers to the spread of infection, filtering out and destroying micro-organisms and toxins. The production of antibodies centers around the lymph nodes. **Lymphosarcoma** is cancer of the lymphatic system, discussed in Chapter 21, "Cancer."

The Blood

A vital component of the circulatory system is the blood. The red blood cells are responsible for carrying oxygen to the tissues. **Anemia** is the condition of having less than the normal amount of red blood cells in the circulation, causing lethargy and fatigue. Normally, the gums and lower inner eyelids will be pink in color, but in an anemic animal, they will appear pale. Anemia can be caused by a decrease in production of red blood cells, an increase in the destruction of red blood cells, or a loss of blood cells through internal or external bleeding. Inadequate production of red blood cells can be due to a tumor in the bone marrow, destroying the center where most red blood cells are made. Anemia will also develop if the animal's diet lacks some of the components of red blood cells, notably iron.

Red blood cells can be destroyed if they truly are abnormal, as occurs in some types of blood cancer, or if the body's immune system incorrectly destroys normal red blood cells, as happens to dogs with autoimmune anemia. High doses of anti-inflammatory medication can help to control autoimmune anemia.

Some microscopic parasites can live in the bloodstream and destroy the red blood cells. **Feline infectious anemia** is caused by the single-celled organism *Hemobartonella*. Similarly, some canine blood parasites such as *Erhlichia* and *Babesia* can cause anemia. Treatment with certain antibiotics will usually help combat or control these diseases.

White blood cells comprise the body's defense mechanism, protecting it from bacteria and other infectious agents. Unlike red blood cells, of which there is only one variety, there are several types of white blood cells. White blood cells are produced in the bone marrow, spleen, and other parts of the lymphatic system.

The number of white blood cells in the body can vary with some diseases. An increase in a specific type of white blood cells usually indicates the body is responding to an infection. White blood cells can also increase in number if there is a tumor in the bone marrow cells that produce them. This is a form of **leukemia**, a malignant disease of the blood-forming organs with cancerous cells in the bone marrow and bloodstream. Alternatively, if the producing cells have been destroyed by a tumor, there will be a drastic decrease in the number of white blood cells.

Bleeding Disorders

Aside from the white and red blood cells, the circulation has components that cause the blood to clot. **Hemophilia** is a bleeding disorder caused by a defect in the clotting system, which can occur in dogs and cats, just as in people. Studies in dogs have shown that certain breeds have an increased incidence of hemophilia. These dogs can be tested to identify and eliminate them from the breeding pool. The best-known type of hemophilia in dogs is **Von Willebrand's disease**. Originally, this was studied in Dobermans, but now it has been found in many other breeds, including German Shepherds and Labrador Retrievers.

Hemophilia has not been studied as thoroughly in cats but it does occur. After I neutered and declawed a domestic short-haired cat, two toes continued to bleed when the bandages were removed the next day (our usual procedure), although surgical adhesive had been applied during the operation. The scrotum was also swollen with blood. The cat was anesthetized again and each toe was stitched closed, as was the scrotum (this is not normally necessary). The cat continued to bleed slowly from several toes and it was necessary to bandage the paws tightly to encourage clot formation. Blood tests showed that the cat's clotting capacity was far below normal. After being given a blood transfusion from another cat to provide the missing components of the clotting system, there was no further bleeding. Periodically, however, this cat still has painful joints with some swelling in his legs, presumably from bleeding into the joint after playing roughly with his feline companion.

Although this is the only case of feline hemophilia that I have documented in my many years of practice, it highlights once more the fact that unexpected developments can occur in even the most routine surgery. Conditions that are not suspected to exist in a patient and that would not be diagnosed in advance can cause unexpected complications.

Blood transfusions can be used in dogs and cats for the treatment of shock, extreme anemia, sudden bleeding from an injury, or hemophilia. Community blood banks for pets are maintained at many emergency clinics and humane societies. Many veterinary hospitals have a blood donor cat and dog; often they are the clinic mascots or the veterinarian's own pets. When blood is needed, a fresh supply can be obtained from the donor.

Although much is still unknown regarding the "typing" of animal blood, there appear to be two main blood types in dogs (A positive and A negative), while cats seem to have only one blood type. Cat blood should be tested to make sure it is negative for the feline leukemia virus before using it for a transfusion. Giving one transfusion to an animal is usually a safe procedure; complications would occur only if a second transfusion were given. Fortunately, a single transfusion is sufficient for most animals in need of additional blood.

Hemorrhage can be caused by eating the rodent poison, warfarin. Rats bleed to death after consuming bait containing this chemical. Unfortunately, dogs and cats are also attracted to most brands of rat bait. Depending upon the size of the pet and the type and quantity of poison consumed, the results can be very severe immediately, or much more gradual. The common sign of accidental warfarin ingestion is bleeding from the gums after the animal eats. Sometimes the pads of a dog's feet will bleed easily if it walks a lot on a rough surface. Very dark stools or blood in the animal's urine are signs of internal bleeding.

The treatment for warfarin poisoning is injection or tablets of vitamin K. Treatment must be continued for several weeks as the poison can linger in the body for a long time. It is important to keep your pet calm while it is being treated for warfarin ingestion to prevent any trauma which could cause internal or external bleeding.

14

Diseases of the Digestive System

The digestive system is comprised of the tract that food follows from the mouth to the rectum, as well as the liver and pancreas.

The Mouth

The condition of an animal's teeth and gums is very important to its health. Bits of food combine with bacteria and saliva to form **plaque**, which adheres to the surface of the teeth. A buildup of plaque causes inflamed gums, which may discharge pus. Minerals in the saliva become deposited in the plaque, forming a brown crusty material called **tartar**. Badly infected gums and tartar-covered teeth are the most common cause of bad breath. Bacteria from severely infected gums can get into the bloodstream and travel to the heart, causing heart disease.

When pets eat dry food, the chewing action keeps their teeth cleaner, stronger, and in better condition than the teeth of pets that receive only canned food. Dog biscuits are also helpful, but nowhere near as effective as the manufacturers would have us believe. This is because most dogs bite the biscuit once or twice and then swallow it without the benefit of the brushing action and gum stimulation that a more complete chewing would provide. Accordingly, dogs and cats, like people, need regular dental checkups and teeth-cleaning. For some animals, the chemistry in their mouths causes a heavy accumulation of tartar, which necessitates frequent teeth cleaning.

More than 80 percent of dogs six years of age and older and 60 percent of cats in the same age bracket have some degree of tartar buildup and periodontal

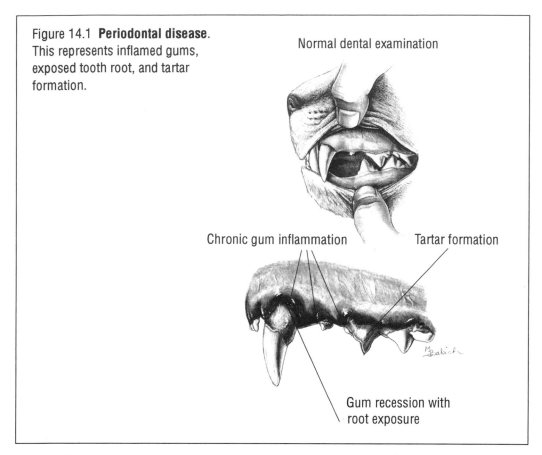

Figure 14.1 **Periodontal disease**. This represents inflamed gums, exposed tooth root, and tartar formation.

Normal dental examination

Chronic gum inflammation

Tartar formation

Gum recession with root exposure

(gum) disease. **Periodontal disease** causes red, swollen, tender gums; bad breath; loosened teeth; and the formation of pus between teeth and gums leading to a generalized blood poisoning. Periodontal disease is illustrated in Figure 14.1. In my experience, dental problems seem to occur more frequently in the smaller breeds of dogs; many Poodles and Chihuahuas become practically toothless even before they reach middle age.

Although dogs rarely develop **cavities**, they are frequently seen in cats. A small defect or cavity develops in the outer surface of the tooth above or just below the gumline. This is a very painful condition; even when the cat has been anesthetized, touching this area will cause movement of the jaw. This defect can extend deep into the tooth, resulting in a fracture near the gumline. The available techniques to repair the damage using a type of glass filling are not always successful. Often the tooth must be extracted to prevent the cat from suffering.

Some gum infections in cats occur as a result of leukemia virus infection or feline acquired immune deficiency. In the case of persistent or recurring gum disease, blood tests should be taken to check for these diseases.

An animal must be anesthetized when dental work is performed. An ultrasonic cleaning machine, similar to that used by dentists, removes the tartar from the teeth and from the roots below the gumline. Teeth that are very loose are extracted and the sockets are flushed with an antibiotic solution. A slightly loose tooth will often become more secure within the socket following stimulation of its root with the ultrasonic cleaner. After the teeth are cleaned, the daily application of an antiseptic solution to the gums may keep gum inflammation, infection, and accompanying bad breath under control.

Veterinarians often recommend that diligent clients brush their pet's teeth to prevent further dental problems. Specially designed toothbrushes for dogs and cats have been developed, although a piece of gauze bandage wrapped on your index finger and then rubbed against the pet's teeth serves almost as well. Toothpaste for pets is available, but the act of brushing is more important than the dentifrice used. Do not use toothpaste meant for people, as it contains a high level of detergent and may make the pet ill. Similarly, baking soda and salt should not be used to brush an animal's teeth; the pet will ingest too much sodium, which could cause kidney problems.

While routine dental cleaning and extractions can be performed by your regular veterinarian, there are also veterinarians who specialize in dental care and provide more elaborate services, such as root canals, filling cavities, applying braces, and replacing missing teeth. One of my patients, an Airedale dog, broke an upper fang; it split the length of the tooth from the tip to the gum. The pulp or center of the tooth was exposed and very sensitive; I referred the dog to a veterinary dentist who saved the tooth by performing a root canal and building up the missing part of the tooth.

The practice of veterinary orthodontics has also progressed with improved techniques. Orthodontic work should be done to improve an animal's bite, but not necessarily to give it a perfect bite. This treatment should never be utilized for a purebred "show" animal that has a congenital or potentially inherited bad bite, unless the animal is spayed or neutered to keep the inherited defect from being transmitted to future generations.

Ideally, a missing tooth should be replaced because its loss causes the adjacent teeth to move out of their sockets. If it is not replaced, more teeth will eventually be lost, due to the improper forces exerted during chewing. A lost tooth can be replaced by a bridge (a false tooth anchored to adjacent teeth). Alternatively, a false tooth can be implanted into the jaw bone. However, the replacement of a missing tooth is still a relatively rare procedure, because it is an expensive procedure requiring specialized expertise and equipment that is not as yet available in many veterinary clinics. This may change as veterinary dental techniques become increasingly sophisticated.

A dog can develop a draining sore on its face due to an infected root of the large first upper cheek (or carnassial) tooth. An infection in the root of any other tooth will drain, usually into the mouth or nose. However, the root of the carnassial tooth extends into a space beneath the eye. When an abscess develops in this root, pus fills this space, resulting in a swelling with or without drainage on the pet's face. Treatment usually requires extraction of the tooth and a brief course of antibiotics.

Tumors can develop anywhere within an animal's mouth. An **epulis**, occurring in Boxers and other large dogs, is a benign growth of gum tissue that can extend down the sides of a tooth. If the epulis is affecting the chewing surface of the tooth or becomes infected, it can be removed surgically.

Tumors can develop in the jaw, and can be either benign or malignant. If your pet is having difficulty chewing, it should be examined by a veterinarian, who will check for tumors as well as other conditions. In my experience, malignant tumors usually grow rapidly and extend from one side of the lower jaw to the other, with very debilitating results. Unfortunately, a jaw tumor is generally inoperable.

A pet whose mouth has a bloody discharge and that is having difficulty eating might have a tumor involving the tongue. Regrettably, most of these tumors are also inoperable.

Sometimes dogs will develop a large saclike soft swelling beneath the jaw, due to a blockage or rupture of a salivary duct causing saliva to back up and fill the salivary gland. If the swollen salivary gland (called a **mucocele**) is merely drained, it will usually fill up again with saliva. X-rays taken after dye is injected into the area will locate the blockage, which can be surgically removed.

The "hard palate" or roof of the mouth may have a crack in it at birth, or it may be split following a blow to the animal's head. A **split palate** is very serious, as when the animal eats, food passes through the opening in the palate into the nose and respiratory system. Choking and pneumonia will quickly develop. For this reason, animals born with cleft palates are usually euthanized. Surgery to close a palate that has been split as a result of an accident must be performed as soon as possible.

The Esophagus

After food is chewed, it passes down the esophagus, or food tube, to the stomach. Some animals are born with **achalasia**, which is a stricture, or narrowing, of the esophagus near the entrance to the stomach. Although liquids can enter the stomach, undigested food backs up in the esophagus and is regurgitated soon after eating. After weaning, the puppy loses weight as the increasing quantitics of food consumed cannot enter the stomach. Regular and barium x-rays will usually pinpoint the problem. Sometimes the puppy can be helped if it is fed a liquified dog food from an elevated food bowl. When it eats with its head raised, gravity will help some food to flow through the stricture into the stomach. When the puppy is older, surgery may be undertaken in some cases to remove the stricture.

The Stomach

Gastric dilatation-torsion complex is a very serious condition involving the stomach. This disease is found particularly in large, deep-chested dogs, such as Irish Setters, Saint Bernards, and Standard Poodles, although I have also seen it in a Dachshund and a Basset Hound. The following is a very simplified explanation of this complicated and not totally understood condition: If a dog consumes a large amount of dry food followed by a large volume of water, the food in the stomach will swell up as it absorbs the water. Gas will be produced, resulting in "dilatation" or expansion of the stomach. This will cause the dog to experience anxiety, and it may swallow a lot of air (called "aerophagia"), adding to the buildup of stomach gases. If the dog is then very active, the stomach, buoyed up by the gas, may rotate upon itself, resulting in torsion. Not only is the gas then trapped in the twisted stomach, but the blood circulation to the area is severely cut off.

A dog experiencing gastric dilatation-torsion complex will be very uncomfortable and reluctant to sit or lie down. It will attempt to release the stomach gas by burping or vomiting, but it will not be successful if the stomach is twisted. Observant family members will notice the dog's stomach enlarging, and the pet rapidly goes into a state of shock and circulatory collapse. This is an **EXTREME EMERGENCY** situation, where time is of the essence in determining whether treatment will save the dog.

Treatment is aimed first at releasing the air that is trapped in the stomach. If the torsion is not complete, the veterinarian might be able to pass a flexible tube through the dog's mouth to the stomach to release the gas. If this is not possible, an incision is made into the dog's abdomen to release the gas directly to the outside. The dog's condition should improve once the gas is released, since the circulation will be restored to some degree. Surgery is then performed to untwist the stomach and sew it to the belly wall to lessen the chance of a recurrence.

It is felt that one way to prevent this dangerous condition is to stop big dogs from drinking large quantities of water immediately after eating a large amount of dry food. Also, feeding a high-quality, highly digestible diet allows the dog to eat less, minimizing the chance of excessive gas formation. Of course, keeping the dog calm after eating will also reduce the chance of torsion.

Garbage gastritis is an inflammation of the stomach resulting from the consumption of rotten or indigestible food, which can occur when a pet gets into garbage. The animal will vomit and perhaps be a little sluggish and subdued. The general treatment is to withhold all food and water for at least twelve hours. If there is no further vomiting, the pet can be offered small quantities of water every hour or two. If there is no relapse, a small amount of bland food such as boiled hamburger and rice can be fed a few times a day. After a few days, the usual food can be added gradually, with normal feeding being resumed within three to four days. If, at any time, the pet vomits again or seems ill, it should be examined by a veterinarian without further delay.

The Pancreas

Pancreatitis is an inflammation of the pancreas common in dogs, although it can also affect cats. Typically, the pet exhibits prolonged episodes of vomiting fluid and bile even when there is no longer any food left to bring up. Even water will be vomited soon after it is swallowed. On physical examination, the veterinarian will detect some pain at the front of the abdomen. The patient will usually have a fever. A blood test, the CBC, will indicate that the body is responding to an inflammatory process. Pancreatitis can be confirmed by finding elevated levels of two chemicals, lipase and amylase, in the bloodstream. The blood sample will usually be "lipemic," which means that it contains a large quantity of fat. For this reason, it is suspected that a high-fat diet contributes to the development of pancreatitis.

Pancreatitis is treated with antibiotics. The animal is not allowed to eat or drink anything for at least twenty-four hours. During that period, intravenous fluids are given to maintain hydration and nourishment. Once vomiting has ceased for twenty-four hours, small amounts of water can be offered every few hours. If this is tolerated, small amounts of bland, easily digested food are given. Over the next few days, the feedings are increased in quantity, and the regular food is gradually added until the animal's usual diet is resumed. The prognosis for recovery from pancreatitis is generally good if the diagnosis is made early and proper treatment is instituted quickly. In rare instances the pancreas will be so infected that it will rupture and **peritonitis** (a generalized infection in the abdomen) will result. In these cases the patient's condition deteriorates very rapidly, with potentially fatal consequences.

In some animals, the pancreas fails to secrete the digestive enzymes that normally allow the body to digest food. This condition, known as **exocrine pancreatic insufficiency**, is most common in young German Shepherds and in dogs that have had several previous bouts of pancreatitis. When not enough pancreatic enzymes are produced to digest the food, nutrients pass out of the body in the stool. These dogs are typically extremely thin with ravenous appetites, and their voluminous stools resemble the food that has been eaten. They will often eat their own stools, which still have some nutritive value.

A lack of pancreatic enzymes can be diagnosed with several laboratory stool tests. The patient can be successfully treated by supplementing the deficient pancreatic enzymes with commercial enzymes added to the food. This drug digests the food; the animal's body needs only to absorb the released nutrients. Control of pancreatic insufficiency is easy; however, the patient must stay on replacement enzymes for the rest of its life.

Aside from producing digestive juices, the pancreas is the source of insulin in the body. When insulin is not produced, **sugar diabetes** results. This is discussed in Chapter 16, "Diseases of the Endocrine System."

The Liver

The liver serves many complex functions and plays an important role in the digestive process. The symptoms of **liver disease** are nonspecific, consisting mainly of vomiting and loss of appetite. In serious or prolonged cases, the animal will develop jaundice, meaning that the whites of its eyeballs, its gums, and sometimes its ears, will have a definite yellow hue. Blood tests and liver biopsies can be performed for diagnosis and prognosis. Generally, symptoms of liver disease are not apparent until about two-thirds of the liver is affected.

There are many causes of liver disease, including viral, bacterial, and fungal infections; trauma; poisons and chemicals; and altered blood flow to the liver due to heart failure and congenital abnormalities.

The liver has a remarkable ability to regenerate after it has been damaged. If an animal has come into contact with a chemical that has damaged the liver, there is a chance that, with only supportive care, the liver will repair itself. Some jaundiced cats have been brought to me with severe liver disease. Supportive care (intravenous fluids and antibiotics) over a period of several days resulted in gradual improvement in their condition. Sometimes special food and medication to aid the liver in its functions will sustain the animal for several years. However, the older pet in generally poor condition is probably suffering from **end-stage liver disease**. In this advanced disease, much of the liver's ability to regenerate is gone and it can no longer adequately perform its functions. Treatment is often unrewarding.

Some cases of liver disease are due to lipidosis or fatty infiltration of the liver. This occurs in middle-aged obese animals when healthy liver tissue is replaced by fat. When the unaffected part of the liver is too small to maintain a healthy animal, liver failure begins.

Hepatitis is inflammation of the liver. In dogs, this can be caused by infection with viruses against which we offer protection in our annual vaccinations. Unfortunately, no vaccine has as yet been developed to protect cats against hepatitis. Supportive care enables many dogs and cats to recover from hepatitis.

Liver cancer can occur in animals. It can be difficult to diagnose even with x-rays and blood tests, and biopsies or exploratory surgery may be necessary to confirm the presence of liver cancer, which carries a grave prognosis.

One condition that has been extensively studied within the last fifteen years is **canine hepatic encephalopathy**. This disease occurs when there is a malformation of the blood vessels between the intestine and the liver, causing ammonia, one of the products of protein digestion, to accumulate in the body instead of being transported to the liver for absorption. After being fed a protein-rich meal, the young animal will become extremely sleepy and might even lapse into a coma. Specialized blood and urine tests can diagnose this condition, and microsurgery can usually repair the defect in the circulation to the liver.

The Intestines

Enteritis is the general term meaning inflammation of the intestine. Both dogs and cats can suffer from a form of enteritis called **distemper**, which is a misnomer as there is no change in the animal's temperament. The causes and symptoms differ between canine and feline distemper.

In **feline distemper**, which is also known as **panleucopenia**, the white blood cells are severely decreased in number. Typically affecting young kittens, panleucopenia causes extreme weakness, vomiting, and diarrhea. The body temperature is usually below normal and the kitten sits all hunched up as if it has severe intestinal discomfort. If diagnosed early, some kittens recover from distemper with a course of antibiotics and good supportive care providing fluids and intravenous nutrition. Vaccination against panleucopenia is usually given annually along with protection against several feline respiratory diseases.

Canine distemper, or **Carre's disease**, typically results in a young dog having severe vomiting, diarrhea, and a fever of 40°C (104°F). This disease is also known as **hard-pad disease**, as the foot pads are often hard like glass. Many dogs with distemper also have severe respiratory disease with heavy coughing and a crusty discharge around the nose. Muscle twitching and convulsions can also occur. Again, treatment with antibiotics and supportive nursing care will assist some dogs to recover, although some nervous symptoms may persist. For instance, there may be "fly biting": the dog will appear to snap at nonexistent flies. The development of full epileptic seizures is also possible, and, while these nervous problems are incurable, anticonvulsant medication is sometimes helpful.

Parvovirus and **coronavirus** also cause enteritis in dogs. Parvovirus causes severe vomiting and diarrhea, often with blood, along with a high fever and weakness. Coronavirus is a less severe form of enteritis, characterized by vomiting and diarrhea, but without blood or fever. Good nursing care, along with intravenous fluids to combat the dehydration from the vomiting and diarrhea, as well as antibiotics and intravenous nutrition, will enable some dogs to recover. Happily, annual vaccinations are now available to protect dogs from both coronavirus and parvovirus infections.

One feline intestinal disease that is occurring with increasing frequency is **inflammatory bowel disease** or **IBD**. In this condition, various sections of the cat's digestive tract can become inflamed, causing diarrhea. In many cases, the stomach is also inflamed, which results in loss of appetite and vomiting even though the animal is not eating or drinking. Feline IBD can be diagnosed through visual inspection and biopsies of affected areas of the digestive tract seen through an endoscope or by way of exploratory surgery. Treatment of IBD in cats consists of daily doses of anti-inflammatory medication; frequently, specialized diets are prescribed. The prognosis for control of this condition is fairly good with lifelong medication.

A specific type of bowel disease, which can develop at any age and is more common in dogs than in cats, is **colitis**, an inflammation of the large intestine. The symptoms are very frequent diarrhea, often with blood or mucus. It may begin as a reaction to certain foods, and with time, many more foods can trigger the diarrhea. The use of x-rays, barium enemas, endoscopic examinations, and intestinal biopsies will help to confirm the diagnosis of colitis.

Colitis can usually be controlled with prescriptive diets: either very bland and easily digestible, to ease the work of the large intestine; or high in fiber, to absorb water within the stools and reduce the fluidity of the stool. Sometimes, other medication is used to prevent bacterial overgrowth in a damaged intestinal environment, or to slow down the passage of food. Colitis is rarely cured; usually, it is controlled with varying degrees of success, through the use of specialized diets and/or drugs.

Intestinal parasites, another cause of digestive system disease, are discussed in Chapter 20, "Parasites."

Intestinal tumors can occur in both dogs and cats. Tumors in the small intestine can cause vomiting and weight loss, while the typical sign that an animal has a tumor in the large intestine is that it will strain to have a bowel movement. The stool is usually loose, very narrow, and ribbonlike. The tumor causes a narrowing of the intestinal wall, and just a small amount of stool is able to pass through. The animal's appetite will be diminished and vomiting might also occur.

Depending upon the size of the tumor, the veterinarian might be able to feel a suspicious mass in the abdomen when examining the patient. Often, x-rays, either plain or with barium, will highlight the area in question. Eventually, exploratory surgery may be needed to examine the mass. If a large segment of the intestine is affected, or if the tumor has spread to other organs, the condition is generally considered to be inoperable, and it is kindest to have the pet euthanized on the surgery table rather than have it suffer from the progression of the disease.

If the tumor can be removed, this will usually help the animal for a variable length of time. I once removed about five centimeters (2 in.) of a cat's intestine containing a tumor. The laboratory diagnosed it to be highly malignant (cancerous). Several months later, when the cat was again showing signs of an intestinal obstruction, I was again able to remove the tumor. About a year later, x-rays showed that yet another tumor had developed, involving a much larger section of intestine. Unfortunately, at this point too much intestine was involved for the cat to lead a normal life, and it was euthanized.

Chronic constipation is also an intestinal disease. Constipated pets either do not pass much stool, or strain a lot to have a bowel movement, eventually passing very large, hard, and dry stools. Frequently, older cats will develop lazy bowels, and have bowel movements only every few days. The intestinal muscles become stretched and lose their strength, thus allowing stools to accumulate in the large intestine. More water is then absorbed back into the body, resulting in even drier, harder stools that will further complicate the condition. The cat may stop eating and start vomiting if the condition is prolonged. Veterinary intervention is usually required to empty the cat's bowels. Occasionally, special stool-softening enemas will be sufficient, but often the animal must be sedated and the rectum emptied.

To prevent this condition, ensure that an older cat receives sufficient fiber in its diet. Prescriptive diets that contain at least 10 percent fiber are definitely recommended in these cases. Fiber increases both water retention, which softens the stool, and fecal bulk, which shortens the time it takes for the stool to move through the intestine. In chronic cases of constipation, stool-softening pills or bulk laxative medications are given to the cat. Bran is a good bulk laxative; cats often like the nutty flavor of bran cereal, or baker's bran can be mixed into the cat's food. Another good bulk laxative is canned pumpkin; cats usually will accept a small amount added to their food. Human laxatives are much too strong to give to a cat, but they are sometimes prescribed by veterinarians in very small doses.

Another type of constipation can occur in dogs that chew bones and swallow the small splinters that break off. In the stomach, these splinters soften and stick together, forming a hard bonelike mass. As the mass moves through the intestines, it may be too large to pass through the anus. The dog will be uncomfortable as it tries to expel this large, hard mass.

Once the dog is sedated, the mass can sometimes be broken down by the veterinarian and removed from the rectum. If this is not possible, or if the mass is trapped in an area that cannot be reached from the rectum, surgery is required to remove it.

Remember, it is *never* acceptable to feed bones of any kind to a dog. Similarly, bones should never be given to a cat.

Long-haired dogs and cats can suffer from **obstipation**, which is an external blockage to the passage of stool. The condition begins when a small amount of stool sticks to long hair around the rectum. With each bowel movement, more stool adheres to the first clump, until there is a large mass literally blocking the passage. The skin beneath the adhering stool will be very inflamed and sensitive. Usually, the pet must be sedated while the area around the rectum is shaved and treated with disinfectants and soothing ointments. This condition can be prevented if the hair around the rectal area is kept well-trimmed.

Two very serious intestinal problems that can occur in young dogs and cats are called **volvulus** and **intussusception**; both involve a twisting of the intestine. In the case of volvulus, a loop of intestine is twisted upon itself and becomes strangulated. Intussusception is a telescoping of a section of intestine into an adjacent section of bowel, thus effectively strangulating it as well. These conditions result from a hyperactive intestine which, in turn, can be caused by a large number of parasitic intestinal worms, or by an inability to digest a poor-quality diet. These diseases cause the animal to vomit, strain to have a bowel movement, and be in obvious abdominal pain. If not properly diagnosed and treated, the animal will quickly go into shock due to circulatory collapse, and die.

Surgery is required to repair the affected area of the intestine. Sometimes, the intestine can be returned to its natural location. However, if the blood supply to the affected area has not been adequately maintained, and that section of intestine is no longer healthy, the damaged tissue must be removed. Even after a successful surgery, there is danger that this serious condition will recur.

Foreign Objects

Foreign objects can become lodged at any point in a pet's digestive tract. If a flat rib-bone becomes lodged tightly against the roof of an animal's mouth, it will paw at its mouth in discomfort. Once the offending object is noticed, it can usually be removed without difficulty by the veterinarian. I have seen animals with open safety pins stuck in their mouths. Fish hooks are another source of trouble for the curious cat or dog, as they can get caught in the lips, tongue, or roof of the mouth. A fish hook cannot be withdrawn because of its barb; the end of the hook must be snipped off and the rest of the hook is then pulled out.

Another source of trouble for cats is thread, which gets looped around the tongue and/or swallowed. Delicate intestinal surgery is required to remove the thread. This situation is discussed further in Chapter 3, "Protecting Your Pet From Harm," under the heading "Swallowing Foreign Objects."

A foreign object can perforate the intestinal wall, resulting in severe **peritonitis** or infection of the abdomen. Surgery is required to remove the object, and a course of antibiotics is prescribed to fight the infection. The chance of recovery is dependent on the degree of contamination of the abdomen caused by the leakage of intestinal contents.

Feline Infectious Peritonitis

One very serious abdominal disease affecting cats is **feline infectious peritonitis** or **FIP**, an inflammation of the peritoneum, which is a sheet of tissue lining the abdomen. FIP usually affects kittens and cats younger than three years of age or over ten years of age.

FIP is a chronic, progressive disease caused by a virus. The onset of FIP may not be noticed for several weeks and may erroneously be thought to have come on suddenly. A cat with FIP will usually appear unwell, have a poor appetite, and be depressed, inactive, listless, and weak. A relatively high fever (generally over 40°C [104°F]) is quite typical; however, these signs are very general and can be due to many other diseases.

There are two distinct forms of FIP, a wet form and a dry form. In the wet form, the abdomen enlarges due to a buildup of fluid produced by the inflamed peritoneum. Typically, the cat will seem to be getting fatter even though it is hardly eating. In fact, just the belly expands; the spine and other bones become more prominent as the cat wastes away. Once the veterinarian suspects that there is fluid in the abdomen, a syringe can be used to withdraw a sample for analysis. If the fluid is pale yellow or golden and has a sticky, egg-yolk consistency, the diagnosis is confirmed. Fluid can also build up in the chest, in which case the cat will have difficulty breathing.

The dry form of FIP is more difficult to diagnose. Instead of producing fluid, the peritoneum produces fibrous bands of tissue that line various organs. The symptoms will vary depending upon the organs affected, but generally the cat will have a fever. Occasionally, FIP will affect the brain, causing nervous signs such as tremors, tilting of the head, or convulsions.

The exact method of transmission of FIP is unknown. I have seen cases in cats from a single-cat household. However, FIP frequently occurs in littermates, or in a mother cat and its young; this suggests the possibility of prenatal infection. FIP cannot be transmitted to humans.

The variety and frequently nonspecific nature of the symptoms often make FIP very difficult to diagnose. A positive diagnosis while the cat is alive is often not possible. Nearly half of all cats with FIP are also infected with **feline leukemia virus (FeLV)**, a further complication in making a diagnosis.

There is a blood test that can supposedly be used to diagnose FIP. However, this test relies on the presence of antibodies to the disease circulating in the bloodstream. If the cat is acutely ill with the disease, it might not have had a chance to develop antibodies, or all the antibodies might be in the tissue fighting the infection and not be in the circulatory system. Thus, a cat that is suffering from FIP may test negative. I do not place great reliance on the results of the test, unless they are positive.

FIP is usually diagnosed by eliminating other treatable diseases that could cause similar symptoms. For example, since FIP does not respond significantly to antibiotics, and most other fever-causing infections do, we can tell that a cat may have FIP if it does not improve when given antibiotics.

Unfortunately, FIP is virtually untreatable and almost always fatal, with most cats dying within two to eight weeks after the appearance of symptoms. Usually, the cat will either die of FIP or it will be so weak and progressively deteriorating that the only humane option is to euthanize it.

In recent years, a vaccine in the form of nose drops has been developed to prevent FIP. Kittens and cats usually accept an "on the nose" vaccine without difficulty. Although the effectiveness of the vaccine has not been conclusively and universally accepted by veterinarians, the product is perfectly safe and, therefore, I feel it is worth trying.

The Rectum and Anus

Large dogs, particularly German Shepherds, can develop two serious rectal problems. **Rectal fissures** (cracks in the rectum) and **rectal fistulas** (deep tunnels through the rectal wall) cause great discomfort during bowel movements. Blood may be visible on the stool, and the anus may appear inflamed and moist with discharge. Very little is known about the causes of these two conditions, which often occur together. The only treatment is to surgically remove the damaged tissue. Infection may set in due to the fact that the surgical site can be easily contaminated, and recovery can be prolonged. Occasionally, in the case of very small fissures, cryosurgery can be performed, whereby liquid nitrogen is applied to the area; the extreme cold effectively "burns" the tissue, causing scar tissue to form, sealing the fissures.

Both dogs and cats can develop **perianal hernias** when the muscles around the rectum split and allow the intestine to protrude beneath the skin. A soft swelling will be noticed on one or both sides of the anus. The prognosis is good if the torn muscles are repaired surgically.

Problems can occur at the anus, which is the actual muscular sphincter at the end of the digestive tract. An animal can have a **rectal prolapse** when the terminal part of the intestine or rectum protrudes through the anus to the outside. The red, wrinkled rectal tissue is visible, and will usually show traces of blood oozing from it. The exact cause of a rectal prolapse is unknown, although it is generally assumed to result from the animal straining severely while having a bowel movement. In young animals, this might be caused by a fiber-deficient diet.

If the prolapsed tissue is healthy, it must be cleaned, reduced to its normal size if it is swollen, and put back through the anus. To guard against recurrence, a "purse-string" suture might be placed around the anus to tighten the area. If the prolapsed tissue is not viable, or has been severely traumatized while outside the body, it must be surgically removed and healthy intestinal tissue must be joined to the anus.

Dogs and cats have two anal sacs, located at about four and eight o'clock if the anus is pictured as a clock face. These sacs store a small amount of very pungent, musky fluid produced by the anal glands. Normally, a small amount of material is released with every bowel movement. Sometimes, however, the ducts leading from these sacs become plugged and the sacs fill up with thick fluid, irritating the animal. This condition is called **impacted anal glands**. In an effort to empty these sacs, the animal will "scoot" or drag its hindquarters on the ground, or lick or bite excessively around the base of the tail. If a pet is showing these symptoms, it should have its anal sacs checked by the veterinarian. Usually, the

Figure 14.2 **Anal sac abscess**.
This represents an enlarged, inflamed anal sac on the left, and a ruptured anal sac abscess on the right.

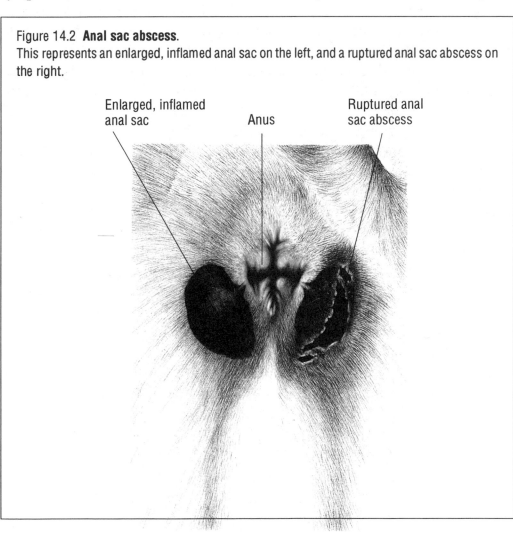

Enlarged, inflamed anal sac   Anus   Ruptured anal sac abscess

doctor will just express or squeeze the material out of the anal sacs. If the anal gland material indicates that an infection is present, the veterinarian will put some liquid antibiotics directly into the openings of the glands.

The frequency with which the anal sacs should be emptied depends on the rate at which the material accumulates. Some animals need monthly attention, some may go from two to three months without any problems, while many dogs and cats are never bothered by this problem. The anal glands and sacs can be surgically removed if absolutely necessary, as they are not believed to serve any purpose in domesticated pets. The surgery is quite delicate in a small dog or cat, where damage to the anal sphincter could result in the patient becoming anally incontinent.

Animals with frequent anal gland problems seem to improve on a high-fiber diet. Either a commercial high-fiber diet, or the addition of bran or mucilose (a fiber product available at pharmacies) to the pet's food, may ease the pet's anal gland problems.

An **anal sac abscess** (depicted in Figure 14.2) is extremely painful and looks like a red boil just to the side of the anus. After sedating the pet, the veterinarian will lance the anal sac abscess, clean it out, and disinfect it. The pet will usually be sent home on antibiotics to fight this abscess.

A **perianal tumor** is a solid growth that can occur around a dog's anus. It may grow slowly or rapidly and its surface may become raw. Since this tumor is found only in unneutered male dogs, it is a sex-linked trait and the dog should be neutered at the same time that the tumor is removed. Small perianal tumors can be surgically removed, or "frozen off" with liquid nitrogen.

15

Diseases of the Urogenital System

The urinary, or excretory system, and the genital, or reproductive, system both terminate in the same area of the body. They will therefore be discussed together. The female urogenital system is illustrated in Figure 15.1 and the male urogenital system in Figure 15.2.

Urinary System

Within the urinary system, liquid waste is filtered by the two kidneys, passes down a narrow tube (the ureter) to the bladder, travels from the bladder through the urethra, and is expelled through the penis (in males) or the vagina (in females).

Kidney Disease

The kidneys filter the liquid waste products from the blood and retain the water that is needed by the body. Kidneys that are not functioning properly will allow protein to leave the body in the urine, which will also contain too much water and not enough waste products. **Kidney failure** is the inability of the kidneys to adequately perform their functions. Kidney disease can strike cats and dogs of all ages. Acute, or sudden, kidney failure is a life-threatening disorder. In contrast, chronic kidney failure develops over several months or years and is a leading cause of death in older pets.

The causes of acute kidney failure include: blood loss, heart failure, shock, surgical stress, trauma, severe dehydration, poisons, drugs, and obstructed urine flow. Chronic kidney failure has various causes including: inherited defects, infections, poisons, nutritional factors, and immune system deficiencies.

Generally, the early signs of kidney failure are increased thirst and urination. This is a natural compensatory mechanism: as large quantities of water leave the body in the urine, sufficient waste products will also leave to allow the animal to live without any symptoms of illness. As time passes, the animal may start to lose weight, lose its appetite, and lack energy. It may continue to drink excessively and vomit fluid or bile.

As kidney disease progresses, the animal's condition deteriorates. Physical examination will reveal a depressed, lethargic animal that has lost weight. If a fold of skin is pinched, it will retain the crease for a prolonged period of time, revealing moderate to severe dehydration. In chronic kidney failure, the kidneys fail to produce a hormone that regulates the production of red blood cells. The gums and inner eyelids will be pale, due to the low number of red blood cells. The body temperature will usually be below normal, indicating a very weakened animal. The patient will often have a urinelike odor to its breath because the high levels of waste products in the bloodstream diffuse into the mouth.

The tests to confirm the existence of kidney disease are a CBC (complete blood count), blood chemistry screen, and urinalysis. The CBC will often show a decrease in red blood cells as well as dehydration. In advanced kidney disease, a blood screen will show a significant elevation in blood urea nitrogen (BUN) and creatinine, two chemical by-products of protein metabolism that are normally maintained in low levels in the circulation. Some other chemicals, such as calcium and phosphorous, will also show abnormal values. A urinalysis will usually reveal the presence of protein in a very dilute urine.

Once a diagnosis of kidney disease has been confirmed, the probable cause and prognosis should be considered. Certain poisons, particularly antifreeze or methanol, can damage the kidneys even when ingested in very small quantities. In the case of a poisoning, the quantity of poison ingested and the size, age, and general health of the animal will help to determine whether the patient will survive.

The general treatment for kidney disease is fluid therapy. The animal is given large quantities of fluids to combat dehydration as well as additional fluids to force the kidneys to excrete some of the accumulated waste products along with the excess fluids. Fluids are given either subcutaneously (under the skin) or intra-

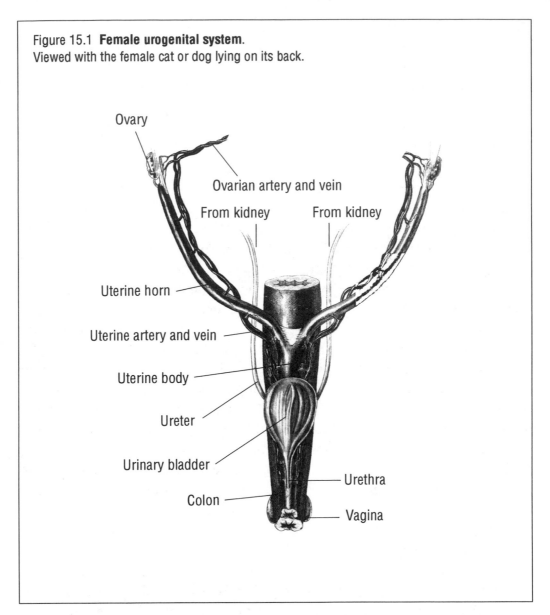

Figure 15.1 **Female urogenital system**.
Viewed with the female cat or dog lying on its back.

Ovary

Ovarian artery and vein

From kidney   From kidney

Uterine horn

Uterine artery and vein

Uterine body

Ureter

Urinary bladder

Colon

Urethra

Vagina

venously (in a vein in a front leg or the neck). Although intravenous fluids will be more beneficial to the animal, the pet must be closely supervised. If the animal bends its leg, the site of fluid administration will be compressed and the flow of fluid will be interrupted. On the other hand, fluid that is running too rapidly can cause severe heart problems. In contrast, subcutaneous fluids are deposited under

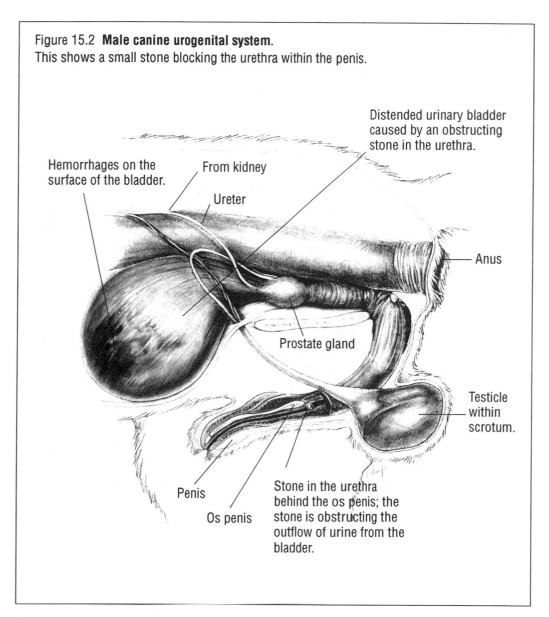

Figure 15.2 **Male canine urogenital system**.
This shows a small stone blocking the urethra within the penis.

Distended urinary bladder caused by an obstructing stone in the urethra.

Hemorrhages on the surface of the bladder.

From kidney

Ureter

Anus

Prostate gland

Testicle within scrotum.

Penis

Os penis

Stone in the urethra behind the os penis; the stone is obstructing the outflow of urine from the bladder.

the skin in several sites several times daily and are absorbed by the body at a more constant rate.

If the animal is not vomiting, its nutritional requirements can be met if it is fed a concentrated food in paste form. If it will eat on its own, special low-protein diets will be beneficial. If it refuses to eat, or if it vomits in spite of treatment even without eating, the outlook for recovery is not promising. On the other hand, if kidney disease is detected in the early stages through routine geriatric or presurgical tests, the progression of the disease can be delayed considerably if the animal is fed a prescriptive kidney diet.

Leptospirosis

Leptospirosis is an infectious disease of the urinary system of dogs, and particularly affects the kidneys. The microscopic organisms that cause the disease are usually acquired from the urine of other dogs recovering from the disease. The onset of signs is often sudden and consists of vomiting and diarrhea, which quickly result in dehydration, along with a fever, depression, and refusal to eat. The patient is reluctant to walk and exhibits pain by moving with very short steps. Pain is also reflected by tenseness of the abdominal muscles, which gives the dog a "tucked up" appearance. It might develop jaundice as evidenced by a yellow hue to the eyeballs.

If leptospirosis is present, blood tests will usually show a high white cell count, indicating a severe infection, and the BUN value will be high, showing kidney failure. A urinalysis will indicate a serious kidney infection. If the disease is diagnosed early, it can be cured with antibiotics.

Protection against leptospirosis is available through annual vaccinations. However, this vaccine is not always given unless the disease is prevalent in a particular area; I have never actually seen a case of leptospirosis. It is important to note, however, that this disease can also affect people. When canine leptospirosis is diagnosed, the owner must take precautions to prevent the spread of contaminated urine. Organisms are shed in the urine ten to fourteen days after the onset of the illness, and shedding may continue for as long as a year unless the carrier animal is properly treated.

Kidney Tumors

A kidney with a tumor will be larger than normal. This may be detected by gently feeling the abdomen, and can be confirmed by an x-ray. The enlarged kidney will not usually be functional, and will not filter out a special dye injected into the bloodstream during a radiographic procedure called "an intravenous pyelogram," or IVP. In a kidney biopsy, a small piece of kidney is removed and examined under the microscope, to identify the cause of the enlargement. The kidney and its tumor can be surgically removed if the tumor has not already spread to other parts of the body. An animal can live a normal life with only one kidney, so long as that kidney remains healthy.

Hydronephrosis

An enlarged kidney may be nonfunctional when an animal has hydronephrosis, a condition in which the filtering mechanism has become a fluid-filled cavity. This is frequently caused by a blockage in fluid outflow from the kidney, causing fluid backup and subsequent tissue destruction through increased pressure. Exploratory surgery and a biopsy are usually needed to differentiate between a kidney tumor and hydronephrosis. Treatment for hydronephrosis is removal of the affected kidney.

Avulsed Kidney

If an animal has sustained a severe trauma to the back, such as being struck by a car or falling from a great height, one of its kidneys might be torn away from its normal location against the spine. An avulsed kidney is a very serious medical emergency. There will be extensive internal hemorrhage (bleeding) if any of the blood vessels to the kidney have been torn. If the ureter leading from the kidney has been severed, the filtered waste products (urine) will be discharged directly into the abdomen. This is one of the reasons why, following a severe trauma, an animal's urinary system should be carefully examined by a veterinarian. If an x-ray shows that the abdomen is full of fluid, the withdrawal of a fluid sample from the abdomen (called a "tap") might show the fluid to be blood. However, the source of the bleeding would remain unknown until exploratory surgery locates and hopefully repairs it. An avulsed kidney can be removed, as an animal can survive with only one functioning kidney.

Ectopic Ureter

The most common medical condition affecting the ureters is a structural abnormality called ectopic ureter. This condition occurs only in female dogs, most frequently in Huskies. Instead of opening into the base of the bladder, one of the ureters (rarely both of them) empties directly into the vagina. Urine dribbles steadily from the vulva instead of pooling in the bladder and later being released outside the body. The animal is totally unaware of the soiling.

The symptoms appear very early in life. At the first veterinary visit, the family may not report any problems with urine control, thinking that it is "normal" for a puppy to be wet. However, the veterinarian may notice the abnormal urine staining of the fur around the vagina, and suggest further investigation.

An ectopic ureter can be definitively diagnosed with an IVP x-ray. After being filtered by the kidneys, the dye will be visible in the ureters and terminate either in the bladder or in the vagina. Microsurgery can be performed to move the termination of the ureter into the bladder, and the prognosis for full recovery is excellent.

Infection of the Bladder

Both males and females, dogs and cats, can suffer from **cystitis**, or **lower urinary tract disease**, which refers to an infection of the bladder. The basic symptom of a bladder infection is hematuria (blood in the urine), visible if a dog urinates on the snow outside, or if a cat or dog urinates in an unusual place in the house. Frequently, the pet will strain or try very hard to urinate but not pass much urine. People with cystitis report a severe burning sensation when urinating. Presumably this is the same in animals, and this causes the patient to stop urinating; once the discomfort eases, the pet attempts to urinate once more. Even when the bladder is empty, the irritated bladder lining makes the pet feel as if it needs to urinate again, and so it continues to try to pass urine.

Physical examination might reveal a fever, a tender abdomen, and perhaps some lethargy. Even if the urine does not appear to be bloody to the naked eye, microscopic examination could reveal a large number of white blood cells, red blood cells, and bacteria.

The indications of cystitis, namely blood and bacteria in the urine as revealed in a urine test, could also be caused by bladder stones, although in the latter case, bacteria are usually less numerous. The veterinarian must differentiate between these two conditions through the use of x-rays and possibly ultrasounds. Several times, I have seen cats that were not responding to treatment for cystitis as prescribed by other veterinarians, who had examined but not x-rayed the cats. As part of my examination I took x-rays which showed numerous small bladder stones. Therefore, although a urine test is the first step in diagnosing a urinary problem, an x-ray and possibly an ultrasound should be taken in all cases of urinary discomfort.

If no stone is found, the problem is most probably cystitis, and a course of antibiotics will be prescribed for the pet. Sometimes a urine sample will be cultured to identify the exact type of bacteria causing the infection and to determine the most effective antibiotic. However, since this procedure can take two to three days, most veterinarians will prescribe an antibiotic that is usually effective for cystitis pending the culture results, and, if necessary, change the drug when the results are available. Once the pet is on medication, there should be a noticeable improvement within a day or two.

Bladder Stones

As stated above, a bladder stone (a **cystic calculus**) can cause symptoms similar to cystitis: blood in the urine, pain, and partial or complete obstruction of urine flow. A female dog with a bladder stone may squat to urinate for a long time but then, after taking a few steps or lying down, will pass some urine. This can be explained by imagining the bladder to be a sink, and the stone as a free-floating cork. When the animal tries to urinate, the flow of urine will stop when the "cork" blocks the drain. As the animal moves around, the "cork" will become dislodged and the urine can flow again for a short time until the stone once more blocks the urine flow.

A bladder stone is a hard mineral mass similar to a regular stone found outside. The surface can be smooth or rough, and can range in size from very small, like large grains of coarse salt, to over two centimeters (1 in.) in diameter. There can be a single stone, or numerous stones can fill the bladder like a bag of marbles! One small Pug that I examined had such a large quantity of bladder stones that she was unable to hold her urine for any length of time; her bladder could not stretch any farther to allow urine to be retained.

Dogs and cats can develop four different types of bladder stones: struvite or triple phosphate, calcium oxalate, ammonium urate, and cystine. Some dogs (notably Dalmatians, Dachshunds, Scottish Terriers, and Irish Terriers) are born with an inability to metabolize certain protein components, which leads to cystine bladder stone formation. Ammonium urate stones are found only in Dalmatians. The other types of stones can be found in any breed.

It is not known why some individuals develop stones, why they get the type of stones they do, and why other animals do not form stones at all. However, bacterial bladder infections and foods containing high levels of protein and minerals such as magnesium, phosphorous, and calcium have been linked to bladder stone formation.

Of the four types of bladder stones, only the two most common, struvite and calcium oxalate, are visible on plain x-rays. The other types of stones are visible by ultrasound. Some specialists state that an increasing number of cats are developing oxalate stones. It is felt that this can be attributed to a change in the mineral composition in commercial cat foods as pet food manufacturers attempt to control a cause of urinary blockage in male cats.

Bladder stones can be surgically removed. The stone can then be analyzed, and based upon its composition, a dietary change may be suggested to prevent recurrence. However, there is also a special prescriptive diet that, when fed exclusively for six to eight weeks, should cause a struvite stone to dissolve; in this case, surgery can be avoided.

Although a bladder stone usually only causes the animal some irritation and discomfort, a small stone can solidly block the exit from the bladder and totally obstruct the release of urine. In dogs, a complete obstruction of the urethra is much more common in males than in females, due to the longer, narrower urethra in males. In addition, male dogs have a bone in the penis (the os penis), which cannot expand as soft tissue can, so most obstructions occur there, as depicted in Figure 15.2. If the animal strains repeatedly and is not seen to pass any urine, an emergency situation is developing. I once had a male Lhasa Apso patient where the stone moved out of the bladder and lodged within the penis. This stone, covered with sharp spines, was gripped by the lining of the penis, blocking the flow of urine. Delicate surgery was performed to remove the stone. A female Bichon Frise, whose stones were seen on x-rays, succeeded in passing them on her own (the owner was able to recover them!); this is not the typical outcome in cases of bladder stones.

Feline Urologic Syndrome

Feline urologic syndrome (FUS) is a very serious urinary problem that can occur in cats. Up to 10 percent of all cats admitted to veterinary hospitals in North America are affected with FUS, which, in male cats, is a life-threatening condition. Researchers are attempting to identify the exact cause of this condition. At this point, it is believed that among risk factors predisposing cats to FUS are alkaline (nonacidic) urine and a high urinary concentration of magnesium and other minerals. A measure of the ash content in food refers to its total mineral level, but it is the level of magnesium that plays an important role in the development of FUS. High urine levels of magnesium come from: high dietary magnesium content, infrequent urination due to a dirty litter pan, and reduced water intake. If the urine is slightly acidic, the crystals will tend to remain dissolved; however, when the urine is less acidic, the minerals will crystallize. Factors that contribute to an alkaline urine include: the size and frequency of meals, the type of food eaten, and bacterial bladder infections. In summary, certain foods will cause the urine to be less acidic; others contain too much ash. Both of these will increase the chance of crystal formation.

Both male and female cats can be affected by FUS, but the disease is much more serious in male cats because of their longer, narrower urethra. The wider urinary passageway in females permits crystals to flow out in the urine. The cat might strain to urinate, or it might urinate in unusual places. If a urine test shows the presence of crystals, a prescriptive diet formulated to dissolve crystals will be recommended. If a larger stone has formed in the bladder, or if there is evidence of a bladder infection, the treatments described below would be instituted.

In my practice, I have found an increase in the number of male cats with FUS in the spring and fall, particularly when the weather is cold and damp. Since

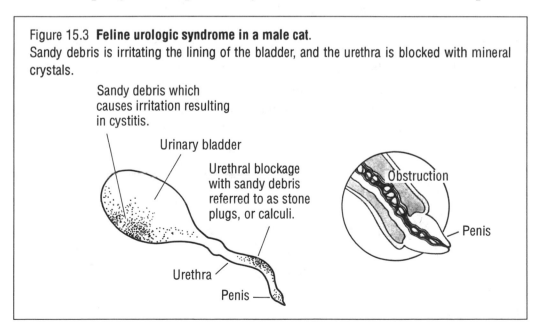

Figure 15.3 **Feline urologic syndrome in a male cat.**
Sandy debris is irritating the lining of the bladder, and the urethra is blocked with mineral crystals.

Sandy debris which causes irritation resulting in cystitis.

Urinary bladder

Urethral blockage with sandy debris referred to as stone plugs, or calculi.

Obstruction

Penis

Urethra

Penis

most of these are indoor pets, it is difficult to explain any connection between the weather and FUS. Some researchers feel that a virus plays a role in the development of the condition. However, in multicat households where one cat has FUS, the other cats usually do not develop this condition, indicating either that the virus is not contagious, or, if it is, other pets can develop a resistance to it.

Figure 15.3 depicts FUS in a male cat. Crystals in the bladder resemble tiny grains of sand, composed of struvite, a material containing magnesium, ammonium, and phosphate. When the cat urinates, the crystals are carried down the urinary passageway, causing extreme discomfort as they dig into the urethral lining. This results in a spasm that reflexively closes the passageway. The crystals and mucus can also form a physical plug in the urethra or penis. In either case, the obstruction makes urination impossible. The cat becomes increasingly uncomfortable and may repeatedly lick its penis. It will resent having its belly touched, and may attempt to urinate outside of the litter pan, or go repeatedly into the litter pan and strain without producing any urine; this must be differentiated from severe constipation!

As a result of the obstruction, wastes that are normally expelled in the urine build up in the body, causing life-threatening changes. As urine backs up from the full bladder, the kidneys will begin to fail. At this stage, the cat usually will not eat very much, have some degree of dehydration, and may vomit. It may seem to be unable to lift its hind end and will become progressively weaker. If no urine is passed, the cat will be in a coma within twenty-four hours and within forty-eight hours it will probably be dead. For these reasons, a male cat suspected of being "blocked" is in an emergency situation. Its chances of recovery diminish greatly with each passing hour that it remains unable to urinate.

I never cease to be amazed at the length of time some owners will wait before seeking medical attention for a blocked cat. I have even seen some cats that were already comatose when they were brought in. The importance of seeking prompt veterinary attention when a pet seems to be uncomfortable or in distress cannot be overemphasized.

The basic treatment for a blocked cat is to re-establish urine flow. Depending upon the patient's condition, a tranquilizer may be necessary for this procedure. A flexible plastic tube or catheter is passed up the penis to dislodge the blockage. In cases where it is extremely difficult to move the obstruction, a prognosis for complete and rapid recovery is not likely. When the catheter reaches the bladder, the urine can be removed. Usually, the cat is given fluids, either intravenously or under the skin, to restore its level of hydration and to help the kidneys remove wastes from the bloodstream. The catheter may be left in place for a day to drain the bladder and to permit monitoring of kidney function by measuring urine production. If there is a bladder infection, the cat will be given antibiotics. In addition, antispasmodic drugs can be given to relax the urinary passage. Special food can be given to help dissolve the crystals and prevent their reformation.

After the catheter is removed, the cat is closely monitored for a day or two to ensure that it does not block again. Some cats have such a large quantity of crystals that within hours or days of removing the catheter, they will reblock. If the cat blocks repeatedly, an operation is usually recommended to reduce the chances of a relapse. The most frequently performed surgery, called a perineal urethrostomy, involves removing the tapered end of the penis and opening up the urethra. The larger urinary opening allows any remaining crystals to pass without causing a blockage. The success rate of this surgery is quite high; even if the cat occasionally still develops a bladder infection, it should not develop a life-threatening blockage.

If a male cat urinates in many locations around the home, or is passing blood in the urine, but is not blocked, the prognosis is more favorable. Most likely this cat has a bladder infection, which can be controlled with antibiotics; however, it would be very prudent to feed such a cat special food to reduce the danger of crystal formation.

Bladder Tumors

A tumor can develop on the bladder lining and fill part of the bladder, making the pet unable to retain its urine for long periods of time.

A urinalysis might reveal abnormal cells, and a special x-ray (a cystogram) taken with contrast material injected into the bladder would reveal a "filling defect," meaning that the contrast material does not fill the entire bladder due to the presence of the tumor. Exploratory surgery is often needed to see the exact extent and location of the tumor, and to determine whether it can be removed. Often, by the time a bladder tumor is diagnosed, it is so large that its removal would greatly diminish the bladder's capacity to store urine. This means that the animal would no longer be suitable as a pet due to the poor quality of life it would have; the decision is usually made to euthanize the pet during surgery.

Genital System of Female Cats and Dogs

The genital or reproductive system of female cats and dogs is comprised of the ovaries, which produce eggs; the uterus; and the vagina. After fertilization, the eggs develop in the uterus for sixty to sixty-three days, until birth. The normal reproductive cycle is described in Chapter 9, "Breeding Your Pet."

Tumors of the Ovaries

Tumors in the ovaries cause the animal to have extremely irregular heat cycles. This condition, which occurs most frequently in older animals, can be diagnosed by x-rays or exploratory surgery. The prognosis following surgical removal ranges from guarded to fair, depending upon: the type and extent of the tumor; whether the tumor was completely removed; and whether it might already have begun to spread through the bloodstream to other organs.

Infection of the Uterus

After an animal has been in heat, the uterus can become infected and fill up with pus; this is known as a **pyometra**. During the heat period, the cervix (the entrance to the uterus) is open, and a bacterial infection can easily enter from the vagina and ascend through the cervix to the uterus. After the heat has terminated, the cervix closes again and the infection is trapped within the uterus. As the infection develops, the uterus fills with pus, and four to six weeks after the heat is over, the animal is very ill. Symptoms of pyometra include increased thirst and urination for a while, followed by appetite loss, weakness, vomiting, and fever. There may be a smelly vaginal discharge or staining of the fur surrounding the vaginal area. This means that some of the infection has been leaking outside the body; these animals are generally not as ill as those in which the infection is tightly contained within the uterus.

Blood tests and x-rays are used to diagnose a pyometra. The best treatment is to surgically remove the infection by spaying the pet. However, the animal is at much greater surgical risk in this condition than if it were being spayed when healthy, as its body has been weakened by the infection and possibly by kidney failure and blood poisoning, which often occur at the same time. On one occasion, I operated on a small 3.5-kilogram (8-lb.), twelve-year-old cat; the grossly infected uterus weighed one kilogram (2 lb.)! Having to remove an enormous infected uterus from a large Saint Bernard dog can be a veterinarian's nightmare.

Infection of the Vagina

Young female animals can develop **vaginitis**, a minor infection that appears as a sticky vaginal discharge. It can usually be controlled with antibiotics. Some veterinarians suggest allowing a female dog that has had repeated episodes of vaginitis to have a heat cycle before being spayed. During the heat period, the body's natural defenses will strengthen the vaginal walls and increase its resistance to further infections.

Vaginitis can also occur in dogs and cats that have been spayed, but this is not common. Usually, antibiotics will eliminate the problem.

Tumors can develop in the walls of the vagina. These would be noticed visually as disfigurations of the vagina. Depending upon the nature of the tumor and its extent, surgery might allow its successful removal.

Mammary Glands

The mammary glands or breasts, although not directly a part of the reproductive system, are influenced by the female hormones. The mammary glands of an unspayed pet may develop lumps or **tumors**; this possibility increases as the unspayed pet gets older. Mammary tumors can be of varying size, and the skin over a large tumor can become raw.

The usual treatment for mammary tumors is a mastectomy (surgical removal of the breast). Since the development of breast tumors is related to the presence of female hormones, many veterinarians suggest having the animal spayed at the same time as the mastectomy to reduce the risk of further tumors. Even so, tumors frequently reoccur, and since they often spread, a preoperative chest x-ray will disclose any tumors in the chest. In such cases, the prognosis will be very guarded.

If the tumor is large, or if several tumors are being removed, complications can occur. The surgical site can become infected and drain. The more active the pet, the greater the tension on the stitches, and the greater the risk that they will pull out and leave the incision open. This means that following the surgery, the pet must be closely supervised.

Mammary tumors can also occur in male animals, appearing as a small nonhealing sore near a nipple. The prognosis is very poor if, upon removal and biopsy, the tumor is found to be malignant.

The mammary glands can become infected when a mother cat or dog is nursing its litter. This is known as **mastitis** and can usually be controlled with antibiotics. Mastitis is discussed further in Chapter 9, "Breeding Your Pet."

Genital System of Male Cats and Dogs

The male genital or reproductive system consists of the testicles, prostate gland, and penis.

Tumors of the Testicles

Testicular tumors are fairly common in unneutered older dogs, with the average age of affected dogs being about ten years. Testicular tumors are rare in cats, partly because most male cats are neutered at an early age.

The testicle with a tumor will be enlarged, while the other one will usually be reduced in size. One type of testicular tumor can upset the hormone balance in the dog's body and result in hair loss on the abdomen, chest, and thighs. The animal may be lethargic, have enlarged breasts and nipples, and the sheath surrounding the penis will droop.

The removal of both testicles through castration is the usual treatment for testicular tumors. While some testicular tumors are benign, most are highly malignant. Therefore, a thorough preoperative battery of blood tests and x-rays is needed to determine whether the tumor has spread and to evaluate the prognosis for the patient.

A complication to discovering a testicular tumor arises when the testicle is retained within the abdomen, having failed to descend into the scrotum within the first few months of birth. Male dogs with undescended testicles are ten to fifteen times more likely to develop testicular tumors than are normally developed dogs. When a retained testicle develops a tumor, it is not noticed until the tumor has spread and symptoms become readily apparent. Again, the removal of both the retained testicle with its tumor and the descended testicle is the preferred treatment.

Diseases of the Penis

The penis is contained within a sheath of skin. During sexual arousal, it extends from the sheath in an erect state. A structural abnormality can narrow the end of the sheath; once the erect penis is extended, it is trapped and cannot be withdrawn back into the sheath. This is **paraphimosis**, a very serious condition; the penis can be easily damaged in this exposed condition, and the restricted blood flow to the penis results in rapid tissue damage. Surgery is required to enlarge the opening of the sheath so that the penis can be withdrawn.

Male dogs, particularly unneutered ones, frequently develop **balanoposthitis**, an infection of the sheath and shaft of the penis. Although the dog may be oblivious to this problem, the owner will likely notice an unsightly, thick green or yellow discharge and the accompanying staining on household furniture. I have found it very difficult to totally cure balanoposthitis. Improvement might be obtained by putting mild antibiotic solutions into the sheath, but oral antibiotics are generally ineffective. If the condition is severe, the dog can be sedated and the affected area scrubbed with a cleansing antibiotic solution. Frequently, the only thing a family can do is to keep the fur trimmed from the end of the penis sheath and wipe away the discharge as needed.

Diseases of the Prostate Gland

The male's prostate gland, a secondary sex gland located around the base of the bladder, empties into the urethra. When infected, the prostate gland becomes enlarged, restricting the flow of urine. The dog will have some discomfort when urinating; it may pass only small quantities of urine, which may contain blood. The enlarged prostate gland can also put pressure on the rectum, situated directly over it, causing the dog to have difficulty passing stool, which will appear narrow and ribbonlike in shape.

Benign prostatic hyperplasia, an enlargement of the prostate gland occurring most frequently in middle-aged and old dogs, is the most common canine prostate disorder. Up to 80 percent of unneutered male dogs over five years of age may be affected. Prostatic disease is rare in cats.

Prostatic disease can be diagnosed by feeling the gland through the rectum. Abnormal tumor cells from the prostate or signs of infection might be found in a sample of prostatic fluid, obtained by catheterization. X-rays can sometimes show an enlarged prostate gland.

Antibiotics are used to control a prostate infection. Female hormones are sometimes given to shrink the prostate gland and make the dog feel more comfortable, although the use of hormones in this type of case is controversial. Surgical removal of the prostate gland in dogs is much more difficult than the procedure in humans, and this operation is not always suggested, or successful. However, as neutering will cause the prostate gland to shrink slowly, castration is often suggested as an adjunct to medical treatment for prostatic disease.

Rectal Growths

Another condition of male dogs that is hormone-dependent is the development of **perianal adenomas**, benign growths around the rectum. These tumors range from small, pea-sized, solitary nodules to larger raw masses.

Surgery is the treatment of choice for perianal growths. Due to the location of the surgical site, the area must be kept clean and free from infection. The patient must be watched closely to ensure that it is not licking the area, as this action might open the stitches. Cryosurgery is sometimes used on smaller rectal growths to "burn" them off through freezing with liquid nitrogen. Neutering the dog at the same time may reduce the risk of recurrence.

16

Diseases of the Endocrine System

The endocrine system consists of glands that produce chemicals (hormones), which travel through the bloodstream to other parts of the body and control other body systems. Some endocrine diseases are very rare; this section discusses only the most common ones. In some cases, several endocrine diseases occur simultaneously, making the diagnosis and treatment quite complicated.

Diabetes

Diabetes mellitus, or **sugar diabetes**, occurs when the pancreas does not produce enough insulin to allow sugar to be digested and absorbed by the body. This sugar remains at a high level in the bloodstream and is also passed through the kidneys into the urine.

Diabetes occurs in both cats and dogs, perhaps slightly more frequently in middle-aged females. As with people, the typical symptoms of diabetes in pets are increased thirst, urination, and appetite, and progressive weight loss. Diabetes can remain untreated in some animals for a while. In other cases, if left untreated, the patient can slip into a dangerous diabetic coma.

Diabetes can be diagnosed with blood and urine tests. Once a diagnosis is confirmed, a decision about treatment must be made. In some mild cases, diet management may sufficiently control the disease. This means giving the exact same food, in the exact same amount, at the same precise time every day.

However, most diabetic animals must be given insulin injections. Medically controlling a diabetic dog is neither a very difficult nor a very expensive undertaking; however, it does require that the family be committed to being very regimented in treating the patient. Insulin is given by injection under the skin, either once or twice daily. In the case of cats, we usually prescribe a fixed dose of insulin, and adjust it occasionally, based on repeated blood tests. The amount of insulin required by a diabetic dog will vary with the amount of exercise it has, the outside temperature, the degree of stress to the animal, and so on. A urine sample taken first thing in the morning is tested using a commercial kit, to measure the amount of sugar present. The dose of insulin is adjusted based upon the previous day's dosage and the current sugar-level in the urine. After the insulin is injected, the patient is given a fixed amount of food. Twelve hours later, another fixed quantity of food is given.

The timing of the insulin injections and feedings is critical to the animal's well-being. If the pet receives too little insulin, its symptoms of diabetes may worsen. On the other hand, if too much insulin is given, the animal could become very weak and even lapse into a coma. In such a case, a source of sugar, such as corn syrup, must be put into the pet's mouth immediately, and then veterinary attention must be sought.

Once diabetes is initially diagnosed, the patient is usually hospitalized for several days to determine the correct insulin dosage and to stabilize the blood-sugar level. When the patient is ready to go home, the owner should have a training session on how to give the pet insulin. The injection is given anywhere under the skin with a very fine needle; the animal rarely even notices it. I have had families maintain a diabetic dog in good health for over five years. Cats can be more difficult to regulate and often other problems, such as kidney failure or liver disease, develop, but I have known of diabetic cats being treated for upwards of seven years.

In some cats, diabetes can be temporary. These particular individuals require insulin for up to several months and then recover, for unknown reasons. The veterinarian will determine whether insulin is still required, based on periodic blood tests.

A new development in the treatment of diabetic animals is the use of tablets to stimulate the body to produce more insulin. These hypoglycemic (meaning "sugar-lowering") tablets have been used for people, and if they prove to be successful in animals, the need for insulin injections will be eliminated.

Insulinoma, a type of tumor, can develop in the insulin-producing area of the pancreas, causing the same symptoms as those that occur when too much insulin is given: basically, a very weak animal that might become comatose following muscular twitchings and convulsions. The symptoms will worsen after eating, since the presence of food in the digestive tract will stimulate the tumor to produce insulin. Initial treatment with a high-calorie diet may be necessary to prevent a coma. Tests will reveal very low blood-sugar levels even after calories are administered. Although surgery can be attempted to remove the tumor (which would cause the animal to become diabetic due to a lack of insulin), these tumors often have already spread to other organs by the time they are diagnosed.

Another type of diabetes, called **diabetes insipidus**, results from a problem in the hormonal control of the kidney's urine-concentrating mechanism. This disease causes the patient to drink and urinate a lot, but no sugar is passed in the urine, in contrast to diabetes mellitus.

When an animal has excessive thirst and urination, a urine test should be performed. If the urine is very dilute and contains no sugar, diabetes insipidus is among several conditions to be considered. To confirm the diagnosis, a water deprivation test is performed to measure the concentration and quantity of urine produced by the pet while it is deprived of water until it loses 5 percent of its body weight. In healthy animals, the kidneys will respond by concentrating the urine to the normal range.

Diabetes insipidus is not easily treated. Some drugs can be administered to lower the animal's thirst and reduce its urine output. Although this is not always totally successful, some improvement may be achieved, but the patient may continue to drink and urinate a lot.

Cushing's Disease

Over each kidney there is an adrenal gland, which is a very important source of hormones. The core of the adrenal gland, called the adrenal cortex, produces a chemical called cortisone, which regulates many diverse functions. If too much hormone is produced, **hyperadrenalcorticism**—Cushing's disease—results.

The typical symptoms of Cushing's disease are increased thirst and urination. Normal dogs drink from five to thirty milliliters (0.25–1 oz.) of water per five hundred grams (1 lb.) of body weight per day. Excessive amounts of cortisone can increase this amount by four to five times. A dramatic increase in appetite is also common, along with behavioral changes such as increased begging and raiding garbage cans. Sometimes, muscle tone is diminished and the pet develops a "pot belly" appearance. The skin becomes very thin and parchmentlike. The hair coat can become very patchy and sparse, and often there is hair loss on each side of the body. There may be small firm raised bumps noticeable on the body, due to calcium deposits in areas just beneath the skin.

A urinalysis and some biochemical blood tests will help to confirm the diagnosis of Cushing's disease. The urine is examined for signs of urinary tract infection, for sugar content, and for excessive cortisone levels. The veterinarian can perform tests to determine why there is too much cortisone in the bloodstream. It can be caused by a tumor in the pituitary gland at the base of the brain sending too strong a signal to the adrenal glands to produce cortisone. Alternatively, the problem can be a cortisone-producing tumor in one or both of the adrenal glands themselves.

If hyperadrenalcorticism is confirmed, treatment consists of pills given daily to destroy the adrenal cortex, and good results are usually obtained. If the patient's condition has improved after about ten days (that is, it is drinking less water), the pills can be given on a weekly basis.

Since hyperadrenalcorticism is caused by excessive cortisone production, similar symptoms occur when high doses of cortisone are given as an anti-inflammatory drug. Although cortisone is very useful for treating many conditions, the usual side effects are increased thirst and urination and, often, increased appetite as well. Very high doses of the drug for long periods of time can result in medically induced Cushing's disease. The side effects of cortisone can be lessened by using a slowly reducing dosage schedule until the lowest dose that will control the disease is found. Often the side effects can be greatly reduced with "alternate-day therapy," which means giving the pet a double dose of cortisone every other day.

Addison's Disease

Hypoadrenalcorticism—Addison's disease—occurs if the adrenal cortex fails to produce enough hormone to allow the body to respond to stress without going into a state of shock. Addison's disease is very rare in cats but I usually see several cases every year in dogs. As long as a small amount of adrenal cortex hormone is produced, the signs of Addison's disease can be nonspecific, such as vomiting and diarrhea. However, a life-threatening condition will develop if the patient is subjected to a stressful situation and the adrenal gland cannot produce enough hormone. The lack of adrenal cortex hormone causes the chemicals in the bloodstream to be totally out of the normal range: potassium is too high, sodium is too low. The animal will be very weak and may collapse into a coma. Examination will show that the animal is in a state of shock with low body temperature and a very slow heart rate. An electrocardiogram may show some specific changes when the potassium level in the blood is high.

Once this disease is diagnosed, and the correct treatment is instituted, recovery is rapid. Intravenous fluid is given to combat the state of shock, and this also dilutes the dangerous level of potassium in the blood; adrenal cortex hormone is given, and sodium is supplemented in the intravenous fluids.

Addisonian patients must be given adrenal hormone for the rest of their lives. The size of the pet and the resulting cost will help to determine whether treatment should be by tablet or injection. A very small tablet can be given daily, while an injection is usually given every four weeks. In addition, salt must be added to the dog's diet, and under conditions of stress, such as visiting the grooming salon or boarding, a cortisone tablet might also be given.

Addison's disease can also occur as a chronic progressive disability, with recurrent episodes of diarrhea and vomiting. Routine blood tests might reveal abnormal potassium and sodium levels, as well as changes in the complete blood count. Although the patient is not in a state of acute crisis, this might develop by the mere stress of hospitalization. I recall a dog that was hospitalized to investigate its chronic diarrhea, vomiting, and lethargy. Blood samples were taken on admission; when we made rounds a few hours later, the dog was comatose. Although the blood results had not yet been received, I recognized the symptoms and immediately began providing the required therapy; the animal rapidly improved.

Following an acute Addisonian crisis, dogs can develop a **gastric ulcer**. This is because a dog's stomach and intestine respond to stress, whereas in cats the respiratory system is the target of such situations. When an ulcer develops, the dog begins to get weak again, in spite of therapy for Addison's disease. Diarrhea recurs, and often the stools are black. As well, the patient will vomit, and blood might be seen. If a fair amount of internal bleeding occurs, the gums will be very pale and the dog will be weak.

Ulcer treatment in dogs is the same as in people: strong antacids; no food for a day or two; and drugs to lower the production of stomach acid. After a day or two of intravenous feeding, a bland diet is gradually introduced, with medication to protect the stomach lining. Further ulcers should not occur if the Addison's disease is kept under control.

Hypothyroidism

The thyroid gland, located in the neck, produces hormones that regulate the basic activity level of the rest of the body. In cases of hypothyroidism, a subnormal quantity of thyroid hormone is produced. Although any breed of dog or cat can develop hypothyroidism, Golden Retrievers and Dobermans are the most frequent sufferers of this condition.

The hypothyroid animal will lie near sources of heat, such as a hot air register or oven, and will try to avoid cold environments. Animals that have not been neutered or spayed will have decreased reproductive activity. It will gain weight very easily, even on a reduced-calorie diet, and will be very lazy and inactive. In fact, two Golden Retrievers that were thought to be such excellent, calm patients, were shown a year or two later to be hypothyroid. They were just too calm! Often a hypothyroid dog will develop a "worried look" with a wrinkled brow and hanging jowls. It will also have a depressed heart rate, thickened greasy skin, a dry brittle coat, symmetrical hair loss on both sides of the body, greasy ears, and often a subnormal temperature. Blood tests can be taken to measure the basic level of thyroid hormone in the bloodstream.

If a patient is hypothyroid, treatment consists of thyroid hormone replacement tablets. The facial expression and the lethargy usually improve with several weeks of medication, although occasionally the "worried" look persists. Blood tests are repeated to adjust the dosage of thyroid hormone, as too much hormone is more dangerous than too little.

Hyperthyroidism

Hyperthyroidism, which occurs almost exclusively in cats, has a very gradual onset when too much thyroid hormone is produced. The general symptoms are a very "hyper," nervous, active animal. The cat is constantly hungry but does not gain weight, and often will lose weight. An enlarged thyroid gland can sometimes be felt. Hyperthyroidism is diagnosed by finding an elevated level of thyroid hormone in the bloodstream. A hyperthyroid cat has a very rapid heart rate and is in danger of suffering from a damaged heart and from heart disease.

If a cat is hyperthyroid, radiation can be utilized to kill part of the thyroid gland, but this is undertaken only at specialized veterinary centers. Alternatively, the enlarged thyroid gland can be surgically removed, and then the cat is treated with thyroid hormone supplementation, but this surgery can be difficult to perform. Recently, medication has become available to selectively stop the production of the thyroid hormone. This tablet is given two or three times daily for two to three weeks, which should return the thyroid hormone level to normal. The hormone level will be retested and the dosage adjusted, if necessary. If the hyperthyroid condition has damaged the heart, medication for this problem will also be given.

Hyperparathyroidism

The parathyroid gland is located near the thyroid. One of its functions is to regulate calcium and phosphorous metabolism, and maintain a specific balance between these two minerals in the bloodstream. Young cats can develop secondary nutritional hyperparathyroidism when they are fed a lot of meat, especially horse meat, which is very high in phosphorous and low in calcium. As the circulatory system absorbs the phosphorous from the intestine, the parathyroid gland, in an effort to maintain the balance between these minerals, becomes overactive. As the only readily available source of calcium is in the skeleton, the hormone of the parathyroid gland causes calcium to be reabsorbed from the bones. A young animal with this disease will often be lame and uncomfortable when moving because its weakened bones develop cracks and hairline fractures (or worse) very easily. Lameness will shift from one limb to another on successive days as old injuries heal a little and new ones occur. The pet usually responds well to an improved diet supplemented with calcium.

Both dogs and cats can develop hyperparathyroidism as a result of chronic kidney disease. When diseased kidneys lose their ability to eliminate sufficient phosphorous, the result is an increased level of phosphorous and a decreased level of calcium in the bloodstream. The lowered calcium level stimulates an increase in production of the parathyroid gland hormone. As a consequence, calcium is released from the bones, resulting in a very fragile skeleton. Treatment is directed at the underlying kidney disease.

17

Diseases of the Bones, Muscles, Paws, and Nails

The muscles, in conjunction with the tendons and ligaments that join them to the bones, enable an animal to move. This chapter discusses problems and conditions of the bones, ligaments, and muscles. Since the paws and nails also play an important role in an animal's mobility, they are included in this chapter.

Fractures

If a bone is subjected to sufficient force, it will fracture or break. A broken limb will usually be at an unusual angle and the animal will not put its full weight on it. Fractures can be diagnosed by carefully feeling and moving the limb, and by taking x-rays.

A **greenstick fracture** (a "crack") does not extend across the entire bone; in a **complete fracture**, the break extends across the bone; and in a **compound fracture**, some bone protrudes through the skin.

Fractures usually occur in normal bones as a result of trauma, such as a car accident or a fall from a height. However, bones that are weakened by disease can break with normal activity. Bone cancer, or "osteosarcoma," eats away at the bone until it may snap easily. Similarly, "nutritional hyperparathyroidism" causes calcium resorption from bone that becomes so weak that normal activity will cause a crack or a complete fracture.

A fractured bone can heal if the broken ends are very close to each other, and there is no movement of the fracture site until healing is complete. Various "coaptation devices" can be used to keep the fracture site immobile, depending upon: the amount of interdigitation (fitting together) of the ends of the fracture; whether any small fragments of bone are broken off; the age and anticipated healing capacity of the patient; and so on.

Splints are firm plastic strips attached to the skin with tape; they are used to treat greenstick fractures and some complete fractures. If more support is needed, a plaster cast can be put on the fractured limb. For a splint or a cast to be effective, the support must extend from one joint above to one joint below the fracture. It is imperative to follow the veterinarian's directions regarding follow-up visits to check a splint or cast, to ensure that it has not slipped and is not too tight. Usually the animal's toes are left uncovered to permit monitoring of any swelling or change in their temperature.

It is very important that moisture not get inside the cast or splint. If this happens, the skin quickly becomes infected from the buildup of warmth and moisture, and a large open sore will result. Keep moisture away by placing a small plastic bag over the cast or splint when the animal goes outside, but *always* remove it when the animal is inside.

Splints and casts are applied while the patient is either heavily sedated or anesthetized because of the painful process of setting the fracture to place the broken ends of the bone in the correct position. Rechecks can usually be done without sedation.

When the fracture site is smooth and there is little interdigitation of the bones, the bone ends will have a tendency to slip away from each other. In these cases, internal fixation or coaptation methods are used to stabilize the fracture. The animal is anesthetized and the broken bones are surgically exposed. After the bone has been set, a metal implant is attached. An intermedullary pin is a metal rod, usually threaded at one end, that is placed down the core of the bone, from one end to the other, past the fracture site. Sometimes a metal plate, which is a flattened piece of metal with several holes in it, is screwed onto the broken bone to immobilize it.

Another metal fixation device, which is not totally internal, is called a "Kirshner-Emer apparatus." This consists of small metal rods applied perpendicular to the skin from outside the body and anchored in each fractured piece of bone. Another rod, parallel to the skin and perpendicular to the first set of rods, is attached to the ends of the first stabilizing set of rods, to keep them in the desired location. Although this apparatus may seem cumbersome, it is useful when there are several fractured pieces of bone and insufficient room to apply a plate. Most animals adapt quite well to it.

In general, internal fixation devices enable quicker healing and more mobility than external support devices. Several implant methods can be used at the same time.

Bones heal by producing a bony callus, or new bone growth, which bridges the fracture line. The progress of healing is monitored with occasional x-rays, and once healing is complete, the metal implants are removed during another minor surgery.

Delayed union or nonunion means the fracture has not healed as expected, due to infection, too much movement at the fracture site, or the pet's poor nutritional state. A bone graft can be used to stimulate healing in such cases. A piece of bone is taken from another site, usually the hip, and placed at the fracture site. As the graft grows, the fracture heals.

There are cases where it is impossible to repair a limb with severe multiple fractures. This is common following a crushing injury—for example, from a leg-hold trap. If there is an insufficient amount of intact bone to use internal fixation devices, the limb may have to be amputated. It is amazing how well amputee pets can manage in everyday situations. My assistant adopted a cat whose front left leg had to be amputated at the elbow following injury in a leg-hold trap. This cat now runs around the house, jumps up on window ledges, and even holds onto its toys or swats them with its little stump.

Dislocations

Trauma to a bone can also result in a dislocation or **luxation**, meaning that the bone has been pushed out of its socket. Diagnosis of a dislocated shoulder or hip can usually be made through physical examination and x-rays. If a dislocation is suspected, prompt attention is very important, since putting the limb back in place becomes increasingly difficult as time elapses; a matter of hours can make all the difference between success and failure. The pet must be anesthetized to allow relaxation of the muscles, and the veterinarian must use skill (and strength) to pop the limb back into place. This can be a very difficult procedure on a large dog with solid muscles! A bandage may be applied to keep the limb flexed up against the body for a week or so to prevent another luxation.

Patella Luxation

Another area of the body where luxations can occur is the "patella," commonly known as the kneecap. Most often seen in small dogs, a luxating kneecap causes the animal to suddenly become three-legged when it is running. This happens when the kneecap slips out of its shallow groove in the bottom of the thigh bone, causing the leg to be held up. At this point the ligaments relax enough to allow the patella to move back into its proper place and the leg can again be used.

Surgery can be performed to deepen the groove in which the kneecap is located. If this condition is left untreated, there is a good chance of arthritis setting in and causing the pet discomfort when it gets older.

Ligament Injuries

Trauma can cause an animal to limp from a sprained muscle or strained ligament. In the case of injury to soft tissue (muscles, tendons, and ligaments), it is important that the animal rest and have only very restricted exercise so that the injured tissue can recover. Liniments are sometimes used to stimulate blood flow to the area and hasten recovery, and anti-inflammatory medication may also be helpful.

One of the more common ligament problems involving dogs is the rupture or tearing of the "anterior cruciate ligament," which is located in the knee, and runs from the front of the end of the thigh bone to the back of the top of the shin bone. This ligament can easily be injured by a sudden twisting of the hind leg; in the human realm, this is a common football injury.

An animal with an injured cruciate ligament will not put full weight on the affected leg. There may be some evidence of pain when the pet walks, and going up stairs will be more difficult than going down them. Careful examination by the veterinarian may reveal a looseness in the knee joint, and x-rays may be needed to rule out other injuries.

If the cruciate ligament has been stretched, the pet should have lots of rest and only restricted exercise for several weeks, until the damaged ligament has healed. More commonly, however, the ligament is torn and surgery is needed to rebuild it. Very strong synthetic material may be used to reconstruct the torn ligament, or, in smaller animals, strong fibrous tissue may be transplanted from the thigh. Prognosis for recovery from a cruciate injury is generally good; however, if the animal is overweight, which frequently is the case, it will be putting additional stress on its good leg to protect the injured leg. Consequently, the uninjured leg may develop the same injury shortly after the first leg has been repaired!

Arthritis

A common condition affecting the joints in animals, as in people, is arthritis. By definition, arthritis is an inflammation of a joint, and appears as lameness, usually intermittent, in one or more limbs. Although arthritis generally affects middle-aged or older individuals, a joint that has been injured or has had surgery will be predisposed to developing arthritis at an earlier age.

Careful examination by the veterinarian will pinpoint the joints that are causing the animal discomfort. Sometimes, x-rays are taken to ascertain the degree of inflammation, determine whether the bones are deformed, and rule out other conditions.

The symptoms of arthritis can be eased somewhat with anti-inflammatory medication. In my experience, these tablets can be given when the patient seems uncomfortable, rather than on a regular basis. In this way, the animal's body does not have a chance to build up a tolerance to the drug and the benefits are more pronounced.

An arthritic animal can be soothed if you gently massage the tender area. Liniments are sometimes helpful. Avoid prolonged bouts of intense exercise with older dogs; instead, give them regular, moderate exercise. It is important to dry the animal thoroughly after it has been out in damp weather, or after bathing it. For cats, keep the food and litter pan on the same floor of the house, so that the cat does not have to climb stairs repeatedly during the day. It is amazing how often this suggestion is ignored by cat owners.

Diseases of the Hip

Hip dysplasia is a specific hip problem, generally found in large breeds of dogs, such as German Shepherds and Golden Retrievers. Hip dysplasia is a looseness in the ball and socket joint of the hip. When the socket of the pelvis is very shallow, the ball at the top of the thigh bone is not held securely, and arthritis or degenerative disease of the hip joint will develop. In severe dysplasia, the ball at the top of the leg bone is deformed, usually flattened, and very rough around the edges. Hip dysplasia is depicted in Figure 17.1.

Figure 17.1 **Hip dysplasia**.
This is a representation of an x-ray of a dog's hips, taken with the dog lying on its back with its legs extended. The normal hips have the rounded head of the femur (leg bone) well seated in the hip socket (acetabulum). In moderate dysplasia, the acetabulum is more shallow, and the head of the femurs are flattened. In severe dysplasia, the femurs are almost luxated out of the acetabulum.

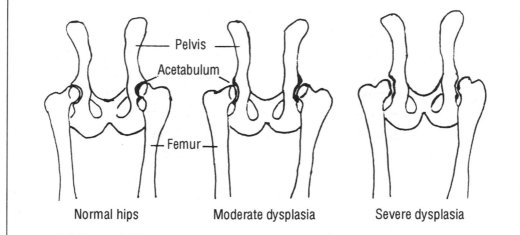

Pelvis

Acetabulum

Femur

Normal hips   Moderate dysplasia   Severe dysplasia

Among the symptoms of hip dysplasia are: difficulty standing up; a hopping or swaying gait; pain and stiffness; and a wasting of muscle in the hindquarters. The dog may carry its head low to shift its center of balance away from the rear, and it will sometimes have periods of lameness, especially following rigorous exercise. An x-ray of the hips can be compared to the standard good hips. The differences will be rated on a scale of I to IV, with IV being a severely deformed hip joint.

We do not know the exact cause of hip dysplasia. Although the condition is largely controlled by genetics, other factors exist. The condition occurs when an animal has a genetic predisposition to developing dysplasia, coupled with either too much or too little exercise, too much or too little calcium in the diet, and so on. When a veterinary radiologist certifies both the mother and the father dog as being free of hip dysplasia prior to breeding, the offspring's risk of developing the condition later on in life are minimized. Although two certified "normal" dogs will produce a greater percentage of healthy puppies than two parents showing symptoms of hip dysplasia, normal dogs can still produce some offspring that carry the genes for hip dysplasia. Dogs must be twenty-four months of age or older to be eligible for certification, because research has shown that dogs graded normal as youngsters may still develop hip dysplasia as they mature. Hip dysplasia certification can be done by board-certified radiologists at veterinary colleges in Canada, and by the Orthopedic Foundation for Animals (OFA) in the United States.

There are various treatment options for dogs with hip dysplasia, depending upon their size and age. Anti-inflammatory drugs can be given when the dog seems most bothered by its hips. If this is not successful, surgery can be performed. One procedure, called a "pectineus myotomy," involves cutting a muscle on the inside of the thigh near the groin. While this procedure does not prevent or correct the hip deformity, it frees the leg bone from the discomfort of being pulled tightly into the hip socket, thereby providing immediate relief from pain.

Another operation to help a dog with hip dysplasia is called an "excision arthroplasty," or "femoral head excision." The deformed ball at the top of the thigh bone is removed. With no contact between the thigh bone and the hip socket, the source of discomfort is gone. Although there is no longer any bone-to-bone contact, the ligaments and muscles in the area tighten up, and after a relatively short period of convalescence the patient will be able to use the leg with just a slight limp.

Perhaps the most favorable way to deal with severe hip dysplasia, but, unfortunately, the most expensive, is the replacement of the deformed joint with an artificial hip joint. The success rate for this surgery is very high.

It should be emphasized that an animal with signs of hip dysplasia should not be used for breeding. Our goal is to eliminate dysplasia, and selective breeding will help to achieve this goal.

A condition occurring in small breeds of dogs, similar to hip dysplasia, is **Legg-Perthes disease**. Most commonly seen in young animals, this disease causes varying degrees of lameness in the hind end. X-rays will show severe "eating away" of the rounded top (ball) of the thigh bone. The treatment of choice is the removal of the ball from the top of the thigh bone (excision arthroplasty).

Other Bone Diseases Causing Lameness

Several developmental problems of the elbow joint in dogs can cause lameness. One of these is called **ununited anconeal process**, seen most often in German

Shepherds and Basset Hounds, between the age of four months and one year. The ulna, a long bone of the front leg, ends in the anconeal process, which forms part of the elbow joint. The anconeal process normally attaches to the ulna when the pet is about five months old. However, when this does not happen, arthritis may develop in the elbow. The affected dog usually has a history of intermittent front leg lameness on either or both sides, with progressive severity. During exercise, the elbow is not fully extended, and the lameness is particularly severe following exercise. On examination, the animal will be sensitive to having its elbow completely bent or extended. X-rays will show the anconeal process as a small piece of bone, either completely free or still attached to some degree, in the elbow joint. When the bone fragment is surgically removed, the dog should make an excellent recovery.

Another cause of lameness in dogs, known as **osteochondritis dissecans**, can occur in any joint, although it is most commonly seen in the shoulders of large dogs. It is caused by a bone chip becoming detached from the joint surface and moving within the joint space. Again, x-rays should detect the offending bone chip, and it can be removed. The prognosis for full recovery is excellent.

Panosteitis is inflammation of the leg bones in young dogs of large breeds, resulting in pain and severe lameness. This condition usually disappears following treatment, which consists of anti-inflammatory medication and strictly restricted exercise for two to three months.

Bone Tumors

Osteosarcoma or bone cancer usually destroys the ends of the long bones, such as those found in the leg. A persistently lame middle-aged or older dog might have bone cancer, and confirmation would be obtained with x-rays. I recall a Standard Poodle with a lame hind leg being brought into my clinic. My assistant had to run up and down a flight of stairs about ten times with the dog before I was able to localize the source of the problem! Repeated x-rays were inconclusive, and the patient did not improve on anti-inflammatory medication. Unfortunately, after several weeks the x-rays did indicate the presence of a bone tumor.

Bone tumors readily spread to the lungs, so the chest would also have to be x-rayed prior to deciding on a treatment. If the tumor has not spread, amputation of the affected limb, combined with radiation or chemotherapy, would be the treatment of choice. If the cancer has spread, the prognosis is extremely grave, and euthanasia is recommended.

Muscle Problems

Myositis or inflammation of a muscle will cause an animal to show sensitivity and swelling in the area of the affected muscle. The patient will have a high fever, and may be reluctant to move or eat. Antibiotics and anti-inflammatory agents will usually alleviate the problem.

Myositis of the chewing muscles is an unfortunate condition that is seen in both sexes of German Shepherds, usually less than four years of age. All of the chewing muscles suddenly become swollen and the dog develops a "foxlike" facial expression. The lower jaw usually hangs open to some degree. There is great difficulty in seizing and chewing food, and the animal becomes progressively debilitated. Following an acute phase of two or three weeks, there may be a period of remission. Recurrent attacks occur with increasing frequency, and the muscles involved will lose their ability to expand and contract. Unfortunately, there is no known cure for this condition, and even anti-inflammatory medication is of very limited use.

Problems with the Paws and Nails

Although the pads on the paws are fairly thick and tough, they can easily be cut if the pet walks on a sharp object. A cut pad may bleed profusely, and a bandage must be applied. Even after bleeding has stopped, the pad might start bleeding again when the animal begins to walk on it.

After washing and disinfecting a cut pad, the veterinarian must decide whether stitches are needed. If the pad is stitched, a very large needle must be used to get through it, leaving large holes, which will weaken the pad. Once the suture is tied, it may become untied or abraded when the animal walks. For this reason, it is often sufficient to bandage the pad securely after cleansing it. After a day or two, the bandage can be changed or removed. Sometimes I will use surgical glue in an attempt to seal the cut if the surface is dry enough for the glue to hold.

When a foreign object is embedded in the pad, it can be impossible to remove if it is buried beneath the surface. However, if the paw is soaked in warm water a few times a day, the foreign object may come to the surface, where it can then be removed. If this does not occur, heavy tissue will develop around the offending object to wall it off. Sometimes the swelling, complete with the foreign object, can then be surgically removed.

Pets can develop cracked or broken nails, which may bleed. The pet may lick at the broken nail and be lame on that paw. The usual treatment for a broken nail is to remove it by cutting the nail back to the quick. Since freezing the area will be as uncomfortable as actually performing the procedure, the nail can just be cut close and then cauterized without any painkillers. In a way, this is similar to a persistent tender hangnail in a person; there is sensitivity just until the hangnail is removed. Often the paw is bandaged for a day or two to guard against infection.

Cats' nails will usually fall off if they get very long, or the cat may bite them off. In the case of dogs, the nails will get worn down if the animal walks on pavement or concrete. However, the nails on some cats and dogs may continue to grow and become embedded in the pad of the paw. This terribly painful condition is one which I see regularly. The pet may lick the area and be lame on that paw. The ingrown nail must be cut short, the pad must be disinfected, and the pad must be bandaged if it bleeds profusely. When senior dogs and cats walk with an altered gait due to age-related muscle stiffness, some nails might not get worn down, resulting in them becoming ingrown and infected. Careful attention to your pet's nails, and periodic trimming should prevent ingrown nails from hurting your pet.

Dogs and cats can develop a condition known as **paronychia**, a bacterial infection of the nail and surrounding tissue. Usually, a discharge or dry crust can be seen around the nail base. The animal will lick the affected area and will show some tenderness when walking. The diseased nail must be surgically removed to allow the infection to drain, followed by a course of antibiotics. In most cases, the nail will grow back.

18

Diseases of the Nervous System

A mammal's nervous system channels information obtained through the senses (hearing, smell, taste, touch, and sight) along nerves to the brain, and then down the nerves of the spinal cord to the various muscles. This chapter begins with problems of the sense organs, followed by diseases of the brain, and finally, conditions involving the nerves of the spinal cord.

The Senses

Hearing

Infections of the ears are discussed in Chapter 19, "Diseases of the Skin," since the ears are lined with skin.

Dogs and cats have a very well-developed sense of hearing, and can respond to sound frequencies beyond the range of human hearing. The ear openings are sealed in newborn dogs and cats until they are fourteen to seventeen days of age. Some animals are born deaf; this is often the case in white cats with blue eyes and dogs with "merle" or silver-blue coats. To test an animal's ability to hear, make a loud sound, such as calling its name or clapping your hands, while it is asleep. A pet with normal hearing will show a startled reaction; a pet with a diminished sense of hearing will not respond. As an animal ages, its hearing will deteriorate somewhat. Although this does not usually cause a problem, owners should be especially careful about supervising hearing-impaired pets while the animals are outside.

The hearing organ has a "vestibular apparatus" or inner ear, which maintains balance. A kitten can develop a vestibular problem and suddenly lose its balance. It will hold its head tilted on an angle and may fall over when it tries to walk. The exact cause of this condition is unknown. Over the following days or weeks, the cat will learn to adjust to this balance disturbance and the symptoms will gradually subside without treatment, although there may be some residual balance problems. Similarly, older dogs and cats can develop a sudden problem maintaining balance. This condition, called **geriatric vestibular disease**, is discussed more fully in Chapter 10, "The Senior Years." If an animal shows any balance problem, it should be immediately examined by a veterinarian.

Smell

A cat's sense of smell is very well developed; in fact, it may not eat its food if its nostrils are blocked by a respiratory infection. Of course, the sense of smell in dogs is legendary. For proof, just watch a dog following the trail of a rabbit or sniffing areas where other animals have urinated.

Problems with the smelling mechanism are rare in pets. However, one of my feline patients suffered from a chronic respiratory infection that permanently destroyed its capacity to smell. It was taken to an internal medicine specialist and a neurologist, and elaborate testing revealed a deficiency in the functioning of the nerve endings in the nose. The cat could survive only so long as it was being force-fed.

Taste

The sense of taste is well developed in dogs and cats. Be aware that the appealing taste of some harmful substances can attract animals. For example, dogs like the sweet smell and taste of antifreeze and are also attracted to slug bait, both of which are extremely poisonous substances.

Touch

The sense of touch in dogs and cats is not as keenly developed as it is in humans. However, a cat's "vibrissae"—its whiskers—help it to maintain balance and to pass through narrow openings. Many dogs have their whiskers shaved when they are groomed, without suffering any consequences.

Cats with **feline hyperesthesia syndrome** have an increased sensitivity over part of their body. The skin along the cat's back ripples if it is touched, and the cat may appear to attack its own skin by biting and chewing at it. The few mild cases that I have seen were left untreated; in more severe cases, control with medication can be attempted.

Sight

The eyelids of newborn kittens and puppies normally do not open until they are ten to fourteen days of age, although there is no cause for concern if they remain closed until the animal is twenty-one days old, at which point they can be opened in a minor surgical procedure. Any discharge from a very young animal's eyes, whether open or shut, indicates a serious problem, usually an infection.

At the part of the eye nearest the nose, dogs and cats have "nictitating membranes" or third eyelids, visible when the animal is very tired or has been sedated. A foreign object can become trapped under this eyelid. If your pet is squinting or rubbing one of its eyes, it should be examined by a veterinarian right away, as a foreign object could severely irritate and damage the eye. Usually a drop or two of anesthetic will freeze the eye and eyelids so that the veterinarian can find and remove the foreign object.

The gland located behind the third eyelid produces some of the tears. Occasionally, this gland will become enlarged and bulge from behind the third eyelid, appearing as a reddish swelling, known as a **cherry eye**. This can occur in any breed of dog and occasionally in cats, but it is most common in young Cocker Spaniels and Bulldogs. Surgery is required to correct a cherry eye. Left untreated, it can cause chronic irritation to the eye and interfere with the normal production of tears.

Tears are needed to keep the eyeballs moist. There are two drainage channels for excess tears located near the nasal side of the eyelids. When excess tears are produced, or when the drainage system is plugged, the tears overflow near the nose. Runny eyes occur quite frequently in certain breeds, including Shih Tzus, Poodles, Maltese dogs, and Bichon Frises, as well as in Himalayan and Persian cats. Tears will cause a brown stain on the fur beneath the eye in light-colored animals.

If moisture around the eyes turns from a clear, thin liquid to a thicker green or yellow-colored substance, or if the eyelids are inflamed or swollen, there may be an infection known as **conjunctivitis** or **pink-eye**. Dogs can have one or more extra eyelashes, which rub the surface of the eye, causing infection and discharge.

Extra eyelashes must be surgically removed. Frequently, cats suffering from a severe upper respiratory virus also have eye infections. A veterinarian should examine any unusual developments in your pet's eyes and determine whether antibiotic eye drops or ointment are needed.

Some dogs with insufficient tear production develop **keratoconjunctivitis sicca** or **dry eye**. Although the fluid component of the tears is insufficient, the mucus component is still produced, causing a buildup of thick, sticky material around the eyes. As the surface of each eye becomes chronically irritated by dryness, it will lose its sheen and become pigmented and perhaps quite bumpy. English Bulldogs, American Cocker Spaniels, and Pugs are prone to this condition. Treatment with frequent application of artificial tears, obtainable at a pharmacy, will help to control dry eye. Recently, a new medication containing the drug "cyclosporine" has shown a great deal of promise in treating this condition. Delicate surgery can also be performed to move the duct leading from one of the salivary glands in the mouth to a position near the eye. Whenever the dog eats, or drools, the saliva will flow over the eyeball and prevent it from drying out.

Pigment can also cover the surface of the eyeball in a condition known as **pigmentary keratitis**. This can result from a chronic irritant such as an ingrown eyelash rubbing the eyeball. German Shepherd dogs are prone to a specific form of pigmentary keratitis called **pannus**, which is characterized by new pigment and blood vessels growing over the surface of the eyeball. Both of these conditions can usually be controlled with strong anti-inflammatory eye drops, which must be administered for the life of the animal. A long-lasting anti-inflammatory medication can also be injected directly beneath the eyeball's surface. Although this procedure might sound very dangerous, it is well tolerated by dogs with just a mild sedative or local anesthetic eye drop.

A pet with a **corneal ulcer**—a defect in the surface of the eyeball—will squint and/or rub at its eye frequently. Among common causes of corneal ulcers are: a scratch, damage from a foreign object (a speck of dirt), and the hot airflow from a hair dryer pointed at an unblinking animal after being bathed.

If, during a careful examination, a foreign object cannot be found on the eyeball, the doctor will stain the eye with a few drops of fluoroscein solution. This yellow-green dye will be absorbed into, and highlight, any damaged areas of the eye surface. Any excess dye will show up on the animal's nose with the tears that run from the inner corner of the eye, and will disappear within a few hours. I remember a client becoming very excited that her dog was going to have a green eye following my examination, as she was Irish and I examined the pet on St. Patrick's Day!

A corneal ulcer is usually treated with antibiotic ointment or eye drops, and vitamin A capsules given orally; left untreated, the ulcer will keep growing deeper and the eyeball may eventually burst. If a deep ulcer is not healing, minor surgery can be performed to scrape the damaged tissue from the eye to stimulate healing. The eyelids or the third eyelid might be stitched closed to protect the healing eyeball. Most pets tolerate this procedure well and, after a couple of weeks, the veterinarian will remove the stitches and the ulcer will have healed. If a white scar remains after an ulcer has healed, anti-inflammatory drops may then be used to shrink it.

Aside from damage to the surface of the eye, blunt trauma can cause the eye to come partially or totally out of its socket. This happens easily in dogs with prominent bulgy eyes, such as Pugs and Pekingese. It might be possible to successfully replace the eyeball following such an accident if the dog is taken quickly to a veterinarian. If, however, following trauma or a severe disease process, the eyeball "dies" (that is, it becomes nonfunctional and shrinks in size), it might have to be removed, since a dead eyeball could become a source of infection. In this operation, called enucleation, the eyelids are sewn together to hide and protect the socket, and the animal rapidly adjusts to having vision from only one eye. In animals with furry faces, such as Sheepdogs or Lhasa Apsos, the fact that one eye is missing often goes unnoticed!

Older dogs often develop a hazy bluish hue to their eyes. This is not cataract development, but **nuclear sclerosis**, which is a loss of moisture from the lens in the center of the eyeball, changing the reflection of light from the lens. The dog can see through this lens, and no treatment is needed for this normal part of the aging process.

On the other hand, a true **cataract** is a complete opacity of the lens, which appears white. The pet cannot see through it. Although most common in older animals, some young pets can develop **juvenile cataracts**. Surgical removal of cataracts is more difficult in animals than in people, but can be successfully carried out by specialized veterinary eye surgeons.

Animals can develop **glaucoma**, which is an increase in the pressure within the eye due to decreased drainage of eyeball fluid. Glaucoma usually follows some sort of eye trauma or cataracts, eye tumors, or infections. The pet with glaucoma may have a protruding eye with a large pupil in the center that will not constrict in light, and there may be inflammation of the white part of the eyeball. The animal may rub the eye. Left untreated, glaucoma damages structures within the eye, causing blindness. Glaucoma is diagnosed by testing for increased pressure within the eyeball using special instruments.

A veterinary eye specialist, called an ophthalmologist, should be consulted whenever glaucoma is suspected. Although an eye with glaucoma will eventually go blind, drops may be prescribed to decrease production of fluid within the eyeball and increase its drainage. These drugs may make the animal more comfortable and must be continued for life.

If a pet appears to suddenly go blind with no obvious change in the appearance of its eyes, the problem will lie either with the nerves running from the eye to the brain, or with the visual center in the brain itself. This is a serious condition usually requiring a referral to either a veterinary neurologist or ophthalmologist. Your veterinarian can test the pet's vision by tossing wisps of cotton towards it. Cotton balls should capture the animal's attention if they are seen, but do not produce any wind to alert the animal. A finger might also be moved rapidly toward the pet's face to see whether the animal reacts.

The Brain

Problems in the brain can sometimes be evident in very young animals. An increase in the pressure within the skull, seen most often in Chihuahuas and other toy breeds, will cause the head to develop a domed shape with an unusually high forehead. While this may make the animal appear cute, it might be mentally retarded, since **hydrocephalus (water on the brain)** prevents the brain from growing in a normal fashion. The animal may be very quiet, sleepy, uncoordinated, have seizures, and be stunted in its growth. Delicate surgery can be performed to place a tube to drain the excess fluid into the abdomen, but as the young animal grows in size or if the drainage tube becomes blocked, this surgery will have to be repeated.

Dogs and cats can develop **epilepsy** when the brain sends out an overload of messages causing the muscles to contract in an uncoordinated fashion. Epilepsy may be caused by scar tissue in the brain after a dog has recovered from distemper, or by brain damage during birth, or it may be inherited. Other causes include: certain poisonous substances, such as lead (from paint), slug bait, and strychnine; chemical imbalances in the body, such as milk fever in a nursing bitch, or kidney failure; and other rarer conditions, such as brain tumors. If all blood test results are normal and exposure to toxins has been ruled out, the animal has **idiopathic epilepsy**, which means "not caused by another disease." This is the most common type of epilepsy found in pets.

In a "grand mal" epileptic seizure, the pet may first act as though it hears or smells something unusual, and it may seek its family's attention as if anticipating that something is about to happen. During the seizure, the pet is not aware of its surroundings, and will usually fall onto its side and paddle with its feet. It will drool and chew with its jaws; frequently, it will lose control of its bowels and bladder. The seizure can last from several seconds to several minutes and can be very upsetting to witness. The pet may remain in a dazed state for a variable period of time afterwards.

It is important to avoid trying to open the pet's mouth during a seizure; do not worry about the possibility of it swallowing its tongue. It can severely damage your hands in its unconscious seizuring state. Make sure that the pet does not bang its head against any furniture. You can talk quietly to it, and stroke it gently, so that it will be reassured as the seizure terminates.

A single seizure is not immediately life-threatening. However, if the animal has continual repeated seizures, it may become totally exhausted from the seizure activity, with serious medical consequences.

Seizures can usually be controlled with anticonvulsant medication, which often has initial side effects of sluggishness and increased appetite or urination. Once medication is begun, it must be continued for the rest of the pet's life. If the medication is stopped, there is a very real danger of a rebound effect resulting in increased seizure activity. For these reasons, I generally am not anxious to start a patient on anticonvulsant medication immediately. I suggest that the family keep track of the frequency and duration of seizures. If they occur every month or so, and are not increasing in duration or severity, it is better to wait before beginning medication; however, if they worsen in any way, anticonvulsant treatment will be started. The dosage or type of drug may have to be changed from time to time to control the seizures. While we may not be able to totally eliminate them, we hope to minimize their frequency and severity.

Rabies is a very serious brain disease. It is a contagious and fatal viral infection that can affect people and all warm-blooded animals, including skunks, raccoons, foxes, bats, ferrets, coyotes, and domestic farm animals. The virus can be transferred by a bite, or through a break in the skin, in a completely nonaggressive way, such as when the rabid animal simply licks skin that has a very minor abrasion. The virus then travels along the nerves, eventually reaching the brain. From the moment of infection until the appearance of symptoms can be from two weeks to six months. In dogs and cats, death invariably occurs within ten days after the first appearance of symptoms.

There are two types of rabies in animals—"dumb" and "furious" rabies. In the "furious" or "mad" form of rabies, an animal becomes overly aggressive for up to seven days, and may attack and bite any other animal or person, rapidly spreading the disease. Other signs characteristic of furious rabies include excitement, pacing, incoordination, irritability, and seizures. The subsequent course of the disease may include aberrant behavior, lethargy, and paralysis.

In the absence of aggressiveness, a rabid animal has the "dumb" form of rabies, in which paralysis is an early and predominant sign. Such an animal may be totally oblivious to its surroundings and just sit and do nothing; an animal sitting still in the middle of a busy highway may be too sick with rabies to seek safer shelter. The sign most often associated with "dumb" rabies is frothing at the mouth, caused by paralysis of the lower jaw and the swallowing muscles, which results in the animal being unable to swallow its saliva. Other signs of dumb rabies may include difficulty breathing, changes in voice, lameness, and progressive limb paralysis, followed by death within two weeks.

Rabies may cause wild animals, such as foxes and skunks, to lose their natural shyness and appear quite fearless. At this stage, they may attack livestock or pet animals. Pets exposed to rabid wild animals then encounter and infect people.

If you are bitten or scratched by a suspected rabid animal, or contact is made with the animal's saliva, two steps should be taken without delay. First, the affected parts of the body must be washed thoroughly with soap, and flushed with lots of water for several minutes to dislodge virus particles. A physician should be consulted to determine whether antirabies treatment, consisting of five injections of vaccine given over a period of one month, should be undertaken. Although at one time these injections were given in the stomach, they are now given in the arm. For most people, there are no unpleasant side effects from this treatment.

Second, the local medical officer of health should be informed. The name and address of the person exposed to the animal, the time and place of the incident, and any other information that would assist in finding and identifying the animal, will be of great help. Once located, the suspected rabid animal, if a dog or cat, will be quarantined for a minimum of ten days. If signs of the disease appear during this period, the animal should be euthanized and tested for rabies. Unfortunately, the most reliable test can only be conducted on the brain of a dead animal.

As a pet owner, you can help to prevent rabies in your community by following these guidelines. Have your dog or cat routinely vaccinated against rabies and repeat the vaccinations yearly or as advised by your veterinarian. Obey leash and licensing laws in your community. Keep your pets indoors at night, since many night-roaming animals, notably skunks, carry and transmit the disease. Report stray dogs to the local animal control authority. Do not approach or attempt to play with stray cats or dogs or other animals. Teach children to avoid strange animals, particularly wild animals, especially when you are camping. Do not touch any animal that is dead or that you suspect of having rabies unless it is absolutely necessary. If you must touch the animal, wear leather gloves, and wash them with a disinfectant after use. Do not keep wild animals for pets, as there is no licensed rabies vaccine that is proven safe for use in wild animals.

A specific liver disease known as **hepatic encephalopathy** can affect the brain in dogs. If the problem is caused by a defect in the blood circulation through the liver, it can be corrected with surgery. Otherwise, keeping the dog on an extremely low-protein diet may alleviate some of the symptoms. This condition is discussed further in the section on liver disease in Chapter 14, "Diseases of the Digestive System."

The Spinal Cord

The spine consists of a series of small bones known as vertebrae, between each of which is a small cushion or disk. Within the spine is the major nerve cord of the body, known as the spinal cord.

A **slipped disk** is a common problem of the spine. When a disk moves out of place, it causes inflammation and varying amounts of damage to the spinal cord. This is illustrated in Figure 18.1. Although cats seldom have back problems, many breeds of dogs do have disk problems. Dachshunds, Cocker Spaniels, and Poodles

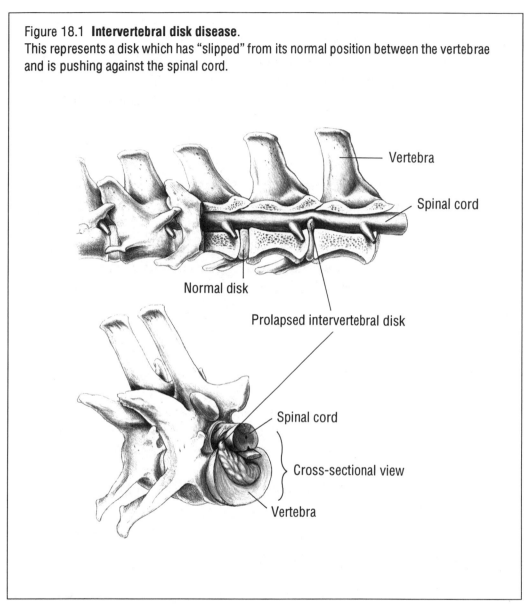

Figure 18.1 **Intervertebral disk disease**.
This represents a disk which has "slipped" from its normal position between the vertebrae and is pushing against the spinal cord.

Vertebra

Spinal cord

Normal disk

Prolapsed intervertebral disk

Spinal cord

Cross-sectional view

Vertebra

are particularly prone to this type of problem, although any purebred or mixed breed animal can be affected.

There are three basic stages in the progression of disk disease. With the early symptoms of a slipped disk, an animal shows some discomfort by arching its back to some degree when it is walking. There will be a reluctance to jump up onto the furniture and perhaps even to climb stairs. If the offending disk is in the neck region, the animal will attempt not to move its neck.

The next stage of a slipped disk causes the pet to "knuckle under" when it walks. In effect, the brain does not "know" the position of the paws; when the dog walks, the front surface of the paws will touch the ground instead of the pads of the paws.

The advanced stage of a slipped disk is paralysis; the animal will be unable to move its front legs (if a disk in the neck is the problem) or its hindquarters (if the offending disk is in the abdominal section of the spine). If there is to be any hope of recovery for an animal at this stage, there must be immediate and aggressive treatment.

Disk disease can be diagnosed by testing the animal's reflexes and location of sensitivity. X-rays can localize the offending disk and identify any other potential disk problems. A special x-ray, called a "myelogram," will identify the exact location of the problem after dye is injected into the spine and flows along the spinal cord.

The usual treatment for a slipped disk begins with high doses of anti-inflammatory drugs. The aim here is to reduce the inflammation and bruising of the spinal cord caused by the disk. Clients often ask whether painkillers can be given if the dog appears to be in discomfort. My answer is "no"; if the animal is a little uncomfortable, it will rest quietly, which will help the healing process. If it has no discomfort, it will move around to such a degree that further damage to the spinal cord can occur.

Prognosis for recovery is good in the first two stages of disk disease. However, if the animal is completely paralyzed, other problems relating to bed sores and urine scalding will occur. For this reason, the dog must be kept on a heavily padded surface. An indwelling urinary catheter is used to drain urine away from the animal. Physiotherapy may be begun to strengthen the animal's hind legs once some voluntary movement has returned. The best form of therapy, depending upon the size of the patient, is to have the dog swim in a bathtub of water. If the dog has good bladder control but remains paralyzed due to permanent damage to the nerve cord, it can learn to get around in a wheelchair known commercially as a "K-9 Cart." The dog's hindquarters are placed in a support that rests between two wheels; harness-type straps run to the front around the dog's neck. The practicality of this depends upon the size of the dog and the devotion of the family to maintaining it in spite of its paralysis.

Back surgery can be performed if medical treatment does not provide relief, or if the condition recurs frequently. One operation actually removes the disk, while another procedure removes some of the bone from the vertebrae adjacent to the affected disk or disks, allowing the nerve cord to swell without becoming compressed against the bone. Both of these procedures are delicate, but the chance of recovery is quite good if the damage to the nerve cord is not extensive.

A further condition of the nerve cord, called **wobbler syndrome**, is seen only in large dogs, particularly Dobermans and Great Danes. This condition results from nerve cord damage caused by a looseness in the joint between the base of the skull and the very first neck vertebra. The dog is very uncoordinated when walking and it will sometimes cross its front legs when it turns in a tight circle. Severe forms of the disease, which can be progressive, can mimic the symptoms of a slipped disk, with discomfort in the neck region or even paralysis of the legs. Surgery can be performed on a wobbler dog to strengthen the first intervertebral space and prevent the nerve cord from being compressed in that area.

An animal's back might be broken if it has been hit by a car or has fallen from a great height. The nerve cord is usually extensively damaged or severed, and will not heal. Sadly, euthanasia is usually the only option for an animal with a badly fractured spine and severed nerve cord.

Tumors can develop within the spine. Arising either from the bones or from the nerve cord itself, these tumors will put pressure on the spinal cord, causing serious problems. Diagnosis of a "space occupying mass" in the spinal cord is easiest with a myelogram. Surgery to remove the mass can sometimes be attempted, depending upon its extent and location.

A very serious and life-threatening infection of the area surrounding the brain and the spinal cord is **meningitis**. The usual symptoms are a high fever and severe nervous signs. A definitive diagnosis can be made only after a spinal tap has been taken, where a sample of the fluid surrounding the spinal cord is withdrawn and analyzed. If an infection is present, treatment with antibiotics is needed.

The entire nervous system of animals is so very complicated and broad in scope that veterinary neurologists are frequently consulted to help diagnose and treat diseases in this area.

19

Diseases of the Skin

Dermatology is the study of diseases and conditions of the skin. Many skin diseases cannot be cured, but medication can keep them under control and in remission. Referral to a veterinary dermatologist is sometimes necessary when a diagnosis, cure, or successful treatment is difficult to achieve. This chapter will review the most common skin conditions affecting dogs and cats. Parasites affecting the skin (such as fleas) are dealt with in Chapter 20, "Parasites."

Diagnostic Methods

Several methods of closely studying the skin can help diagnose a particular condition. Skin scraping involves rubbing a surgical blade along the skin to catch microscopic parasites and to see fungal elements. Minimal restraint is needed as this procedure is well tolerated. A skin biopsy involves taking a small circle of tissue (smaller than the size of a pea) from a lesion with a "biopsy punch." A local anesthetic might be sufficient for this procedure. If a lesion has a raw surface, a glass slide can be held against it to obtain an impression smear. When stained and examined under the microscope, particular types of cells may be seen, signifying certain diseases. Hair, plucked from around a lesion, can be examined and cultured to detect fungal elements. Discharge from a lesion can be cultured to detect the presence of bacteria and determine the appropriate antibiotics to be prescribed.

Diseases of the Ear

The outer ear is a continuation of the skin. There are many causes of **otitis** (inflammation of the ear), including ear mites, which are more common in cats than in dogs. The treatment of ear mites is discussed in Chapter 20, "Parasites."

Most animals produce a small amount of wax in the ear canal. Glance inside your pet's ears, and also check for any odor, at least once a week. As a wax buildup invites infection, regular ear-cleaning should be part of your pet's grooming routine. The ear canal makes a right angle turn before the eardrum is reached, so a cotton swab can be used, providing you are gentle and do not probe too deeply. If you can see where the cotton joins the stick, you are within the safety zone. Dampen the swab with hydrogen peroxide or rubbing alcohol, as these products have some disinfectant properties. Avoid water or edible oils such as olive oil, which could increase the risk of ear infection. A cotton ball wrapped around your finger may be useful to remove heavier wax accumulations from dogs with large ear canals.

Regular ear examinations allow you to spot problems early. An infected ear will have a foul smell and a buildup of moist, glistening debris. The pet will have discomfort and paw at the ear or rub it against the carpet. Although cats can develop ear infections, certain breeds of dogs—particularly Poodles and Cocker Spaniels—are notorious for having infected ears. In these floppy-eared dogs, the heavy ear flap hangs down and prevents air circulation to the ear canal, creating a warm, moist environment that is ideal for the rapid growth of bacteria. However, dogs with erect ears are not immune to developing ear infections.

Many different medications are available to treat ear infections, and new drugs are being introduced all the time. Sometimes, after a drug has been effective for a time, the animal builds up a resistance to it, thereby eliminating its effectiveness. Each ear can have a different infection, requiring a different medication. Cultures can be performed to ensure that the most appropriate medication is selected. Unfortunately, the animal must be off all medication for at least five days before a culture is taken. Medication can be started while waiting for the culture results, which will take at least two or three days, and then the medication can be changed if necessary.

If an internal medical condition causes greasy skin and waxy debris in the ear, the veterinarian must diagnose and treat both the internal condition and the ear problem. A prime example is **canine hypothyroidism**, which causes the ears to become greasy and easily infected.

In cases of severe otitis that is resistant to medication, surgery can be performed to open the ear canal to the outside. This serves three purposes: air can circulate into the ear canal, preventing the buildup of warmth and moisture; any discharge can drain out; and medication can be applied closer to the infection.

My recommended method of cleaning and medicating ears is described in Chapter 4, "Your Pet and Your Vet," in the section on "Medicating Your Pet." Once an ear infection has been controlled, the occasional use of various drying agents, as required, will keep infection away. A little alcohol or hydrogen peroxide will change the acidity in the ear and reduce the ability of bacteria to grow there.

Hematoma of the Ear

A soft swelling on the inner surface of the ear is an **ear hematoma**, or **blood blister**. A cat or dog with a chronic ear infection or ear mites will scratch its ear excessively, causing bleeding which is contained between the ear cartilage and the skin. Surgical repair is required since the hematoma will form again if the blood is merely drained. The operation opens the hematoma, drains it, and tacks the skin to the cartilage to prevent the hematoma from reforming. Some animals repeatedly develop ear hematomas.

Ringworm

Ringworm is a superficial fungal skin infection, which derives its name from the shape of the lesion. It is not a worm! Although ringworm can afflict mature animals, it primarily affects young ones, on the head and forequarters. It appears as small roundish areas of hair loss; the skin is usually flaky and the lesion may be itchy. A lesion may be solitary, or there may be several sores in the same area or on different parts of the body. A cat grooming a ringworm lesion on its head, for instance, may spread the infection to its front legs. Some cats are carriers of ringworm, even though they show no visible signs.

Ringworm is passed between animals and between animals and people mainly through direct contact. In my experience, washing your hands carefully with soap and water after handling or treating affected animals will generally prevent human infection. I did see a case where the owner of a kitten with ringworm had facial lesions; the woman slept with the kitten curled against her face! Frequently, when a person has been diagnosed with ringworm, the physician will suggest that all household pets be checked by a veterinarian to determine the source of infection. However, I generally feel no need to treat a pet that has no signs of hair loss or lesions, since the human infection might be from another source.

Many types of ringworm will fluoresce a greenish color when a lamp with a specific wavelength (called a Wood's light) is shone at the lesions. The presence of a fungus can also be discovered by microscopic examination and culturing of some hairs taken from the edge of the lesion. As a fungus culture can grow very slowly, it takes six weeks to confirm the absence of ringworm.

Ringworm can be treated with creams or solutions applied to the lesions two or three times daily. The medication must penetrate down to the infection. If this is difficult to do, or if more than one or two lesions have to be treated, the animal can be treated with griseofulvin tablets once a day for six weeks.

When treating ringworm, remember that the hairs surrounding the visible sore are already infected. The original lesion will appear to get larger as the damaged hair continues to fall out for a time. However, after a few days, new hair will begin to regrow from the center of the lesion.

Allergic Skin Conditions and Atopy

There are four types of allergies: **parenteral allergies** (insect bites and drug reactions); **inhalant allergies** or **atopy** (breathing in the offending substance); **ingestion or food allergies**; and **contact allergies** (direct skin contact with the offending substance, such as shampoo, plastic, rubber, and so on). Some animals may suffer from any combination of these allergic conditions.

Many pets are allergic to flea bites. When a flea bites a cat or dog, it injects a small amount of saliva, which can trigger an allergic reaction, known as **flea bite dermatitis**. The pet will chew and scratch at itself, sometimes making open sores, and pulling out its hair. Red pinpoint sores, the actual flea bites, will be seen on the pet's body. The intensity of the reaction to flea bites varies between individuals. Some pets can be covered with many fleas and not react severely, while sensitive individuals will become extremely itchy in the presence of just a few fleas. As flea bite dermatitis resembles other allergic conditions, it can be difficult to diagnose unless a flea is actually seen on the patient. A flea eradication program must be undertaken (see Chapter 20, "Parasites"). Any open sores will be treated with salves. Anti-inflammatory medication will make the pet more comfortable; however, this will not get rid of the fleas!

The main symptom of allergies to substances breathed from the environment is itchiness; the animal continuously rubs, scratches, or licks at its feet, groin, underarm regions, and at its face—particularly the eyes and the nose—with varying degrees of self-trauma and inflammation.

Many allergies begin early in life on a seasonal basis. Some animals are allergic to new foliage in the spring, while others react to dying vegetation in the fall. Other pets are worse in the winter if they are allergic to molds in the heating system filter. As the pet ages, its allergies may extend to other seasons. A pet that is allergic year-round is reacting to substances it encounters regularly, such as wool carpets, other animals, food, or household dust.

Allergy tests can determine the exact cause of a pet's allergy. Some laboratories can do this by analyzing blood samples. Although some experts question the reliability of this method, it is constantly undergoing refinement and improvement. The usual way to test for specific inhalant allergies is by means of "intradermal" testing. An area of the abdomen is shaved and injected with a series of substances derived from items in the environment, such as grass, plants, mold, dust, wool, flea extracts, and so on. The degree of reaction around each of these injection sites can be interpreted to indicate the extent to which each substance causes an allergic reaction.

The most important thing to remember about allergies is that there is no easy cure! We try to control the animal's chronic itchiness and discomfort, but there will be periods of improvement and relapse. Ideally, we should prevent the pet from inhaling the allergy-causing substance, but this is rarely practical. Avoidance is much easier with contact allergies involving removable substances, such as plastic food bowls and wool. Keeping the animal indoors most of the day is partially effective in the case of allergy to pollen. Air conditioners also will limit pollen exposure. Molds can occur outside, as well as in basements, houseplants, aquariums, pillows, and mattresses. Rooms with carpeting, kapok-stuffed furniture, or houseplants can cause severe reactions in dust-allergic pets.

Once the allergy-causing substances have been identified, a hyposensitization program, similar to that used for hay fever sufferers, can be undertaken to lessen the animal's sensitivity to the substances. The concept is simple: once the body gets used to receiving small amounts of the allergy-producing substance, its reactions to the substance will get progressively milder. A small amount of extract of the allergy-inducing substance is injected under the skin every week, in increasingly larger doses. Many veterinarians report up to 75 percent success with these programs, even to flea allergies, but six to eight months of injections might be required for the benefits to be evident. Hopefully, up to several months can then elapse between injections, although in certain seasons more frequent treatments might be necessary.

Bathing the allergic pet is an excellent way to relieve itchiness, but the effect is short-lived. Animals should be bathed in cool water with an appropriate medicated shampoo, selected based on the animal's coat condition. Antihistamines have been reported to relieve some itching in one-third of patients. Drowsiness is one of their few side effects, but this may help a pet get a good night's sleep instead of scratching incessantly. As with all medications, antihistamines should be given only on the advice of a veterinarian, and in the prescribed dosage.

For an allergic pet, the veterinarian may also recommend dietary supplements, including specific essential fatty acids (known as omega 3 and omega 6 fatty acids). These prescription items, which are different from fatty acid supplements designed to make the coat glossy, have some anti-inflammatory properties and are completely safe. They are effective in up to 20 percent of allergic pets.

Anti-inflammatory drugs (cortisone) are very effective in relieving itchiness, but they have possible side effects, including increased appetite, thirst, and urination. These side effects are less pronounced in cats than in dogs. Injectable cortisone is useful in cats, but less desirable for dogs as once they are administered, the dosage cannot be reduced if an animal seems to be very sensitive to it. Some products contain low levels of cortisone in combination with antihistamines.

Food allergy is a very common cause of allergic dermatitis in dogs, and can also occur in cats. Although food allergy usually causes itchiness and bumpy skin, the symptoms can be extremely variable and can mimic other skin conditions. Interestingly, the timing and severity of the symptoms is unrelated to the time that the offending food is eaten. Food allergy is acquired over time; about 70 percent of dogs that develop food allergy have been on the same diet for at least two years prior to developing symptoms. It is of no benefit to simply switch diets, since the allergy is to specific ingredients (such as beef, soy, or corn) that are present in many brands of food; the allergy, therefore, is not to a particular brand of food.

Food allergy is best tested by feeding a hypoallergenic diet of lamb with rice or potatoes for a minimum of four weeks. Lamb is used since food allergies are acquired, and the pet cannot be allergic to ingredients it has never had. Of course, lamb would not be suitable for this test if the pet has eaten lamb meat in the past; in this case, a chicken-based diet might be helpful. Although commercial hypoallergenic diets are available, these diets should not be used for testing purposes since 10 to 20 percent of documented food-allergic animals have reactions even when fed these diets.

Food allergy is best controlled by removing the offending ingredient from the diet. If the animal improves dramatically on the trial diet, "challenge" its body by adding one new ingredient every five days (e.g. beef, milk, soy, corn, wheat) until the offending substance can be identified. Most animals are allergic to one or possibly two food substances. Select a commercial diet that does not contain these ingredients.

Urticaria (**hives**) is a sudden, severe allergic reaction to some stimulus. One evening, my dog Aimée came in from the backyard after I had sown some grass seed, and she began rubbing her face. After a few minutes her jowls and eyelids were so swollen that her eyes were barely visible. Her abdomen broke out in large red raised welts, and she was itchy all over. Some animals can react in this fashion to an insect bite; some to one of the components in a vaccine; others, like Aimée, to contacting something unusual in the environment.

Hives are treated with antihistamine injections alone or in combination with anti-inflammatory drugs. Emergency treatment should be sought, because this type of reaction, if severe enough, can cause the throat to swell up and choke the animal.

Hair Loss

There are many causes of **alopecia** or hair loss. External conditions (flea allergy, for example) can result in patchy hair loss. An internal hormonal condition usually causes the areas of alopecia to be identical on both sides of the body. For example, Cushing's disease (hyperadrenalcorticism) and hypothyroidism can cause symmetrical hair loss. A Sertoli-cell testicular tumor also results in bilateral symmetrical hairlessness. When alopecia is a result of hormone-related internal diseases, improvement in the hair coat usually follows resolution of the underlying condition.

Conditions Affecting Fur Color

The fur color of dogs and cats can sometimes change without significance. For example, if a dark-coated animal has received a deep wound or skin laceration, the fur around the injury frequently grows back lighter or darker than the rest of the coat. On a dark-coated pet's body, an area that has been shaved before an operation will sometimes grow back white.

If a light-colored animal continually licks an area of its coat, the saliva may turn the area a rusty brown color. Runny eyes may also cause brown-stained areas on the fur beneath the eyes. This frequently occurs in white Persian cats or white Toy Poodles. A careful application of undiluted hydrogen peroxide may help lighten the stain. Products to remove this discoloration are also available at pet supply stores.

Autoimmune Skin Diseases

Within the last fifteen to twenty years, a new group of autoimmune skin diseases, also known as **pemphigus**, has been investigated. In these diseases the body reacts to itself in an unusual manner, typically forming small blisterlike swellings, or crusty scabby sores, at the margins of the lips or rectum, where the smooth lining tissue joins the outer skin. Diagnosis can be confirmed by skin biopsy. Pemphigus is treated with high doses of anti-inflammatory medication, and reasonably good control can usually be obtained. However, lifelong therapy will be necessary.

Skin Conditions Particular to Dogs

Collie Nose

Solar nasal dermatitis, or **Collie nose**, affects the nose of Collies and Shelties more than other breeds, although Retrievers and Cocker Spaniels can also be affected. The disease results in a gradual loss of pigment from the nose, nostrils, and, sometimes, the eyelids. These areas will suffer severe sunburn, and may ooze and bleed. In severe chronic cases, the affected areas become eaten away, and there may be a greater risk of skin cancer than in unaffected areas.

Treatment of Collie nose is not very successful. Keeping the pet out of direct midday sunlight may help. Dark dye may be injected into the area to replace the lost natural pigment. The application of sun-blocking agents might help if the dog doesn't lick them off right away. Research is continuing to develop drugs that can be given orally to control this condition.

Skin-Fold Pyoderma

The brachycephalic (short-faced) dog breeds frequently develop **pyoderma**—infections in the skin folds on their heads. Pugs, Boston Terriers, and Shar-Peis are among the breeds that have a deep fold of skin over the bridge of the nose. Warmth and moisture are easily trapped in this fold and a foul-smelling discharge of pus can develop. Skin-fold pyoderma can also develop in the deep fold of skin around the base of the tail in many of the same breeds. Treatment of pyoderma with hydrogen peroxide, alcohol, or diaper rash cream for babies might be effective in keeping the areas dry. The only effective way to eliminate the problem completely is by performing surgery to remove the folds of skin. This is the animal's version of a "face-lift"!

Many breeds of dogs have deep folds of skin on their lower lips, which can become infected. This infection, called **cheleitis**, can be very painful. Aside from the discharge of pus, there may also be some bleeding and crusting. This condition is difficult to treat because the pet will rapidly lick off any applied medication. Although antibiotics can be given and topical drying agents can be tried, surgery is the treatment of choice.

Skin Infections

Folliculitis, a condition affecting many short-coated dogs, particularly Dobermans and Great Danes, occurs when the follicles, or base of the hairs, become infected. This disease may cause moderate itchiness and is characterized by numerous small bumps on the dog's back and sides. Sometimes the hair will fall out from the lesions. This disease can be treated with frequent medicated antibiotic baths and oral antibiotics. There may be occasional recurrences in some patients.

A more severe form of bacterial skin infection, **furunculosis**, is a deep follicular infection with the development of a large, very tender, cystlike boil. Treatment consists of drainage and antibiotic therapy.

Juvenile or **puppy pyoderma** is a mild skin infection that appears as small nonitchy pimples in the groin of young dogs. Gentle cleansing of the area, and sometimes the application of an antibiotic salve, generally suffices. Recurrences occur with decreasing frequency as the animal matures.

An uncomfortable skin condition that can develop very rapidly is called **acute moist dermatitis** or **hot spot**. It occurs most frequently in warm humid weather and affects dogs with thick, heavy coats, such as Golden Retrievers. When the dog is not thoroughly dried after it goes swimming or is bathed, the skin remains damp on top of the animal's head, around its neck and around its tail base, even when the dog shakes itself off. Normal skin bacteria begin to multiply rapidly on the moist skin. As a result, a red moist infection develops which, within hours, expands in size and becomes an oozing inflamed hot spot.

Usually the dog must be sedated for treatment of a painful hot spot. The hair is clipped to allow air and medication to reach the sore. Gentle cleansing with a mild antibiotic soap will remove the pus, and drying agents and healing salves are applied for a few days. The dog is usually given antibiotics.

Seborrhea

Seborrhea refers to an abnormal oil gland activity, resulting in scaling, crusting, hair loss, and, at times, oiliness of the skin. It frequently affects Cocker Spaniels. The cause is unknown in the majority of cases, but certain endocrine diseases, such as hypothyroidism, can be contributory. Two types of seborrhea are **sicca** (a dry form) with dandruff and flaking of the skin, and **oleosa** (an oily form) with rancid-smelling greasy skin. Seborrhea usually worsens in the winter, and affected skin is susceptible to bacterial infections. Ear infections often occur with seborrhea oleosa, as the greasiness and bacterial infection extend into the ear.

Treatment of seborrhea is generally symptomatic unless an underlying cause can be determined. Shampoos that dry out the skin can be used to alleviate oleosa, and moisturizing baths and sprays can soothe sicca. **Staph dermatitis**, a frequent secondary bacterial skin infection accompanying seborrhea oleosa, is treated with antibiotics. Animals with seborrhea should not be used for breeding purposes, as there may be an inherited component in the disease.

Lick Granuloma

Dogs can develop a lick granuloma when, for an unknown reason, they begin to lick at an area on either the front of a front paw, or the side surface of a hind leg. The persistent licking soon results in a hairless raw area. Boredom may have a role in causing the dog to traumatize itself. Treatment with various injectable drugs, or covering the area with bad-tasting products, tends to be marginally effective. Recently, the application of dimethylsulfoxide (DMSO) seems to help, as it is a deep-penetrating anti-inflammatory agent with drying properties and a bitter taste to stop the dog from licking the area.

Interdigital Cysts

Interdigital cysts, which can be solitary or multiple, are raised, blisterlike, tender swellings occurring both on and between the toes of dogs. The dog will lick the cysts and may even limp. The cause might be foreign object penetration (grass awns, grains of sand), ingrown hairs, or bacterial infections of the hair follicle. In my experience, these cysts occur most frequently in Lhasa Apsos, Pugs, and Shar-Peis, so the length of the pet's coat does not seem to matter. These cysts generally must be opened and allowed to drain and dry. I have had frequent success using dimethylsulfoxide painted onto the cyst; this dries it out even if the cyst has not been opened, and the bad taste usually prevents the patient from licking the area.

Sebaceous Cysts

One type of skin growth is a sebaceous or **inclusion cyst**. These growths can be found anywhere on dogs middle-aged and older. They appear as slightly raised bumps within the skin, about the size of a green pea, although they can grow larger. If they break open, they discharge a thick cheesy material, which is an accumulation of wax normally released from the sebaceous glands onto the skin's surface. A dog may have numerous cysts at any one time.

I take a conservative approach in dealing with a sebaceous cyst. I recommend leaving it alone if it is not infected and discharging, if it is not growing rapidly, if it is not bothering the dog and being licked or chewed at, and if it does not offend the family. However, you should always consult your veterinarian to rule out a more serious condition, such as a skin tumor (see Chapter 21, "Cancer"). If the cyst is growing rapidly, or if, by its location, it interferes with the dog in any way, then it should be removed. If the patient is anesthetized for another procedure, such as for teeth cleaning, this would be a good time to remove any cysts, although once a dog has started to develop sebaceous cysts, it will usually continue to do so.

Skin Conditions Particular to Cats
Feline Acne

Feline acne is characterized by one or more pimples or blackheads on the cat's chin. I have seen this condition in both male and female cats, and more frequently in short-haired breeds. It does not seem to result from bits of food blocking the pores, as acne occurs in cats fed dry food as well as those fed moist food. If there are just a few blackheads, they can be treated by scrubbing the area with a disinfectant soap and then applying either hydrogen peroxide or alcohol to dry them up. In more severe cases, when the entire chin is swollen and tender, more aggressive treatment is required. The cat must be sedated and the area thoroughly drained.

Home care includes antibiotics and astringent soaks for the chin. Some of these cases may take several weeks to clear up.

Feline Eosinophilic Granuloma Complex

Feline rodent ulcer—eosinophilic granuloma complex—is a condition that affects the lip area of cats. The upper lip appears as a flattened, raw area with raised borders, as some tissue is missing from the lesion. The involved area can extend up towards the nose, and include both sides of the upper lip.

The cause of feline eosinophilic granuloma is not certain. Many veterinarians believe it is either caused by, or at least aggravated by, continuous licking of the area by the cat's rough tongue. It may be an autoimmune reaction, meaning that the cat's body attacks itself. There may be an allergic component as well, as some cats improve when changed to a hypoallergenic diet. Anti-inflammatory medication, given either by injection or tablets, will usually control the condition.

Another type of raised reddish swelling, resembling a cold sore, can appear very suddenly in the center of the lower lip. This is a type of **localized lymphoid reaction** and does not seem to bother the cat at all. Left without treatment, the swelling will gradually subside over a period of a few days. Sometimes an injection of anti-inflammatory medication will hasten recovery, but recurrences are common.

Lick Dermatitis

Cats can cause skin irritations through excessive licking. This **feline neural lick dermatitis** can result in large areas of fur loss from the groin area, the inner side and down the back of the hind legs, around the base of the tail, and from the posterior abdomen. The exact cause of this condition is not known. However, if a cat licks repeatedly at an area for some reason, its rough tongue soon removes the fur and irritates the skin, which causes the cat to continue licking the area, thus setting up a "vicious circle." This condition may also be related to food allergies or to feline eosinophilic complex.

Treatment of feline neural lick dermatitis can be frustrating. "Elizabethan" collars can be placed around the cat's neck to prevent it from licking the area, but this does not address the cause of the problem. Hypoallergenic diets are sometimes helpful. Treatment with female hormone tablets is often beneficial, but there may be severe side effects, including a tremendous increase in appetite and subsequent weight gain. Long-lasting anti-inflammatory medication given by injection is frequently the best treatment.

Miliary Dermatitis

Miliary dermatitis is a form of seborrhea found in cats, seen as extensive scaling and crusting over large sections of the body, including the head. These areas may be oozing or covered with scabs, making the sensation of patting such an animal very unpleasant. It is generally accepted that this condition is caused by an allergy, perhaps to something in the diet or a severe reaction to fleas. Treatment with medicated shampoos is generally helpful. A hypoallergenic diet should be given, and anti-inflammatory drugs may be necessary.

Abscesses

An infected bite, causing an abscess, is a problem frequently occurring in cats allowed free access to the outdoors, although indoor cats in multicat households can occasionally have abscess-producing fights with one another. Cats that tend to develop abscesses on the front half of their body are usually the aggressors, while animals with abscesses on their hindquarters have usually received their wounds while fleeing.

A day or two after the fight, even if no puncture wound remains visible, an abscess develops in the skin. An abscess is a large, soft, swollen pocket of pus, resulting from bacteria trapped beneath the skin's surface and white blood cells fighting the infection. The cat usually develops a high fever. If left untreated at this stage, there is a danger that an internal abscess might develop, which is a serious condition.

If the abscess is fairly superficial, the overlying skin may rupture and the pus will drain. Occasionally, it will then appear to heal when the skin closes over. However, if the area has not drained completely, a new abscess will form from the remnants of the first infection, with the same results. To prevent this needless suffering, veterinary attention should be sought. Usually the cat must be sedated so that the abscess can be opened, drained, and disinfected. The wound is generally left open and home care includes applying warm compresses to the area a few times a day to encourage drainage. The cat is also treated with antibiotics. Occasionally, the veterinarian will remove the abscess whole without breaking it and close the wound with stitches. In this case, compresses would not be necessary. Recovery is usually rapid; however, some cats will get into repeated fights and develop abscesses on a regular basis.

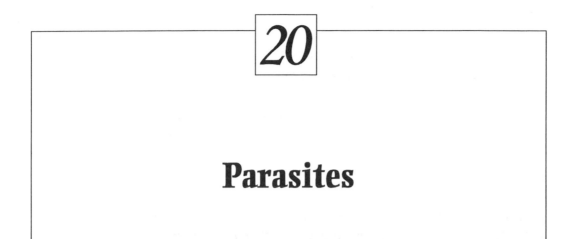

Parasites

Parasites are organisms that survive by living off other animals. Cats and dogs can play host to many types of parasites, which fall into two broad categories: internal parasites that live inside the body; and external parasites that are found on the body.

Internal Parasites

The majority of internal parasites, commonly referred to as **worms**, live at least part of their lives in the host's intestine. Many pet owners believe that if a dog or cat "scoots" or drags its hindquarters along the ground it must have worms. While scooting may indicate that worms are present, it may also signify an irritation of the anal glands. (See the section on anal glands in Chapter 14, "Diseases of the Digestive System.") Intestinal parasites can cause loose and/or mucus-covered stools, with or without blood. Sometimes the pet will seem unhealthy, not be gaining weight as it should, and have a dull coat. A young animal might appear pot-bellied; it may lack energy and its gums might be very pale if it has a heavy infestation of blood-sucking intestinal worms.

Of all intestinal parasites, only roundworms and tapeworms are visible with the naked eye. Some people report that they have seen worms in their dog's stool when, in fact, they are seeing fly maggots. As soon as stool is released, flies can lay eggs that develop into maggots within minutes. The speed with which this happens is amazing and I sometimes find it impossible to convince the dog's family that these maggots did not originate within the dog! If you think you see a worm in your dog's stool, pick it up with a piece of tissue and bring it to the veterinary office for proper identification.

The veterinarian will look for the eggs of internal parasites by examining a fresh stool sample under the microscope. While the presence of eggs indicates a parasitic infestation, their absence may simply mean that no eggs are present in that particular sample, or that the sample contains only male worms or immature worms, which are not producing eggs. This explains why a pet may still have worms even though a stool sample has tested negative.

The veterinarian may provide you with a special container in which to submit a stool sample for testing. Alternatively, you can collect the sample by putting a plastic bag over your hand, picking up the sample, turning the bag inside out and sealing it. It does not matter if there is some cat litter in the sample. The sample should not have been frozen, and the fresher the sample, the more reliable the test result. If the doctor wishes to test for some of the hard-to-find parasites that deteriorate rapidly outside the body, you will be given a container with a liquid preservative. A very fresh sample (less than ten minutes old) must be put into the container and submitted to the veterinary office within several hours.

Intestinal Worms

Roundworms (*Toxocara* and *Toxascaris* species) appearing as round spaghettilike white worms, 2.5 centimeters (1 in.) or more in length, are very common intestinal parasites in young animals. They can sometimes be seen on the stool, and occasionally the animal may vomit a number of worms. In a very severe infestation, the roundworms can form a mass in the stomach or intestine and cause a blockage.

Hookworms (*Ancylostoma* and *Uncinaria* species), another common parasite, are tiny white to reddish-brown parasites that puncture the intestinal lining and feed on blood. They can cause diarrhea and life-threatening blood loss.

Adult **whipworms** (*Trichuris* species) are white and 5 to 8 centimeters (2–3 in.) long. They attach themselves to the lining of the large intestine, where they feed on tissue fluids and blood. Whipworms are a common cause of colon inflammation in dogs, and a severe infection can be fatal.

Roundworms, hookworms, and whipworms are commonly acquired when the pet eats the eggs laid by female worms. In addition, the eggs can be passed from a mother to her young while she is still pregnant, or, after delivery, through the mother's milk. Immature hookworms can also penetrate the animal's skin, usually between the toes.

People can be infected with roundworm larvae. This is a serious public health concern. This infection, called **visceral larva migrans**, occurs most commonly in children sixteen to thirty-two months old, as a result of eating dirt contaminated with roundworm eggs. The young worms migrate to a number of tissues, including the lung and liver, but the greatest danger occurs when larvae enter the eye or brain, where the worms can cause blindness and mental retardation. By disposing of animal stools daily, and excluding pets from the play area (yard or sand box) of small children, the risk of acquiring visceral larva migrans is minimized.

Tapeworm infection (*Taenia* and *Dipylidium* species) differs from other worm infections in that an intermediate host animal is necessary for the tapeworm to develop. In other words, if a pet eats a tapeworm, the tapeworm will not develop in the pet. Tapeworms must pass part of their life-cycle either in rodents, wild rabbits, sheep, cattle, pigs, or fleas. A tapeworm will develop in the pet when it eats a flea, mouse, or other animal containing infective tapeworm larvae.

Tapeworms, which may reach a length of 15 centimeters (6 in.), attach to the lining of the small intestine in dogs and cats. The body of a tapeworm is composed of segments that fill with eggs, detach from the rest of the tapeworm, and leave the pet's body through the anus or in the stool. The segments are white and shaped like cucumber seeds or flattened grains of rice, often moving by contracting and elongating. Diagnosis of tapeworm infection is based upon finding these egg-filled segments in the stool, on furniture, or on the animal's coat near the anus.

Deworming medication effectively eliminates worms from dogs and cats. Your veterinarian will select the appropriate drug, based upon such factors as the animal's size, ease of administration, and the presence of other parasites. Several consecutive days of treatment may be necessary. Whatever the treatment schedule, you should submit a stool sample two weeks after the final deworming treatment, to ensure that the worms have been eliminated.

It is also important to remove feces on a daily basis from areas that your pets visit, and pets should not be allowed access to areas where free-roaming animals have bowel movements. Feces should be removed from litter pans daily. The frequency suggested for regular fecal examinations by your veterinarian will depend upon the severity of the worm problem in your area.

Giardia and *Coccidia*

Two other intestinal parasites, which are not actually worms but microscopic one-celled organisms, are *Giardia* and *Coccidia*. Animals acquire these infestations from infected animals, infected feces, or contaminated food and water. *Giardia* and *Coccidia* are often problems in puppies and kittens obtained from pet stores and unhygienic kennels. It is thought that a low number of *Coccidia* can exist in the normal intestine; under stressful situations, however, their number will increase and symptoms will result. It is important to treat all pets in the household to stop the cycle of infection.

Giardia and *Coccidia* usually produce a large-volume, mucus-containing diarrhea. Fresh fecal blood is sometimes present, and the affected animal may be dehydrated. Both of these organisms can be difficult to detect in the stools, as they may appear only sporadically. Therefore, fecal examinations over several days may be required to establish a firm diagnosis. *Giardia* and *Coccidia* can be treated with a short course of medication, although this treatment may have to be repeated.

Toxoplasma

Toxoplasma is a single-celled intestinal parasite with potentially serious public health ramifications. Cats, both domestic and wild, play a major role in the spread of this organism. When a cat eats an infected bird or rodent, the parasite multiplies in the cat's intestinal tract and infective *Toxoplasma* eggs are excreted for a few weeks. When people ingest these eggs, the body's immune system will usually go into action and eventually encapsulate them in scar tissue.

Most cases of human *Toxoplasma* infection go unnoticed. However, people with immune systems that are not functioning properly—for example, those on drug therapy or carrying the Human Immunodeficiency Virus, HIV—can be in serious trouble as *Toxoplasma* infections often cause potentially fatal brain or heart disease. Research has also shown that *Toxoplasma* infections in AIDS patients is due to reactivation of a previous infection because the waning immune system fails to continue to suppress the parasite. To be on the safe side, it is recommended that HIV-positive cat owners wear gloves and masks while changing the litter pan, or have someone else handle the litter.

If a woman who has never been previously exposed to *Toxoplasma* becomes infected during pregnancy, she may have serious problems. While she may feel little or no ill effects, spontaneous abortion, stillbirth, premature delivery, or congenital disease may occur. Children who acquire infection while still in the womb may appear normal at birth but develop problems later on in the form of mental retardation, blindness, and epilepsy.

Cats with *Toxoplasma* infection generally have no symptoms. Occasionally, there may be lethargy, breathing difficulties, poor appetite, vomiting, fever, or abortion.

There is limited value in testing a cat's blood for *Toxoplasma*. A positive test means that the cat has been exposed, but a single test does not reliably tell if the cat is presently contagious and shedding infective eggs. A negative test likely means that the cat has not yet been exposed, was infected so recently that a response has not yet developed, or was exposed but for some reason did not respond.

There are many effective ways to prevent *Toxoplasma* infection. Although some of these involve your cat, it is very important to note that cats are not the only source, and, in fact, are a relatively minor potential source of infection. People who own or work with cats, including veterinarians, have not been shown to be at any greater risk of becoming infected than those who do not encounter cats regularly. On no account, as has been suggested by some of my clients' physicians, is it necessary to get rid of your cat! What little risk there is can be minimized through basic hygiene, even when a pregnant woman or HIV-positive individual is involved.

As the only route of infection for people is oral, always insist that *all* family members wash their hands before eating. Avoid eating raw or poorly cooked meat or drinking unpasteurized milk, especially goat's milk, which often contains infective organisms. If you are pregnant or have a damaged immune system, designate someone else to clean out the litter pan on a daily basis. The litter pan should be disinfected weekly by putting it in boiling water for at least five minutes. This is more effective in killing *Toxoplasma* than most household cleaners. Do not feed your cat raw meat. To prevent infection from the soil and from eating birds and mice, do not allow your cat to go outdoors.

Heartworms

The heartworm, or **Dirofilaria**, lives mainly in the heart and large blood vessels, and is transmitted from dog to dog by mosquitoes. A mosquito ingests immature forms of the heartworm (called "microfilariae") when it takes blood from a dog with heartworms. The microfilariae develop for a while in the mosquito and are then injected into the next dog when the mosquito takes its next blood meal. Over the next six months, the microfilariae move to the heart and adjacent blood vessels, and become adult heartworms capable of releasing microfilariae into the bloodstream, completing the cycle.

Cats are susceptible to heartworm infection but are relatively resistant, although since the first reported case in a cat in 1921, it has been recognized in the United States with increasing frequency. Most heartworm-positive cats do not have circulating microfilariae and therefore the condition is difficult to diagnose. An x-ray offers one of the best screening tests for feline heartworm disease although findings are not conclusive. Other disorders that may mimic heartworm in cats include asthma, cardiomyopathy, and bacterial and parasitic infection. Unfortunately, to date there is no specific licensed prevention for use in cats.

For many years heartworm disease has been a major problem for dogs in areas where mosquitoes live year-round, such as the southern United States and Caribbean islands. Over the last twenty years the disease has spread throughout North America and many other parts of the world. The disease spreads when dogs visiting warmer climates become infected with heartworms, and then bring the infection back home with them where local mosquito populations spread the infection to healthy dogs.

During the early stages of infection, most dogs appear normal. In fact, some dogs may have heartworms for months or possibly years and the family may not be aware of it. Although not all dogs affected with heartworm are critically ill, symptoms will eventually begin to appear in most cases. The heart becomes clogged by twenty-five to fifty large adult worms, each over 15 centimeters (6 in.) long.

The heartworms interfere with blood flow through the heart, as illustrated in Figure 20.1, resulting in congestive heart failure. In an advanced case, the dog may cough, have difficulty breathing, will not tolerate exercise well, and will lack energy. It may lose weight and have a poor appetite and a pot belly. More severe signs include heavy breathing, falling over, coughing up blood, and, ultimately, death.

Heartworm disease can be diagnosed by a simple blood test. A small blood sample is filtered and a microscopic examination will reveal the presence of any microfilariae. This routinely used method is not 100 percent reliable, and will

Figure 20.1 **Canine heartworm disease**.
This represents a heart, cut open to reveal adult heartworms. At right, the way that the presence of numerous heartworms restricts normal blood flow through the heart is shown.

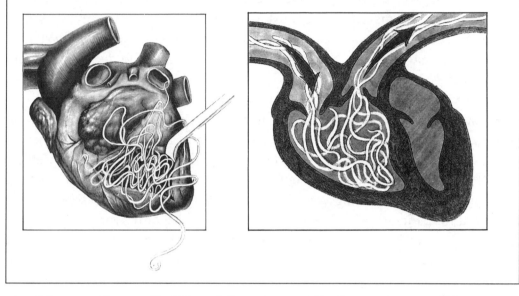

give false negative results if the adult worms are all of one sex or are all immature. Chest x-rays, electrocardiograms, and immunological blood tests may be used to confirm suspicious cases.

If an animal is treated for heartworm disease while it is still relatively healthy, it should tolerate therapy fairly well. However, the risk of complications increases as heart and lung damage becomes more severe. It is also important to assess the condition of the liver and kidneys before beginning the treatment, because the drugs used are toxic and can damage these organs.

The treatment for heartworm disease follows three stages. In the first stage, the adults are killed by injecting thiacetarsamide (an arsenic compound) intravenously, twice daily for two days. It is best to hospitalize the patient to monitor any toxic reactions, such as vomiting, acute depression, loss of appetite, jaundice, or fever. If few complications occur, and if the patient's attitude and appetite are good, it can usually recuperate at home before the next phase of treatment. Confinement and exercise limitation must be strictly enforced, usually for a minimum of four weeks, to allow the heart and lungs to recover, and also to prevent the dead heartworms from forming a mass in the lungs.

Several drugs are available for the second phase of treatment, in which the microfilariae are killed. This can be done four to six weeks after the first phase.

The third phase, directed at preventing reinfection, is the same as the prevention treatment given to all dogs that test negative. Numerous drugs are available to prevent heartworm disease; some must be given daily, some monthly; they may be tablets, chewable flavored cubes, or syrups; some are combined with drugs to prevent intestinal parasites. Your veterinarian will recommend the most suitable product for your pet.

It is very important to make certain that your dog does not have heartworm infection before giving the prevention treatment. These drugs can make a dog very sick, even causing death, if given to a heartworm-positive dog. Even though you may feel that you have been very diligent in giving the heartworm prevention as directed during the summer months, never begin the tablets again the next summer without first having your dog tested. There are several reasons for this important rule. First, if you missed the medication once, or if your pet spit up the drug or vomited after it was given, that one time might have been enough to allow heartworm infection to occur. Second, as with all medication, there is a possibility that your pet's dosage requirement might be different than that which was previously calculated by the veterinarian.

The length of time the heartworm prevention must be given varies with the duration of the mosquito season in your area. Depending upon the type of medication used, it may be necessary to start a month before the mosquito season begins, and end one month after the season ends. In the southern American states, dogs must have year-round prevention. Even these dogs should be tested for heartworm infection at least every six months. To reiterate, it is critical that all dogs be heartworm-tested and be negative before commencing any prevention.

External Parasites

Ear Mites

Ear mites (*Otodectes* species) account for most ear problems in cats and also affect many dogs. They are easily transferred between pets by direct contact, and can live in the environment for several months before infesting a pet. Although all dogs and cats in a household may be affected, the most serious problems occur in puppies and kittens.

At first, there may be few signs of ear mite infestation except a dry, dark, waxy debris in the ear canals. This results from the mites irritating the glands that produce earwax, causing them to produce more thick reddish-black wax. Intense itchiness causes the cat to constantly shake its head and scratch its ears; the back of the ear flap may be scratched raw.

If you suspect that your cat has ear mites, place some ear debris on a dark surface. The mites, which look like tiny white particles, may be seen moving about. The veterinarian will confirm the diagnosis by examining the ear debris under the microscope.

Ear mite infestations are not usually difficult to treat. The veterinarian will clean out your pet's ears and then give you medication for home treatment. Some drugs will kill the adults but not the eggs, so treatment may have to be repeated after two weeks to kill the newly hatched adults before they can reproduce. All pets in the household should be treated.

It is important to note that ear mites can occur on other parts of the pet's body. When a kitten sleeps with its tail near its ears, the ear mites can move to the tail. Even if the ears are treated to kill the mites, the kitten's tail may be a source of reinfection. For this reason, the animal's entire coat should be dusted or sprayed with an insecticide prescribed by your veterinarian.

Fleas

A major problem in both cats and dogs is fleas, which are blood-sucking parasites that live on the skin. Only adult fleas are found on pets. After ingesting blood from an animal, a female flea lays eggs in cracks and crevices inside the home or outside on damp ground. Over her life span, several hundred eggs may be laid. Immature fleas, called "larvae," hatch within two weeks and live in cracks and crevices. Under warm, moist conditions, the entire life cycle may occur in as little as sixteen days, or it may take as long as a year under unfavorable conditions. This aspect of the life cycle explains how fleas survive from year to year in harsh climates.

In the temperate regions where I have practiced, the flea problem is worse in late summer and fall. It is felt that in the cooler evenings, outdoor fleas seek the warmth of an animal's body. Then the pet goes inside the home, and that is where the fleas spend the winter. Fleas can survive for a long time, even in an environment without animals. When people move into a house that has been uninhabited for a time, the fleas will sense the vibrations of their movements. In the proper temperature and humidity, the fleas will hatch from their dormant phase. The newly hatched fleas need a blood meal before they are able to reproduce; if no pets are around, they will bite people!

It is usually not difficult to discover that a pet has fleas. Some people can tell that fleas are around because they themselves have been bitten, particularly around the ankles. They may be very sensitive to flea bites and react more than their pets. Often fleas can actually be seen on a pet. Fleas are about the size of fruit flies and can be seen jumping quickly through the pet's fur. Roll your pet over and check its lower belly and groin where its coat is thin. If you see a flea and try to squash it, you will find that its firm shell has to be broken with your fingernail. Sometimes you will only see small black specks, similar to pepper grains, in the pet's fur. This is flea dirt. If you brush out these black specks onto a white surface and slightly moisten them, they will leave a reddish residue because they contain a large quantity of digested blood.

It is important to understand that the flea spends less than 10 percent of its time on a pet's body. This means that a proper flea treatment must have two components: treating all household pets and treating the environment. Pets can be treated with powders, sprays, foams, shampoos, and dips. Some products are just "quick kill"; others last for eight days or longer. Whichever product you select, it is very important to follow the directions closely. As a general rule, always start at the animal's head, then work down its body, to drive the fleas off. If you happen to treat in the other direction, the fleas will just move up onto the animal's head or nose, where they will most likely be able to survive the onslaught of flea-control product. Realize as well that flea shampoos are not terribly effective. They will help to kill adult fleas and wash them down the drain, but there will be no residual effect once the shampoo is rinsed off. Also, shampoos are not "instant-kill"; they must soak into the coat for at least ten or fifteen minutes before they can be rinsed off. Flea dips are more effective, because the insecticide is not rinsed off, but left on the animal to air dry, leaving residual flea-killing activity (and, unfortunately, a medicinal smell). It is very important to use a product that is meant for your species of pet. *Never* use dog products on cats, as they are very sensitive to and can die from the chemicals used on dogs.

Flea collars are also not very effective at killing fleas. Most flea collars are embedded with insecticide powder, which is released and carried back over the pet's body as the animal moves. Seldom is there enough insecticide to kill a large number of fleas, although the collar usually will keep fleas away from the pet's neck region, and may make the pet undesirable so that fleas that are in the environment are less inclined to jump onto it. However, I have certainly seen many cases of flea infestation on animals that were wearing flea collars.

Another way of treating fleas is with an oral drug (either liquid or tablet), given to the pet every three days. When a flea bites the animal, it absorbs some of the insecticide and dies. However, each and every flea must bite the pet before being poisoned. Although there may be an initial quick reduction in the number of fleas, total eradication of the flea population may take a week or longer. I have had some clients request this drug and swear that they have found it very successful, while other people have reported poor results with it.

There are old wives' tales of small amounts of garlic powder or brewer's yeast being effective as flea repellents when added to a pet's food. While this has never been scientifically proven, it won't do any harm, and many clients insist that it works.

As stated above, the second stage of flea control is to treat the environment. It is a good idea to start by placing a small amount of insecticide powder inside your vacuum cleaner bag to kill the fleas that will be vacuumed up. Then vacuum the baseboards, and all cracks and crevices, and seal and throw out the vacuum bag. Next, treat the premises with an appropriate insecticide. Every year, new products come onto the market. Some are quick-acting and short-lasting, some last for up to three months, others for up to seven months. Some work by stopping the immature flea from developing and therefore from reproducing, while others slowly release insecticide from microcapsules as the product dries. They may be aerosols or nonaerosol pumps; some are designed for crack and crevice treatment, others for general use over carpeted areas.

Flea control outside the home should be aimed at areas where the pet spends most of its time. Grass and weeds should be mowed and the clippings removed. Within reason, areas where the pet spends its time (under porches, in its dog house, in the yard, and so on) should be sprayed or dusted with flea insecticides.

In the United States, you can obtain insecticide foggers, which will discharge long-lasting flea insecticide into an uninhabited room or outdoor area. However, due to environmental protection laws, the foggers available in Canada only release short-acting insecticide.

The best place to find out which product is best for your situation is your veterinary hospital. The products available there are usually more effective than those at a hardware or grocery store. Also, the veterinary staff can advise you on the safe and effective use of these products.

Ticks

Ticks are a type of parasite that attaches to the skin and sucks blood. Immature ticks look like pea-sized dark-colored warts with four pairs of legs.

Different geographic regions have more significant tick problems than others. Adult ticks lay eggs on the ground in sheltered spots such as in sheds, woodpiles, and under rocks. After hatching, immature ticks wait on grass and shrubs for a host. Ticks are indiscriminate parasites; they may feed on dogs, cats, rabbits, deer, people, and other animals. After feeding on the host for up to ten days, immature ticks fall off the animal to complete the next phase of their life cycle.

Although ticks may be found on any part of the body, they are usually found on the ears, head, neck, and between the toes. Ticks may be small and brown, large and whitish-brown, or any size and color in between, depending upon how full of blood they are. Small seed ticks that look like tiny ink dots can often be found around a tick that is full of blood. The skin where a tick is attached may be reddened and inflamed; ticks injure animals by the irritation of their bites.

Carefully check your pet for ticks on a regular basis, especially after walks in the country. Soak a tick with rubbing alcohol and remove it with tweezers. When there are only a few ticks on your pet, they can be easily removed in this way, since the alcohol will loosen the grip of their sucking mouth parts, and kill them. Under no circumstances should a tick be removed by soaking it in gasoline or kerosene, or by applying a lighted cigarette—the consequences to your pet's skin are too severe.

For heavy or persistent tick infestations, the pet may be treated with insecticidal dips or sprays. To eliminate ticks from homes and kennels, use an insecticide spray intended for ticks. Repeated treatments are often necessary.

Ticks transmit bacteria and viruses between animals. The poisonous secretions of twelve tick species can produce **tick paralysis** in many hosts, including dogs and cats. The affected animal is stricken with incoordination in the hind limbs which, over twenty-four to thirty-six hours, results in the victim being completely immobilized. Recovery within a few hours, with no after-effects, follows removal of the ticks. However, death results when the paralysis reaches the respiratory center in the brain.

Lyme disease, a disorder affecting people and dogs, is caused by a bacteria transmitted by the tick. First reported in 1975, this disease has been found in Europe, Australia, and Canada, although most cases have been in the United States. Mice and white-tailed deer are the main reservoirs of tick infestation, so wooded and long-grassed areas with a high mouse or deer population are the most likely sources for the disease.

In people, Lyme disease causes headaches, weakness, fever, nausea, and painful joints. There is also a visible circular skin rash. In pets, the most notable signs are intermittent fever and painful joints which, if left untreated, may progress to chronic arthritis. These latter signs may not occur for weeks or even months after the tick bite.

Diagnosis of Lyme disease is difficult, although there is a blood test that measures the antibody level. If a diagnosis is made before the joints are badly damaged from arthritis, treatment usually consists of antibiotics for a few weeks.

A vaccine to protect dogs from Lyme disease has recently been developed. If you are taking your dog to an area with a tick problem and reported cases of Lyme disease, discuss with your veterinarian the advisability of using this vaccine. Unfortunately, there is no vaccine to protect humans against Lyme disease.

Lice

The two types of lice that can affect dogs and cats—sucking lice and biting lice—are tiny insects that spend their entire lives on one animal, which makes control easy. They accumulate under mats of fur and around the ears and body openings. Sucking lice cause anemia in the host animal through blood loss, and severe debilitation, while biting lice are extremely irritating and cause intense itching. Although sucking lice do not move rapidly and are easily seen and caught, biting lice may be difficult to see.

Since lice infestation can resemble other skin conditions, a diagnosis is made only when the veterinarian sees the lice and their nits (eggs). Lice can be easily killed with insecticidal powders or sprays prescribed by your veterinarian.

Mange

Mange refers to skin diseases caused by various types of mites. One mite that occurs on the skin of dogs and cats is called *Cheyletiella*. ***Cheyletiella* mange** (also called **walking dandruff**) is easily transmitted from pet to pet, especially between animals less than twelve weeks of age. In young animals, a history of recent contact with other animals followed by the onset of dandruff, scratching, and hair loss suggests a diagnosis of *Cheyletiella* mange. The mites may be seen on the animal by using a magnifying lens. Other diagnostic techniques include scraping the skin or combing the dandruff onto a microscopic slide, or applying transparent tape to the skin so the mites stick to it. The veterinarian will use a microscope to look for mites on the slide or tape.

Cheyletiella mites are susceptible to most insecticides, including powders, sprays, dips, and shampoos. Treatment should be continued for several weeks to eliminate the infestation. Because of the highly contagious nature of the parasite, all animals in the household must be treated whether or not they have signs of infestation. Clean and vacuum the household, and use flea control products to control the problem and help prevent reinfestation.

Two further types of mange are **demodicosis** (also called **demodectic mange**) and **sarcoptic mange** (or **canine scabies**). Demodicosis is an inflammation of the skin of young animals, three to twelve months of age, caused by *Demodex* mites, which are microscopic parasites that live in hair follicles and skin glands. Puppies and kittens are born without *Demodex* mites, but acquire the parasite during the first few days of life while nursing from their mothers. In most animals, these mites exist in low numbers and cause no problems, living as normal skin inhabitants. Some animals, however, have a deficiency in their immune or defense systems, which allows mites to proliferate unchecked and populate the skin by the thousands, causing demodicosis.

Demodicosis is usually suspected when a young animal has hairless areas on its face or front legs. A skin scraping examined under the microscope will reveal any *Demodex* mites. It is necessary to find large numbers of adult mites, immature forms, and eggs in order to establish a diagnosis.

There are two forms of demodicosis with vastly different prognoses: a localized and a generalized form. **Localized demodicosis** is characterized by one or more circular hairless areas, usually around the animal's eyes and corners of the mouth, and on the neck or front legs. The skin in these areas may be red or dark. Treatment of the localized form with an antimite cream applied once daily to the affected areas should control the condition; the majority of cases of localized demodicosis recover in three to eight weeks. However, the daily rubbing required to apply topical medications frequently causes more hairs to fall out from parasitized follicles. The lesion may at first appear more hairless and larger in size after a few days of treatment, but improvement can be expected in two to three weeks as hair growth returns. After this, recurrences are rare.

Compared with the mild clinical disease of localized demodicosis, **generalized demodicosis** is one of the most severe canine skin diseases, and can be fatal. This disease is characterized by patchy, widespread hair loss. The animal's skin may become thicker, develop folds and crusts, change to a reddish or blackish color, and feel greasy. Generalized demodicosis is likely to become infected with bacteria. Scratching is usually present.

Treatment of generalized demodicosis requires very aggressive long-term therapy. All hair on the affected animal should be gently clipped and matted crusts must be removed. Bacterial skin infections are treated with oral antibiotics, topical ointments, and medicated baths. Patients with deep skin infections benefit from whirlpool baths using warm water and mild antibiotic solutions. Various harsh products have been used in the past to kill the *Demodex* mites, but new drugs are being developed. The most recent, "Amitraz" (trade-named "Mitaban"), is used as a dip once a week for three to six weeks; results have been promising. The veterinarian will monitor the success of any treatment for demodicosis by examining skin scrapings at repeated intervals to see whether the mite population has been reduced.

Feline demodicosis is a rare disease that usually affects the eyelids and surrounding area. It is localized and usually disappears on its own. A mild antimite ointment speeds recovery and has a soothing effect on the reddened areas that have lost hair.

Sarcoptic mange (canine scabies) is an intensely itchy, easily spread infestation of the itch mite, *Sarcoptes*, which burrows into the outer skin layers. Sarcoptes mites are transferred from one animal to another by direct contact. Newly infested animals begin to show clinical signs ten days to eight weeks after exposure.

Itchiness and contagion are prominent characteristics of canine scabies, which affects dogs regardless of age, sex, or breed, and can also infest people. Family members frequently develop visible lesions soon after the dog is affected. The mite will temporarily invade the person's skin causing severe itching and red bumps on the arms, above the belt line, beneath watch band and brassiere straps, as well as on other parts of the body. The mite does not burrow in human skin and usually disappears from its temporary host in a few hours. The red bump persists for fourteen to twenty-one days, but no new lesions will appear after the dog's mites are eradicated.

A dog with scabies will scratch itself constantly, leading to hair loss and skin abrasions. Skin lesions are often raised and reddish and may become infected with bacteria. Thick yellow crusts and greasy wrinkly skin develop over time. Lesions may appear anywhere on the animal's body, but occur most commonly on the elbows, ears, stomach, and chest.

A history of recent exposure to other animals followed by intense scratching suggests a diagnosis of sarcoptic mange, especially when family members have concurrent skin disease. Confirmation is achieved by finding mites or mite eggs in skin scrapings examined under a microscope. Even if mites cannot be found, which sometimes happens, the veterinarian may think the clinical signs alone, coupled with human symptoms, warrants treating the pet for sarcoptic mange.

Clipping the coats of long-haired animals facilitates treatment. Antiseborrheic shampoos help remove crusts and scales, and insecticides are used to kill *Sarcoptes* mites. Antibacterial shampoos may be necessary if a skin infection is present, and anti-inflammatory agents may help reduce itching. All pets in contact with an infested animal should be treated to prevent reinfestation.

Feline scabies (or **notoedric mange**) is caused by a different mite, called *Notoedres*, which primarily affects cats, but can live temporarily on dogs and people. Characteristically, this mite affects whole litters of kittens and queens or older male cats, and is highly contagious, spreading by direct contact. The mites are more abundant and more easily found than in cases of canine scabies.

Lesions of feline scabies first appear at the lower edge of the ear; they spread rapidly to the upper ear, the face, eyelids, and neck, and also extend to the feet and rectal area. This probably results from the cat's washing habits, and from sleeping in a curled-up position.

Treatment with most parasiticidal agents is not advisable because of their extreme toxicity to cats, although sulfur in various forms is completely safe. The hair should be clipped from affected areas. The cat is then bathed in warm water and soap to loosen scales and debris. A lime-sulfur dip is used, and repeated ten to twenty days later; a commercial polysulfide solution is applied to the affected areas every three to four days. All affected cats on the premises must be treated.

Flies

Technically speaking, flies are not parasites. There are, however, two types of flies that can produce skin problems in animals. The first of these is the organism known as *Cuterebra*. The egg of this fly is laid in the soil; it is thought that the larva, which is a two-centimeter (3/4-in.) long "grub," penetrates the host's skin directly. The larva must have air to breathe, so it lives in a cystlike structure with a round opening. *Cuterebra* is usually seen in very young kittens, and puppies of breeds with a very dense hair coat, most commonly in July, August, and September.

Diagnosis is made by observing a round opening in the animal's skin. The larva's mouthparts can be seen on occasion as two dark objects in the center of the opening.

Treatment involves enlarging the opening and extracting the grub with an instrument. Care must be taken to avoid crushing it as retained parts may produce allergic reactions. The infected wound should be treated but healing will be slow.

The other skin problem caused by flies is **maggot infestation** or **myiasis**. The adult forms of many types of flies place eggs on the wet, warm skin of debilitated, weakened animals with draining wounds or urine-soaked coats. These develop into highly destructive larvae and produce "punched out" round holes over extensive areas of the skin. The larvae are found under the skin and in the tissues. Favorite locations are around the nose, eyes, mouth, anus, and genitals, or adjacent to neglected wounds. Myiasis is always a disease of neglect, and I have found it to be the most disgusting condition I have had to treat. One case that I vividly remember involved a large male Collie that was very old and so arthritic that he had great difficulty getting up and moving around. The dog lived outdoors, and being unable to raise its hindquarters, it repeatedly soiled itself. When the dog was carried into the office by the family as an emergency case at night because it "suddenly" could not get up, I could immediately recognize the noise of the maggots in its hindquarters. Just lifting its tail revealed several large moist lesions that were seething with maggots. The odor of the soiled and rotten tissue added to the pity I felt for the poor animal, and the disgust for his family. They agreed that they would no longer be able to adequately care for a large dog that was not mobile (in my opinion, they had not "adequately" cared for the dog for some time), since in their home situation the dog had to remain outside. It was decided to euthanize the dog so it would not have to suffer any longer.

In less severe cases of myiasis, treatment requires clipping hair away from the lesions. This is not an easy task as the moist hair and dead skin keep clogging the clipper blades. The lesions then have to be cleaned with a mild antibiotic detergent. The larvae must be meticulously removed from deep crevices and from under the skin. Topical antibiotic dressings should be applied, and daily wound care is necessary. Of course, the patient should be housed in screened, fly-free quarters.

Insect Bites

Dogs and cats can also suffer from the sting of bees, hornets, and wasps. Usually, there is just redness and inflammation at the sting site, although in some cases severe allergic reactions can occur, just as happens with some people. If cardiac and respiratory impairment result, the patient may die.

The stinger should be removed if it can be located. Treatment for allergic reactions includes strong anti-inflammatory agents and antihistamines. Hot compresses may relieve local pain.

A dog that is housed outdoors can suffer from dermatitis caused by stable flies that attack its face or ears, with multiple bites commonly found on the tips of the ears. Redness and bloody crusts are typical lesions. Ordinary insect repellents used for people, flea spray, or pastes made of flea powder applied to the affected skin, help to prevent repeated bites. The patient should be housed inside during the day if possible until the lesions heal. Topical medications may be beneficial. The source of the flies should be investigated, and sprayed with an insecticide every three weeks to help decrease the fly population.

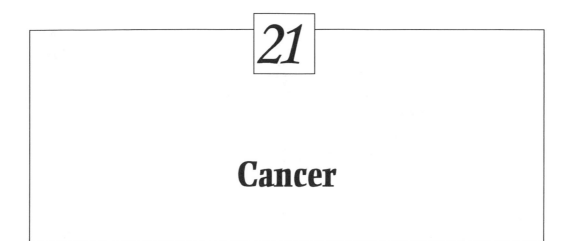

Cancer

Some people are amazed to discover that animals can get cancer. Since the likelihood of getting cancer increases with age, the prevalence of cancer in veterinary practice is increasing as a consequence of the greater longevity of pets in modern times. Veterinary oncology (the study and treatment of cancer in animals) has made great strides in recent years.

Overview

Tumor or **neoplasm** is the general term for any new growth that is unrelated to the function of the tissue in which it is growing. A **malignant tumor** is cancer; it has the potential to spread and invade adjacent tissues, or can travel through the bloodstream to other parts of the body. For example, a malignant breast tumor can spread to other mammary glands, or to the lungs via the bloodstream. A **benign tumor** will not spread in this manner. However, it can recur after being removed, or it can grow to a large size and cause problems. For example, a large benign tumor in an animal's groin can interfere with its ability to walk.

Diagnosis

Some tumors can be detected by seeing a swelling beneath the pet's skin. Others can be felt as masses in areas where such structures should not exist; these are often found when the veterinarian carefully palpates or feels the animal's body. Palpation of the pet's abdomen is a very important part of every physical examination. On several occasions, while feeling the abdomens of older cats that had diarrhea, I detected masses obstructing the intestines. My findings were extremely upsetting for clients who simply thought that their old cats had temporary digestive disturbances.

An x-ray will usually be taken once a tumor has been detected, to outline its size and exact location. Even if palpation has been normal, an x-ray can reveal a suspicious growth in the abdomen or chest. Ultrasound is being used with increasing frequency to pinpoint a mass when it is hidden within an organ such as the liver or pancreas.

A list of the common signs of cancer, applicable to both cats and dogs, has been developed by the Veterinary Cancer Society. These are:

1. abnormal swellings that persist or continue to grow;
2. sores that do not heal;
3. weight loss;
4. loss of appetite;
5. bleeding or discharge from any body opening;
6. difficulty eating or swallowing;
7. loss of stamina;
8. persistent lameness;
9. difficulty breathing, urinating, or defecating; and
10. persistent coughing.

Cancer Treatment

A common and unfortunate problem that veterinarians face is the extremely negative connotation that the word "cancer" carries in our society. A diagnosis of cancer is often equated with a sentence of painful, protracted death. Since one out of every four people will develop cancer at some point, veterinarians and clients alike may have had experiences with family members or friends who have undergone cancer treatment. These experiences, whether positive or negative, strongly influence veterinarians and clients in making decisions regarding cancer treatment for pets. Cancer will not automatically result in the same outcome in every case, and animals may not experience the same side effects as human patients who undergo cancer therapy.

Clear communication between the veterinarian and pet owner is absolutely necessary so that both parties understand the goal in a given case. Some clients will refuse any aggressive therapy with potential adverse side effects, opting instead for palliative therapy aimed solely at controlling pain, with early euthanasia anticipated. For others, prolongation of life while maintaining a reasonable quality of life for the pet is acceptable, allowing for some degree of disability or illness such as may be associated with amputation or aggressive chemotherapy. Clients also need to consider the monetary costs of such treatment, although most animal lovers agree that an animal's health should never be a financial issue.

Once a tumor has been detected, an operation can be performed to examine the mass, determine its exact extent, and identify any involved neighboring structures. This will determine whether or not the cancer can be surgically removed if it has not already spread to other parts of the body. If the tumor is inoperable, I recommend euthanizing the animal during the operation to prevent further suffering.

Many tumors that are confined locally can be cured with complete surgical removal, making this the preferred treatment for many lesions such as skin tumors and breast cancer. The first surgery is always the best chance for a cure.

When the tumor is removed, a biopsy or small piece of the growth will usually be sent for analysis to the pathology laboratory. The veterinary pathologist can determine whether the tumor is malignant or benign and sometimes whether it appears to have been totally removed. I follow the teachings of one of my professors when I was an intern, who said, "If a tumor is worth removing, it is worth learning exactly what it is from a pathologist." To discover that it is benign is great news. If the growth is malignant, the family will know to watch for further symptoms. Further therapy in the form of radiation or chemotherapy can be undertaken following surgery.

A growth may be inoperable by reason of its location. For instance, if a tumor involves a large part of the tongue, surgical removal of the growth would make the pet unable to eat and drink, and therefore, unfortunately, surgery is not a possible option. On the other hand, bone cancer can be removed by amputation of the affected limb if the cancer has not spread, and the pet should get along quite well on three legs.

Some types of tumors are easily destroyed by radiation therapy and others by chemotherapy. In radiation treatment, the area containing the tumor receives repeated doses of radiation designed to kill the cancer cells without damaging many normal cells. Radiation therapy is available only at certain technologically sophisticated veterinary centers and teaching hospitals. One of the problems that arises when using radiation therapy in animals is that the patient must be anesthetized, as it must remain motionless during the radiation session. This means that in addition to the effects of the radiation, the animal will have to recover from frequent doses of anesthetic.

Chemotherapy involves the administration of drugs, usually intravenously, that will kill the cancer cells while sparing normal healthy cells. Chemotherapy is offered at many veterinary practices and referral hospitals. A great deal of experience in the use of chemotherapy has been acquired in veterinary medicine over the years, and many drugs alone or in combination are available to treat a variety of animal cancers.

Some Specific Cancers

Since tumors can develop in virtually any organ or tissue, the symptoms of illness will alert the veterinarian to look for disease in a particular body system. For instance, an animal with severe episodes of vomiting might have a **digestive tract tumor**. If the pupils in a pet's eyes are not equal in size and the pet begins to wander aimlessly or turn in circles, it might have a **brain tumor**. An animal that is experiencing difficulty breathing, frequent coughing, and shortness of breath might have a **chest tumor**.

The spleen is an abdominal organ that drains the lymph, which is a fluid that bathes the tissues and which contains white blood cells. A **hemangiosarcoma** is a tumor that arises in the spleen, greatly enlarging it; the tissue becomes weaker as it is stretched and may rupture, causing severe internal bleeding. The patient will usually have no specific symptoms before the rupture occurs. However, at that point, it will become very weak, its gums will be very pale due to blood loss, and it will rapidly go into a state of shock. Exploratory surgery will determine if the bleeding is from a ruptured spleen, in which case the spleen with its tumor will be removed. An animal can live without a spleen, but it may die from shock during the surgery. However, if the patient is strong enough to withstand the anesthetic and surgery, the outlook is good.

In the case of vomiting or diarrhea caused by an **intestinal tumor**, exploratory surgery will reveal the extent of the growth and determine whether it is operable. In evaluating a **bladder tumor** during surgery, the veterinarian must decide whether, if the growth were removed, enough of the bladder would remain to allow the pet to live a normal life with normal urine control.

Mammary tumors can occur in cats and dogs of both sexes, but are most commonly found in female dogs. If detected early as a small pea-sized lump in a breast, surgical removal of the growth is not complicated. Often, however, the growth is malignant, and spreads first through one mammary gland and then along the chain of mammary glands on one side of the body. Surgery is much more complicated in this situation, as it is difficult to remove all of the affected tissue and still have enough skin to close the incision. Often, mammary tumors spread to glands in the area that are part of the "lymphatic system," in which case the prognosis is not good. Malignant mammary tumors often spread to the chest, causing coughing and shortness of breath.

On several occasions I have removed what I thought were small cysts from the mammary glands of male cats, and the pathologist reported that these were highly malignant tumors. Further surgery was necessary in each case to slow down the spread of the disease.

Tumors can occur as swellings beneath the surface of the skin. Benign fatty growths, called **lipomas**, often occur as lumps along the body. Although diagnosis is not possible without a biopsy, the location of the lump will often suggest to the veterinarian that this is a lipoma. Lipomas will generally grow to a certain size and then stop getting larger, and they usually will not bother the pet. I recommend that the owner check a fatty growth and if it continues to grow, or if the skin over it becomes raw, it should be removed. I once saw an old Scottish Terrier with what I felt was probably a lipoma occupying the entire side of its rib cage. Due to its size and solid attachment, I did not feel comfortable removing it myself. I referred the dog to a veterinary teaching hospital where it was successfully removed in a three-hour operation. It turned out to be just a lipoma, but it weighed more than two kilograms (5 lb.)!

Skin tumors make up at least one-third of the tumors of dogs and about one-quarter of the tumors of cats. Skin tumors can be benign or malignant, and can appear as wartlike skin growths, or as raw open sores that do not heal. Some pets respond well to surgical removal if the tumor is isolated in one small area, but some tumors spread easily and are fatal within several months. A biopsy is the best way to determine the nature of a skin tumor, and the expected course of the disease.

One particular skin tumor in dogs deserves special mention. **Canine cutaneous histiocytoma**, commonly known as a **button tumor** appears as a small domed or buttonlike solitary nodule, usually on the face, ears, or legs of a young animal. This is one situation where a young animal can have a tumor, since half of the cases occur in dogs under two years of age. This benign tumor grows rapidly for one to four weeks, and its surface might be raw if the dog licks it. The usual treatment is surgical removal, which is simple and effective.

The testicles of dogs can develop three different types of tumors. Two types cause swelling in one or both testicles, but they generally do not spread to other areas or cause problems. The preferred treatment is to neuter the dog.

The third type of **testicular tumor**, known as a **Sertoli cell tumor**, frequently occurs in a testicle that has not descended into the scrotal sac. The unaffected testicle is usually smaller than normal, while the diseased testicle is enlarged. Most cases are found in dogs over six years of age, with the average age of occurrence being nine years. However, Sertoli cell tumors tend to occur at an earlier age when they develop in an undescended testicle. This tumor produces an excess of female hormones, which often causes feminization of the male dog. An affected dog will lose hair in its groin, have enlarged nipples (like those of a nursing female), lack the normal male sex drive, and may attract other male dogs. As the tumor grows, the dog will become ill, lose weight, and become depressed. The treatment of choice is surgical removal of the testicles; the female characteristics will quickly regress following the surgery.

Lymphosarcoma is cancer of the lymphatic tissue, which is a network of tiny vessels that filter and return body fluids to the bloodstream. Although lymphosarcoma may occur in any organ, it occurs most frequently in the spleen, liver, lymph nodes, chest, and the digestive tract.

The exact cause of lymphosarcoma in dogs is not known, but a virus is suspected. In cats, lymphosarcoma is associated with the feline leukemia virus complex (FeLV), which is estimated to affect from 2 to 15 percent of the cat population. Diagnosis of lymphosarcoma can be made by feeling the enlarged lymph nodes in the neck or near the shoulder. Tumors of the intestines and of the tonsils can frequently be discovered during a routine physical examination. Blood tests and a bone marrow evaluation are also useful in detecting abnormal cells, as is a biopsy of the enlarged organ.

Lymphosarcoma is not curable in dogs or cats, but therapy can reduce the severity of symptoms and add quality time to the pet's life. Chemotherapy decreases the size of the tumor and alleviates symptoms in up to 80 percent of dogs and over 50 percent of cats. Life expectancy depends upon the degree to which the disease has advanced at the time of diagnosis. Many cats live at least six months after treatment has begun, while dogs may survive up to a year or more.

Leukemia and the Feline Leukemia Virus

Leukemia is a malignant disease of the blood-forming organs, and occurs when cancerous cells invade the bloodstream and bone marrow, rendering them unable to produce normal blood cells. Leukemia can occur in dogs and cats, although only in cats has the feline leukemia virus, or FeLV, been proven to exist.

The **feline leukemia virus** is contagious among cats and is transmitted primarily through saliva. Some cats are resistant to FeLV infection, while a few infected cats do not develop the disease but become healthy FeLV carriers and are a constant source of infection for other susceptible cats.

Besides causing lymphosarcoma and leukemia, the feline leukemia virus can suppress the immune system, making the cat more susceptible to other diseases, including anemia, feline infectious peritonitis (FIP), chronic gum and mouth infections, abscesses and recurring wounds, chronic respiratory infections, and chronic recurring fevers with no apparent cause. More cats die of these immuno-suppression-associated diseases than from lymphosarcoma, which is the most common FeLV-related cancer. In fact, veterinarians now suspect FeLV infection whenever a cat has anything but the simplest of problems!

Blood and saliva tests are available to determine if a cat is infected with the feline leukemia virus. A positive FeLV test indicates only that the cat was carrying the virus at the time of testing. It does not indicate whether the cat is suffering from cancer, has developed immunity, or will develop leukemia-related cancer. Nor does the test predict the lifespan of a leukemia-positive cat.

A negative FeLV test means that the cat had no detectable virus in its blood at the time the sample was taken. However, it might be too early to detect the virus in the blood or saliva. If a negative cat is still negative after a second testing three to six months later, and if it has not been in contact with an FeLV-positive cat in the interim, you can be reasonably confident that the cat is free of the virus. However, a negative test does not mean that a cat is immune to the virus.

The decision about what to do with a healthy cat that has tested FeLV-positive is a most difficult one. Your veterinarian cannot give conclusive advice on the question of whether to euthanize a positive-testing cat or to keep it alive; however, there are several factors to be considered. If the cat is not ill, a rational decision to keep it alive can be made if it has no contact with other cats. If the family of an FeLV-positive cat worries about the risk to other cats, and they cannot keep the positive cat isolated, then euthanasia should be considered if another home for the cat cannot be found.

There is a higher incidence of FeLV-positive cats and FeLV-related cancer in multicat households. If your cat is FeLV-positive but seems otherwise healthy and you have other cats in the household, it is important to have the other cats tested. Those that test positive can stay together as a group, but they must be isolated from the negative-testing cats. Retest the FeLV-negative cats in three months to determine if any of them have become positive. On the other hand, many families do not want to keep their cats isolated from one another, nor do they believe in putting healthy cats to sleep. They take a "laissez-faire" approach and let nature take its course.

If you are a cat breeder, your veterinarian will probably advise you to eliminate all the FeLV-positive cats from your cattery as they are a potential hazard to other cats and will probably produce FeLV-infected kittens.

If your cat dies of an FeLV-related cancer or you have an FeLV-positive cat euthanized and you want to get a new one, some precautions are advised. Do not introduce a new cat to the household for at least thirty days. All items that the deceased cat used, such as the litter pan, food bowls, and toys, should be replaced or disinfected with household bleach. If possible, have your new cat tested before bringing it home, to ensure that you are acquiring an FeLV-negative individual.

There is no conclusive evidence that FeLV is transmissible to humans or other species of animals. Furthermore, the incidence of cancer and leukemia in people with FeLV-infected cats is no greater than in families without cats.

Cats with an FeLV-related cancer can occasionally live for many months even when untreated, although most affected cats die within weeks of the diagnosis. Treatment of leukemia is similar to the treatment of lymphosarcoma, using anticancer drugs. Some anticancer drugs are very toxic and the cat may become more ill at first, and a few cats will be unable to tolerate these drugs at all. Generally speaking, life is prolonged for a few months more than for untreated cats, although, in occasional cases, the treated cat's life is significantly prolonged.

Happily, vaccination against the deadly feline leukemia virus is available. Since kittens are more susceptible to infection than adults, they should be vaccinated. Cats that live in multiple-cat households and catteries are also at risk, and should be vaccinated, along with all breeding animals. Cats that may not need to be vaccinated include those that are strictly isolated (but what happens if the cat has to be hospitalized or boarded?). Pregnant queens should not be vaccinated, as to do so could cause the babies to be stillborn or malformed. Vaccination of an infected cat is unlikely to alter the course of the infection.

In the late 1980s, a new virus was discovered that causes acquired immune deficiency syndrome (AIDS) in cats. The virus has been named the **Feline Immunodeficiency Virus (FIV)**, or **FTLV** for **Feline T-Lymphotropic Lentivirus**. Although closely related to the human AIDS virus, it is very species specific and not capable of infecting people.

The symptoms of feline immunodeficiency virus are quite varied, since the virus' main action is to suppress the immune system. The cat becomes an easy target for disease-causing organisms (bacteria, viruses, fungi, or parasites). Most cats infected with FIV show symptoms of mouth infections, upper respiratory tract infections, chronic diarrhea, and chronic eye infections. As we have seen with the feline leukemia virus, any sick cat, regardless of its actual symptoms, could suffer from an underlying FIV infection, and most veterinarians will test for both these diseases in such cases.

Unlike the feline leukemia virus, the FIV virus seems to be transmitted mainly by cat bites. The virus is very fragile and does not survive outside the cat's body for very long. Young cats living in multiple-cat households and catteries are not at high risk of contracting FIV. The high-risk cat is the free-roaming male over six years of age; these cats are the most territorial, and frequently fight with other cats. It is not surprising that infected males outnumber infected females by three to one in North America. Pets kept indoors and away from free-roaming cats are highly unlikely to contract the disease.

At present there is no cure for cats suffering from FIV, but many of these cats can be maintained comfortably for variable periods of time with supportive medical care.

Risk Factors and Dietary Management of Disease

Good health means more than the simple absence of disease; it also involves the active reduction of risk of future disease. For example, risk factors predisposing a person to heart disease are high blood pressure, high cholesterol level, obesity, and smoking. Identifying and controlling a risk factor (high blood pressure, for example) reduces the chance of developing the disease (heart attack, in this example).

Diet is one of the easiest means of controlling risk factors in pets. This chapter will explain how special diets can reduce the risk of certain diseases, and the diet changes that can control certain medical conditions.

Special Dietary Needs in Controlling Disease

Congestive heart failure results in the accumulation of fluid in the lungs. In animals with existing **heart disease**, dietary sodium (salt) increases fluid retention. Obesity can also increase the chance of developing heart failure. In cats, a taurine deficiency in the diet can lead to heart disease. Therefore, pets with heart disease should be fed prescriptive diets that are low in sodium, low in calories, and, for feline patients, diets that have adequate levels of taurine.

Many age-related changes in the kidneys cannot be prevented. As the dog or cat ages, its kidneys gradually deteriorate, losing the ability to concentrate urine and maintain the normal balance of water, sodium, and other chemicals in the blood. In chronic kidney failure, the breakdown products of protein metabolism are not adequately eliminated by the kidneys, and so these products accumulate in the blood. Any measure that delays the onset and/or slows the progression of **kidney disease** will help the pet live longer. Proper dietary management in kidney disease reduces the workload on the kidneys, while meeting the pet's nutritional needs. In this case, the optimal diet should have a reduced level of protein, to minimize the amount of waste materials passing through the kidneys. Also, the dietary protein should be of very high quality, so that it can easily be used in the body for tissue maintenance and repair. As excess phosphorous can contribute to kidney disease, phosphorous is also reduced in this diet. High blood pressure often occurs in chronic kidney failure, and this is prevented with reduced dietary sodium.

Factors that contribute to **bladder infection** and **stone formation** in dogs include diets with excess protein, magnesium, phosphorous, and calcium. Optimal nutrition should reduce these building blocks for bladder crystals and stones, and produce urine that has an acid content to dissolve any formed crystals. To reduce the risk of these conditions, the veterinarian may prescribe a food with controlled levels of calcium, phosphorous, and protein.

Among the many risk factors for cats with **lower urinary tract disease** (particularly **feline urologic syndrome** or **FUS**) are: diets with excess magnesium, bacterial bladder infections, urine crystals, and alkaline (nonacidic) urine. Once a cat has developed FUS, the probability of recurrence is extremely high unless the diet is modified. To help prevent FUS, the diet should contain a low level of magnesium, thereby reducing the major building block for bladder crystals and stones. The urine formed from such a diet should be acidic, to dissolve any crystals.

Skeletal Problems

Some age-related changes to the skeletal system cannot be prevented. However, the signs of many bone and joint diseases, such as lameness and stiffness, can be prevented, or minimized, when these diseases are discovered early and the health risks are then minimized. Factors leading to the development of arthritis include: advanced age; obesity (which puts added stress on bones and joints); genetics; and improper diet. Excess calcium in poor-quality foods can lead to skeletal problems, especially when misinformed owners feed their pets calcium and phosphorous supplements. All-meat diets are high in phosphorous and low in calcium, and can cause skeletal problems. Pets should be given mineral supplements only on the advice of a veterinarian to treat specific conditions.

In growing animals, high-quality nutrition reduces the risk of skeletal problems developing from excess levels of calcium and phosphorous.

Obesity and Overfeeding

Obesity is a serious condition affecting 25 to 50 percent of all dogs, and 25 percent or more of all cats. Obesity prevention and weight reduction lessen the risks of health problems, prolong life, and improve the pet's appearance. Obesity exists when a pet weighs 15 percent more than its ideal weight, and detrimental health effects begin when an animal is 10 to 15 percent overweight. Check whether your pet is obese by feeling its rib cage. The pet's weight is considered to be normal if the ribs are easily felt. If you can feel fat between the skin and ribs, the pet is overweight. If the ribs cannot be felt, the animal is obese. In some pets, particularly cats, a large abdomen that hangs down or protrudes to the sides indicates obesity. This assessment of the animal's weight should be confirmed by a veterinarian as there are other medical conditions that resemble obesity.

Obesity is more common in older animals, occurs more often in females than males, and is more frequent in neutered pets than in intact pets. As a pet ages, it is very important to prevent obesity and its harmful effects on joints. Obesity can shorten a pet's life and predispose it to medical conditions, including arthritis, respiratory difficulty, high blood pressure, congestive heart failure, liver disease, skin disease, cancer, diabetes, increased anesthetic and surgical risks, and decreased resistance to infectious diseases. Optimal nutrition for middle-aged and older pets avoids excess calories.

The most common cause of obesity is overeating; the pet consumes more calories than it needs. Put simply, the pet has too much food, too little exercise, or a combination of both. Overeating is partly the result of the attractive taste of today's commercial pet foods, but, more often, it is the result of a diet supplemented with table scraps, snacks, and other foods.

Overfeeding puppies and kittens predisposes them to obesity as adults by increasing the number of their fat cells. To prevent obesity, puppies and kittens should be fed all they will eat in ten to twenty minutes, two or three times daily. They should *not* be fed "free-choice" with the food dish continually replenished all day. All puppies and kittens should be fed a growth-type food that avoids excess calcium and phosphorous, and excess calories. Table food and scraps should *never* be fed to pets, no matter how sweetly they look up at you with those expressive and anxious eyes!

The treatment for uncomplicated obesity is to reduce the pet's calorie intake while increasing its exercise. However, merely feeding a smaller quantity of a regular commercial diet may cause a vitamin, mineral, or protein deficiency, and it won't satisfy the pet's hunger. The ravenously hungry pet may become a pest as it seeks other sources of food. Most families will tolerate this type of behavior for only a few days before giving in and resuming the previous obesity-causing diet.

A far more successful plan is to replace most of the fat and some of the digestible carbohydrates in the diet with indigestible carbohydrates and fiber. This is achieved by feeding a high-fiber, low-fat, less calorie-dense diet, available at veterinary clinics and some pet-food stores. This reduces the digestible calories in the diet and allows the pet to eat about the same quantity of food as usual, thus satisfying the pet's appetite.

Every family member must appreciate and accept the necessity for the weight reduction, if the diet is to succeed. Your pet will not be helped if you religiously follow a diet regimen for it, while another family member gives it fattening treats behind your back! For the good of the pet, everyone's total commitment and cooperation to achieving the weight loss is necessary, otherwise the effort may result in wasted time, energy, and resources.

Pregnancy, Nursing, and Convalescence

Another life stage that can have serious consequences on the pet's general state of health is pregnancy and, after the litter is born, lactation, which occurs when a mother nurses her offspring. The mother's milk is rich in calcium and fat; these materials must come either from her body or from her diet. Her caloric or energy needs increase according to the size, number, and age of the litter. By the litter's third week of life, the caloric intake to satisfy the mother's needs and provide adequate milk is two to three times her maintenance needs before breeding. A prescriptive diet formulated for pregnant or lactating animals is higher in protein and fat than regular maintenance food, and provides an adequate level of calcium for the mother.

If the mother does not consume enough calcium to balance that which is leaving her body through her milk, her body calcium reserves may fall dangerously low, resulting in milk fever or eclampsia. Therefore, it is extremely important to give her a special high-quality diet throughout her pregnancy and nursing period.

A high-protein, good-quality food is also needed during a period of convalescence. Patients will benefit from foods with increased levels of protein and calories (energy) while recovering from surgery. Debilitated animals that are being treated for severe intestinal or external parasitic infestations also need extra protein and calories for the body to restore itself to health.

Diets for Senior Pets

A food formulated for seniors provides levels of nutrients based on the pets' need to help delay the onset of diseases common in geriatric animals. Diets for senior animals should have reduced levels of calcium, phosphorous, protein, and sodium to help prevent kidney, liver, and heart disease. Since older animals tend to have drier coats, their food should have increased levels of unsaturated fatty acids, vitamins, and zinc, which help keep the skin and coat healthy. Calories must be controlled to prevent obesity in the less-active older pet. Dietary fiber should be moderately increased to maintain proper digestive system function and appropriate weight.

There is a complete discussion of the needs of senior pets in Chapter 10, "The Senior Years."

Food-Induced Skin Allergies

Dogs and cats that develop a "food allergy" or "dietary intolerance" can have a variety of symptoms involving the skin, digestive system, nervous system, respiratory system, and perhaps even the urinary system. In animals, beef and beef by-products, wheat, and corn are the primary substances causing allergic reactions, while lamb causes the least reactions. The likelihood of allergy development to meat increases in ascending order with: chicken and chicken by-products; fish; pork; horsemeat; and beef. The offending substance can occur in many forms. For example, a reaction to beef may be elicited through kibble, meal, biscuits, bones, rawhide, and so on. In a very highly sensitized patient, even infinitesimal amounts will trigger an allergic reaction.

Adverse food reactions are best tested by feeding a hypoallergenic diet for a minimum of four weeks, and then "challenge feeding" to hopefully identify the element of the old diet that was causing the problem (full details of this feeding program can be found in Chapter 19, "Diseases of the Skin," in the section on allergic skin conditions). Once identified, life-long avoidance of the allergy-causing food—by selecting a commercial diet that does not contain it—should prevent recurrence.

Alternatively, if there is a good response to the hypoallergenic diet, this diet can be used for the rest of the animal's life. A full discussion of allergies is found in Chapter 19, "Diseases of the Skin."

Food-Related Digestive Disorders

Certain intestinal problems can often be controlled successfully through diet. Following virtually any type of **gastrointestinal disease**, from a minor upset with vomiting and diarrhea to an intestinal infection or surgery to remove a foreign object, the recovering patient should be fed a very bland, easily digestible, low-residue diet that is low in fat and high in rice, which serves as a binding agent. This type of diet gives the gastrointestinal tract time to heal.

Some dogs with **colitis** do well on this low-residue diet. I treated an Airedale dog several times for acute episodes of colitis and I always dispensed a supply of the special diet after it responded to medical treatment. The owner did not buy more of the food, as I would have expected, given my instructions that the dog must be fed only this food for the rest of its life. Whenever the dog was brought in for another problem, I would always ask how its digestion was and whether it still had episodes of colitis. The owner invariably said that the dog still was ill from time to time, but he was convinced that this was due to the dog eating something when it would run loose in the park. I could not make this client understand that the dog was unable to digest regular commercial dog food, and that the dog would have fewer problems if it was kept on the special easily digested diet. Some pet owners never learn!

Some types of colitis respond better to a diet with increased fiber, which retains water and adds bulk to the stool, thereby controlling the diarrhea. A large number of cats with the problem of chronic vomiting seem to respond well to a high-fiber diet. A very-high-fiber diet will control chronic constipation in old animals. Also, dogs with recurring anal gland problems seem to do better when fiber is added to their diets.

As research on pet nutrition continues, new specialized diets are being developed to control various conditions. These diets will also reduce the risk of disease and help our pets live longer, fuller, healthier lives.

23

Saying Goodbye to Your Pet

Euthanasia, derived from the Greek word meaning "easy death," refers to the voluntary termination of a pet's life for humane reasons. Other more common terms are: "putting down" or "doing away with" an animal, or putting an animal "to sleep."

As euthanasia is one action in veterinary medicine that cannot be reversed, it is imperative that there be clear communication between the pet owner and the veterinarian. A fellow veterinarian told me that a woman came into his clinic one day carrying a small Poodle, requesting that the dog be "put to sleep," as she was moving away. The dog was taken to the treatment room and euthanized. Several minutes later, when the doctor came back to the reception area to return the dog's leash to the client, she asked him when the dog would wake up. My colleague discovered, to his horror, that the client did not want the dog euthanized; rather, she wanted the dog heavily tranquilized for the long car ride, as it did not travel well! A very sad mistake, but one that always reminds me of the importance of effective client communication. I have clients sign "Surgery Consent Forms" and "Euthanasia Consent Forms," to further prevent misunderstandings.

Making the Right Decision for Your Pet

Euthanasia is a sacred privilege with which pet owners and veterinarians are entrusted, a privilege currently denied to medical practitioners for human patients. It is a means of saving animals from the pain and suffering of prolonged terminal illness or unresolvable distress. In addition, pets are sometimes euthanized when they have severe personality defects and ensuing behavioral problems that cannot be resolved through training.

On other occasions, a veterinarian may be presented with a perfectly healthy animal to be put down because the clients are moving to a place where pets are not permitted, or the clients' work schedules no longer make pet ownership feasible. Many people in these situations feel, perhaps selfishly, that their pets just wouldn't be happy living with anyone else. What should a veterinarian do when a client feels that he or she has no alternative but to end the life of a healthy pet? Some veterinarians will not euthanize animals under such circumstances. My approach is to interview the family and question whether they have truly explored all reasonable possibilities to find a suitable new home for the pet. If I am convinced that there is absolutely no alternative (I often try to find homes for these pets myself), I will, reluctantly, euthanize the animal. I feel that if I were to refuse, the family might simply turn the pet loose in the street or abandon it in an empty building (some clients have actually told me they think their pet would be better off on its own than in another home!). The chance of a loose animal being injured or killed is much greater than the chance of it surviving on its own; at least I can prevent the former from happening.

Many owners are uncomfortable initiating a discussion of euthanasia with the veterinarian. When presenting clients with a grave prognosis regarding the pet's health, I try to help them understand that the pet will not recover from its illness, that its condition will deteriorate, and that it will pass away with or without veterinary intervention. The client usually asks such questions as: "Should my pet be euthanized?"; "If the pet is not suffering, should it be put to sleep right away?"; "Should I wait, and if so, until when?" I cannot be the one to make the decision to euthanize a pet; my role is to present all the facts and answer all of the family's questions in a straightforward manner, so that the family's decision is a fully informed one.

A pet suffers when it cannot function normally. An animal that cannot participate in its normal routine loses self-confidence, self-respect, and, often, even the will to live. While emotional suffering cannot be measured on a precise scale, I have little doubt that pets are aware of debilitating changes and are affected negatively by them. If I am asked what I would do if it were my pet we were discussing, I try to answer honestly, but I do emphasize that the decision is the client's and not mine. This being said, after the decision to euthanize a pet has been made, I will comfort the family with the reassurance that they have made the right decision.

Some clients, however, will refuse to face the inevitable, and say that they cannot "play God." They feel that as long as there is life, there is hope. They will maintain a rapidly failing pet at home, hoping that they won't have to decide to end its life, hoping that it will just pass away in its sleep one night. But nature does not always oblige and sometimes the pet clings to life for a prolonged time, all the while getting weaker and weaker. I can empathize with how difficult it is to make such an important and final decision for a beloved pet, but there are times when I have to point out that keeping the pet alive may be a selfish gesture on the part of the family.

At the other extreme, some families are reluctant to have an ill animal at home and will have it euthanized as soon as a grave prognosis is made, even though the animal might have several months left of quality living. In between these two extremes, other families will choose to maintain the animal as long as it is not suffering. I ask them to evaluate the pet's quality of life: Does it seem to be enjoying its life? Is it eating and eliminating normally, and is it aware of its surroundings? Is the family still enjoying the animal's companionship and not fretting about it all the time? If the answers to these questions are "yes," then I suggest that they wait; I assure them that they will *know* when the "right time" has come even if I can't describe it for them or precisely predict when that moment will arrive. Sure enough, whether it is weeks or months later, they will call and tell me, "Doc, the time has come." They just know when their pet no longer has the will to live.

There are times when an animal's death appears imminent; for example, if it has heart failure. If the animal has been on heart medication, there is always the chance, slight though it might be, that with a change in drugs, the pet might have a temporary remission of its symptoms. There is also the possibility that its condition might not improve at all. Again, different families have different reactions when facing their pet's death. A dog was once brought to me in the terminal stages of heart failure. The family asked me to give the dog injections of medication to make it as comfortable as possible and then they wanted to take it home again. I explained that the medication might briefly ease the respiratory distress but that the pet would pass away within a few hours. Still, they were adamant that that is what they wanted, so I gave it injections to ease its condition and they took the dog home. The next day they telephoned me to say that they were comforted that the dog passed away at home surrounded by the family.

In contrast, a few weeks after that, a similar situation occurred, but this time the family asked that the pet be hospitalized. I explained that hospitalization would just add to the stress for this nervous little Poodle and that all we could do was to monitor its condition during the time between medication administration. The family still insisted that I hospitalize the dog. Several hours later the pet passed away, and when I called the family to give them the sad news, they said that they were relieved that the dog died in a hospital setting rather than at home. I relate these incidents to point out, once more, the importance of clear communication between the family and the veterinarian. We try to accommodate the families' wishes to the best of our abilities.

There is one further point regarding the difficult decision to euthanize a pet. Whenever possible, this decision should be reached after direct discussion between the veterinarian and the pet's family. A case that comes to mind is that of a three-month-old kitten saved from a burning house by a firefighter, who was very quick to offer to "put it out of its misery." The owner was in such a state of distress over the fire that she could not make an informed decision about the pet. A neighbor intervened and brought the kitten to my office, which was only a five-minute walk away, for an evaluation of its condition. After examining it, I felt there was a fair chance the kitten would survive, although its recuperation would be prolonged. Not only was it inappropriate for the firefighter to suggest that the kitten be killed without consultation with a veterinarian (I shudder to think what means he might have employed), but it would also have been against the law for him to kill it. Only if an animal is suffering and it is not possible to obtain a professional prognosis, nor to alleviate its suffering, should other alternatives be considered, with the aim of treating the animal as humanely as possible.

Clients have different ways of proceeding once they have decided to have their pets euthanized. Often they just hand over their pets, sign the euthanasia consent form, and leave. Others wish to see the animal after it is dead. Some clients feel they are abandoning the pet if they are not present at the time of its death. Still others wish to hold the animal during the procedure, feeling that they can comfort the pet in its final moments, or at least be in the room as an intimate witness. Some veterinarians are uncomfortable when the owner asks to stay, in case the client displays a strong emotional response. A client may faint, for instance, forcing the veterinarian to tend to both a dying patient and an incapacitated owner. I even had one client say, in the middle of the administration of the lethal injection, that he "could not go through with it" and wanted me to stop! Such an injection cannot be stopped midway—the effects of even a small amount of the drug are irreversible. Of course, I understood that this was an emotional "reflex" from the client, who apologized for his outburst afterwards.

When I know the client well enough to judge his or her emotional stability, I try to oblige a request to witness the euthanasia. However, I do not encourage this. The pet will often sense the family's apprehension when it is brought in for the last time. Even the veterinarian might absorb the owner's apprehension and feel that his or her skill in administering the injection might be affected by the owner's presence, in which case the family might be asked to wait outside the room until the act is completed.

A final-year veterinary student I knew visited an emergency clinic one evening. He was asked to handle a case under supervision. After performing tests on an old, very ill cat, he had to present a grave prognosis to the elderly couple who owned it. As he discussed the suggestion that the cat be euthanized, he had tears running down his face. The clients ended up comforting *him*; they did not know his reaction was due to a severe allergy to cats that he had recently developed! But aside from that allergic veterinary student, there are times when we all shed real tears when we have to euthanize a special patient. Even if we do not cry on the outside, we cry on the inside; euthanasia is always a difficult task to perform.

In a veterinary hospital, euthanasia is performed by an intravenous injection of a barbiturate overdose. Once the needle is in place, the injection causes virtually immediate death. Clients who witness this procedure are always amazed at the rapidity and painlessness of it, although if an older animal has poor circulation it might take a few seconds for the solution to circulate through its bloodstream before death ensues. The animal just seems to relax its body, fall asleep, and then stop breathing. A "last gasp" may occur, which an owner might easily interpret as a sign of consciousness returning; in fact, it is the final act of life.

The Grieving Process

Some owners will ask to have a few moments alone with the animal after the euthanasia has been completed, to allow them to accept the finality of what has happened. Others want to see the animal to satisfy themselves that the procedure has indeed been done. Media publicity over the use of animals for experimentation has made some clients skeptical that the animal has actually been euthanized. Clients have no need to worry; in most jurisdictions, the bodies of pets euthanized in veterinary hospitals are not used for research, and, in any event, experimentation is not permitted without the owner's written permission.

When owners bid their private farewells to their pets, they sometimes leave flowers with the body, or place the pet on its favorite cushion. Some clients comb the pet one last time; others snip off some fur as a keepsake.

The death of a beloved pet to which you have become emotionally bonded is a traumatic and very sad event in your life. The important role played by pets as "family members" is visible even after the death of a pet. Severe depression and even suicide have been known to occur among bereaved pet owners; one study has found that many pet owners will still weep when discussing a pet's death up to a year after the sad event.

A contributing factor to the intensity of grief felt by some owners is the lack of social and psychological outlets for their feelings (that is, no funeral or personal expressions of sympathy). Often, the veterinarian is the only "outsider" involved in the family's emotional upset. Some people feel embarrassed about letting others know that they are mourning the loss of a pet—they fear they may be ridiculed if they admit to grieving over the loss of an animal. No one should feel this way. It is important to express such feelings and emotions to family and close friends. Grief is a natural and necessary component of the recovery process following the loss of a pet. A relative or friend of a person who has recently lost a pet can provide support by recognizing the symptoms and stages of the grieving process: denial, anger, guilt, and acceptance. These four stages are not always distinct and do not always occur in every case, or in any particular order.

A person who feels sadness and loneliness following the death of a pet demonstrates a capacity to relate to animals and to nature in a meaningful and enriching way. This is a wonderful dimension of a person's character, and usually signifies a capacity for compassion and generosity of spirit, which are qualities that are all too rare in people today. Animal lovers are usually people who care about other living beings—and this is something to be proud of.

Many articles have been written in recent years on the subject of grief and pet loss, and grieving over a beloved pet's death is now generally recognized in most contemporary societies as a normal, legitimate, and healthy process. Several veterinary schools in North America offer courses in assisting bereaved clients, and grief counseling and support groups are also being developed through local humane societies and animal welfare associations. If you are experiencing difficulties in dealing with the death of your pet, be aware that you are not alone. Talk it over with your veterinarian, who can put you in touch with helpful counselors. There are books to help those who need to work through their grief, such as: *Coping with Sorrow on the Loss of Your Pet* by Moira K. Anderson; *When Your Pet Dies* by Jamie Quackenbush and Denise Graveline; and *Pet Loss—A Thoughtful Guide for Adults and Children* by H. A. Nieburg and A. Fischer. These books allow the reader to share the experiences of many other pet owners, and provide sensible advice for coping with the profound sense of loss and despair felt by some people following the death of a pet.

Occasionally, a pet owner will have a more difficult time coping with the death of a pet than is considered normal. The length of the grieving process varies, depending on the individual and the degree of emotional involvement the person had with the pet. If it appears that the grieving process is extending beyond a reasonable time or is preventing the person from functioning in a normal manner, professional counseling by a psychologist specializing in grief recovery therapy may be appropriate.

One reason that the loss of a pet is so traumatic for the owner is that the death leaves a void in the owner's daily routine—the pattern has been interrupted. The ritual of evening walks or play periods has ended. The feeling of grief is particularly strong at these times. At first, try using this time to talk to others or write about your deceased pet. Then try to develop new habits to replace the old routines: exercise, read books, prepare special meals, and so on. While some owners find it comforting to keep the pet's collar, leash, and toys around, or perhaps to incorporate these items into a special memorial display with photos of the animal, others cope more easily if these things are placed out of sight. But don't throw them out hastily, as you may regret your action later on.

For children, the passing of a pet is often their first experience with death. The way in which this experience is handled will have a profound and long-lasting effect on your child. There are booklets available from the American Animal Hospital Association and the American Veterinary Medical Association to help children cope with their grief.

It is a mistake to "put on a brave face" in front of children. They may think you really didn't love the pet, or that their own strong feelings are wrong and inappropriate, based on your example. It is better to talk things through and answer questions; I believe in an open, forthright discussion with the child, as far as the child's comprehension allows, to explain that the pet will no longer be ill or have to suffer. The child should be made to understand that the decision to euthanize an animal is a serious, carefully made, and compassionate one, based on the animal's own good. Emphasize the memories of happy times that were shared with the pet. If the child is deceived or if the onus is put on the veterinarian ("The doctor said we had to put the pet to sleep"), the child may learn to shirk the responsibilities of making important decisions later on in life. Fanciful stories, plain lies, or partial truths ("The pet died at the animal hospital"), though easier in the short term, can be devastating if the child later finds out the truth. The child will also miss out on a valuable lesson about compassion and doing the right thing no matter how difficult it may be. However, it is important to explain to children that euthanasia is only possible for animals, not for human beings. Admittedly, this is a difficult distinction for some people to make.

When a beloved pet has died, there are ways to honor its memory. Donations can be made in memory of the deceased pet to humane societies and shelters, as well as to worthy foundations dedicated to improving animal health through ongoing research projects. Most veterinary colleges have pet trust funds, as do the American Animal Hospital Association (P.O. Box 150899, Denver, CO 80215-0899) and the American Veterinary Medical Association (930 North Meacham Rd., Schaumburg, IL 60196). Show-business personalities often sponsor their own pet foundations, the most famous of which is the "Doris Day Pet Foundation" (P.O. Box 8509, Universal City, CA 91608). When a patient of mine passes away, I make a donation in its name to the Pet Trust of the Ontario Veterinary College (Guelph, ON N1G 2W1) or to the Doris Day Pet Foundation.

Burial or Cremation

When a pet has died, a decision must be made regarding the disposal of the body. There are several choices to consider, each having its advantages and disadvantages. In some areas, it is permissible to bury a pet on private property. This can be a good choice, particularly for families with children, as it is then possible to conduct a small ceremony to help them deal with the death. However, home burial does have a few disadvantages. An adequate grave must be dug. The body must be placed in a thick liner bag and then in a wooden coffin with a tight-fitting lid, to diminish the chance that other animals, attracted by the scent, will dig at the grave site. Also, what happens if the family moves to another home?

Most cities have ordinances prohibiting the private burial of animals within the city limits. For this reason, pet cemeteries, which handle all the arrangements including transportation of the body, remain popular. Most pet cemeteries have several different funeral options, ranging from a basic plan to a very elaborate memorial. Be sure you understand in advance what you are getting and what the final cost will be. Your veterinarian can suggest a pet cemetery where you can choose a fitting and lasting memorial for your pet. Or, check the Yellow Pages in the telephone book.

Cremation, which is usually much less expensive than burial, is a practical choice offered at most veterinary offices. If a pet has passed away at home, you can bring the body to a veterinary office for cremation. Afterwards, the pet's remains are buried. Clients sometimes ask to have their pet's ashes returned to them. To do this, the pet is cremated by itself and, therefore, the cost is much higher than a regular mass cremation. The ashes will be put in a special urn if the client provides one; otherwise we use a plain plastic container with the pet's name on it. Some people keep the urn, while others bury it or scatter the ashes in their pet's favorite area.

Carrying On

The trauma of parting with a pet is less severe if the owner still has at least one other pet. Many pet owners adopt a second young pet when their first pet reaches middle age, to maintain the continuity of having a pet in the home when the older pet passes on. When my old dog, Blue, died, I still had my younger dog, Aimée, at home; I maintained my routine of taking evening walks, giving treats before bedtime, and so on. My grief was alleviated to a greater extent than I had expected, although I still deeply felt Blue's passing.

I am often asked whether animals have the capacity to "mourn" the loss of other animals in the home. If this capacity does exist, the mourning does not last very long.

Owners who have lost a pet will often say that nothing can ever replace their favorite pets and yet they sometimes show up at the veterinary office a few weeks later with a new animal. Occasionally, they express guilt about having adopted another pet. By getting a new pet you are not "replacing" the deceased pet, any more than someone who remarries after the death of a spouse can be said to be "replacing" that spouse. For many people, having a pet is simply an essential component of life and it is wrong to deny yourself the pleasure that comes from the association. True, the grief that is felt when a pet is lost brings much pain. But remember that while no amount of grief can bring the deceased back, there are many more animals that need a good and loving home. They deserve to benefit from your kindness and caring. If you decide to adopt another pet, each animal in your life will have a special and distinct place in your heart.

Some families go out immediately and obtain another pet, while others will wait for a time. Some people will get a new animal of the same breed as the deceased pet, and even call it the same name. In my opinion this will invariably lead to conscious or unconscious comparisons between the two animals, which is unfair to the new pet. I generally feel that a different breed of pet, with a different name, will allow the family to maintain memories of the deceased pet while developing a new and different relationship with their latest pet. After all, it is important to recognize that every animal has its own distinct and special personality. Give yourself a chance to develop a unique rapport with your new pet.

When Pets Outlive Their Owners

Unfortunately, it is not always the pet that dies first. In the event of illness or hospitalization of the owner, particularly in a single-person household, the pet must be cared for. In the short term, friends, neighbors, or pet-sitting services can be called upon. If possible it is best to have the pet cared for by someone with whom it is familiar. It is more difficult for a stranger to step in and care for and comfort the pet.

Because your death or incapacity can occur suddenly, it is a good idea to prepare a "Statement of Intent," setting out your wishes regarding your pet in the event that you are no longer able to care for it. Make sure you have notified relatives and friends as to the location of this document as well as the pet's papers and veterinary information. Plan for a trust fund to cover food and veterinary expenses, to be certain that your pet receives the lifetime care that it deserves. Some clients request that their pets be put up for adoption to good homes. Sometimes a veterinary office can help find a suitable family that will adopt the pet on short notice. Other people instruct that their pets be taken to a "no-kill" shelter for adoption. One of my clients left a large bequest to the shelter on condition that a suitable new home be found for her cat.

Some people insist that their pets be euthanized if they die or if their spouse dies, and demand that the euthanized pet be buried with the deceased. How fair is this to an innocent, healthy animal? These people feel, rightly or wrongly, that their animal could not adjust happily to life with a new family. They feel that they would be saving their pets from the stress and turmoil of being adopted by strangers. Sometimes they may be correct in cases where, for example, the pet is very attached to its owner, or the pet is very high-strung and excitable with strangers, or if an aggressive pet can be safely handled by only one person.

A client might feel that his or her deceased spouse's pet should be destroyed, reasoning that the pet will "pine" incessantly over the loss of its owner, without giving the animal any chance to prove otherwise. Perhaps this view is related to the grief felt by the surviving spouse over the death, or perhaps the spouse just wants to get rid of the animal. In any case, while it is true that pets are likely to be affected by the mourning behavior and emotional distress of the bereaved person, the effect usually passes. One of the strengths of animals is their great adaptability to changing circumstances.

Although I am against euthanizing healthy adoptable animals, I recognize the desire on the part of the deceased's family to fulfill the deceased's wishes. Fortunately, many pets turn out to be more adaptable (and adoptable) than we might expect. On occasion, I have convinced the people bringing in the pet on behalf of the deceased to allow a trial period in a new home. It is a good feeling when this succeeds and I know that a pet's life has been saved.

Further Reading

Allan, Eric, and Rowan Blogg. *Every Dog*. Melbourne: Oxford University Press, 1983.

Edney, Andrew. *The Complete Cat Care Manual*. Pleasantville: Reader's Digest Books, 1992.

Kay, William J. *The Complete Book of Dog Health*. New York: MacMillan, 1985.

Margolis, Matthew, and Catherine Swain. *The Dog in Your Life*. New York: Random House, 1979.

Nemec, Gale. *Living with Cats*. New York: William Morrow Publishers, 1993.

Nichol, John. *The Complete Guide to Pet Care*. London: Christopher Helm Publishers, 1988.

Pinney, Chris. *The Illustrated Veterinary Guide for Dogs, Cats, Birds, and Exotic Pets*. Cornwall: TAB Books, 1992.

Taylor, David. *You and Your Cat*. New York: Knopf Publishers, 1986.

Taylor, David. *You and Your Dog*. New York: Knopf Publishers, 1986.

Vine, Louis. *The Common Sense Book of Complete Cat Care*. New York: William Morrow, 1978.

Vine, Louis. *The Total Dog Book*. New York: Warner Books, 1971.

Viner, Bradley. *The Cat Care Manual*. Woodbury: Barron's Publishers, 1986.

Index